# EUROPEAN COMMUNITY LAW

## A Practitioner's Guide

Second Edition

AUSTRALIA
The Law Book Company
Brisbane • Sydney • Melbourne • Perth

CANADA
Carswell
Ottawa • Toronto • Calgary • Montreal • Vancouver

Agents:
Steimatzky's Agency Ltd., Tel Aviv;
N.M Tripathi (Private) Ltd., Bombay;
Eastern Law House (Private) Ltd., Calcutta;
M.P.P. House, Bangalore;
Universal Book Traders, Delhi;
Aditya Books, Delhi;
MacMillan Shuppan KK, Tokyo;
Pakistan Law House, Karachi, Lahore

# EUROPEAN COMMUNITY LAW

## A Practitioner's Guide

Second Edition

by

**William Rawlinson**
C.B.E., M.A. (Oxon), of the Inner Temple, Barrister

and

**Malachy Cornwell-Kelly**
LL.B. (London), A.K.C., Solicitor of the Supreme Court

Foreword by the Rt. Hon. the Lord Woolf of Barnes

LONDON
SWEET & MAXWELL
1994

First Edition 1990 by W. Rawlinson and M. Cornwell-Kelly

Published in 1994 by
Sweet & Maxwell Limited of
South Quay Plaza, 183 Marsh Wall, London E14 9FT.
Computerset by Wyvern Typesetting, Bristol.
Printed and bound in Great Britain by
Butler and Tanner Ltd,
Frome and London

No natural forests were destroyed to make this product;
only farmed timber was used and replanted

A CIP catalogue record for this book is available from the British Library

ISBN 0 421 50320 3

The index was prepared by Hélène Plant

# FOREWORD

It is four years ago now that in my foreword to the first edition, I welcomed the publication of this book. I pointed out that it could not be better timed and that whether you were a novice seeking a first introduction to the subject or an expert requiring a clear and concise textbook to check the accuracy of your recollection, it was ideally suited to meet the challenge which Community law creates. The authors had managed to distil into a remarkably small package an immense amount of information with clarity and precision.

However, law, and European law above all, does not stand still and the authors have conscientiously ensured that the wide audience who, like myself, have come to rely on the first edition of this book are provided with a thoroughly up-to-date second edition.

The same sensible and practical manner of marshalling material has been retained for the second edition. It has proved an appropriate structure into which to interweave the many changes which have occurred over the past four years. The European Union Treaty and the much debated subject of "subsidiarity" receive the matter-of-fact and sensible treatment which is the hallmark of the work as a whole. The significance of *Francovich*[1] is fully recognised. Dealing with the decision under the heading *"Community Tort"* neatly demonstrates its impact.

One of the most important developments which has taken place over those four years is the enactment of a Community Customs Code and the accompanying Implementing Regulations. This is an area where the authors are particularly well qualified to assist the reader because of their wealth of practical experience of the subject while members of the Office of the Solicitor to Her Majesty's Customs and Excise. For an understandable description of the changes which have been made, I doubt whether you can do better than to refer to Chapter 4 of this edition.

There are many other changes and improvements to which I could refer. It is not necessary for me to do so. Those who are already familiar with the first edition will know the high standard that they can expect. Those who refer for the first time to the second edition will soon find out for themselves this book's undoubted virtues. Having examined

[1] [1991] I E.C.R. 5357, [1993] 2 C.M.L.R. 66.

proofs of this edition I am left with only one question unanswered. Will the third edition be entitled "*European Union Law*"?

Lord Woolf
July 26, 1994

# PREFACE TO THE SECOND EDITION

Since the first edition of this book was published in 1990, the European Economic Community has, while changing its name to the "European Community", acquired cousins in the areas of police and judicial co-operation, common action in foreign affairs and the beginnings of a common defence programme and of a monetary union. These newcomers, who are not subject to the corpus of European Community law, join the Euratom and Coal and Steel Communities, still separately in existence, to form the present European Union. The plans for a fresh inter-governmental conference in 1996 envisage the discussion of further steps on the road to European integration.

Whether the reader sees all these developments as momentous or as intimidating, he or she will not be able to escape their impact. In the preface to the first edition, we commented that Community law "pervades and overlaps the domestic law of the states to the point at which no lawyer can be said to have an adequate view of any legal topic without a knowledge of the Community law relevant to the sector in question". Now there are subjects, notably customs and international trade, of which it can nearly be said that without a knowledge of the relevant Community law a lawyer cannot be said to have any grasp of the topic at all.

We have therefore seen it as our task to continue to provide a clear and practical guide to the ever-growing body of legislation and case law. For that purpose, we have avoided much discussion of the politically controversial areas associated with the Maastricht Treaty since, as yet, their practical importance for the businessman and his advisers is very limited; by the time of the next edition it may be otherwise. It may be, too, that the new and potentially crucial doctrine of subsidiarity will have developed sufficiently to establish a more coherent distinction between the powers of the Union and those of its constituent States than hitherto. For the moment, the division of functions between the centre and the periphery is characterised by an unnecessary degree of uncertainty.

We record our thanks to Miss Gina Genghi for her valuable assistance with Chapter 5. We have sought to state the law as at January 15, 1994.

William Rawlinson
Malachy Cornwell-Kelly

London, August 1994

# CONTENTS

# TABLE OF CASES

## ALPHABETICAL TABLE OF CASES BEFORE THE EUROPEAN COURTS

## EUROPEAN COURT OF JUSTICE

## UNITED KINGDOM CASES

# TABLE OF LEGISLATION

## EUROPEAN COMMUNITY TREATIES AND CONVENTIONS

1976 Brussels. Act concerning the election of the representatives of the European Parliament by direct universal suffrage (September 20): [1976] O.J. L278/1 ............ 1.14
1985 Treaty of Accession to the European Communities (Spain and Portugal) (June 12): [1986] O.J. L321 and L337 ............ 5.06
Art. 16(3)............ 12.03
1986 Luxembourg and The Hague. Single European Act (February 17 and 28): [1987] O.J. L169/1............ 1.03, 1.08, 1.14, 2.04, 12.27, 14,01, 16.10, 16.11
A.A. 16(3) ............ 12.03
1992 Treaty on European Union (TEU) (February 7) .... 1.03, 1.04, 1.05, 1.06, 1.07, 1.08, 1.09, 1.14, 1.32,

1992 Treaty on European Union (TEU) (February 7)—*cont.*
1.35, 2.04, 9.16, 12.27, 12.44, 16.09, 16.11
Art. A ............ 1.03
Art. F ............ 2.03, 2.42
Arts. G and A ............ 1.03
Art. G.6 ............ 1.32
Art. G.51 ............ 1.30
Art. J.1 ............ 1.05
Arts. J.3 and J.8........ 1.05
Arts. J.4 and J.8........ 1.05
Arts. K.1, K.2 and F 1.06
Arts. K.3 and K.4 .... 1.06
Arts. J.9 and K. 4..... 1.06
Art. L ............ 1.04
Titles V and VI ........ 1.04
Protocol on Social Policy ............ 9.16
Art. 1 ............ 9.17, 9.19
Art. 2 ............ 9.18
(6)............ 9.17, 9.18
Art. 3 ............ 9.18
Art. 4 ............ 9.18
Art. 5 ............ 9.18
Art. 6 ............ 9.19

## REGULATIONS

## DIRECTIVES

# COUNCIL DECISIONS

## NOTICES, RESOLUTIONS AND RECOMMENDATIONS

Notice on State Aids (aids to the motor industry): [1989] O.J. C123 .................................. 14.35
Notice on State Aids (aids to synthetic fibres industries): [1989] O.J. C173 .......................... 14.35
Notice on State Aids (regional aid schemes): [1990] O.J. C40......... .......................................... 14.35
Notice on State Aids (aid schemes of minor importance): [1990] O.J. C40 ............................ 14.35
Notice on restrictions ancillary to concentrations: [1990] O.J. C203/5.............................. 14.17
Notice on concentrative and co-operative operations: [1990] O.J. C203/10..................... 14.17
Notice on State Aids (aids to public undertakings in the manufacturing sector): [1991] O.J. C273 .................................. 14.35
Notice on the clarification of the activities of motor vehicles intermediaries: [1991] O.J. C329/20............................. 14.09
Notice on State Aids (small and medium-sized enterprises): [1992] O.J. C213 .............. 14.35
Notice on co-operation between national courts and the European Courts: [1993] O.J. C39/6......................................... 14.09
Notice on co-operative joint ventures: [1993] O.J. C43/2, [1993] 4 C.M.L.R. 328................. 14.09

## UNITED KINGDOM STATUTES

## STATUTORY INSTRUMENTS AND RULES OF THE SUPREME COURT

# INTERNATIONAL TREATIES AND CONVENTIONS

# ABBREVIATIONS

| | |
|---|---|
| Article | refers (unless otherwise stated) to an Article of the Treaty |
| CAP | common agricultural policy |
| CCT | common customs tariff |
| CFP | common fisheries policy |
| C.M.L.R. | Common Market Law Reports |
| CN | Combined Nomenclature |
| Commission | Commission of the European Communities |
| Community | refers to the EEC unless the context otherwise requires |
| Council | Council of the European Communities |
| Court | Court of Justice of the European Communities (or, where appropriate, the Court of First Instance) |
| E.C.R. | European Court Reports* |
| ECSC | European Coal and Steel Community |
| ECU | European currency unit |
| EEC | European Economic Community |
| EEIG | European economic interest grouping |
| Euratom | European Atomic Energy Community |
| FEOGA | European Agricultural Guidance and Guarantee Fund (common agricultural policy) |
| GATT | General Agreement on Tariffs and Trade |
| MCAs | monetary compensation amounts (common agricultural policy) |
| NAFO | Northwest Atlantic Fisheries Organisation |
| O.J. | Official Journal of the European Communities:<br>C: series containing communications and information<br>L: series containing legislation<br>Spec. Ed.: English special edition of O.J. containing Acts passed before the U.K.'s accession |
| SEA | Single European Act |
| S.T.C. | Simon's Tax Cases |

* C preceding the number of a case indicates that it is before the Court, and T that it is before the Court of First Instance.

| | |
|---|---|
| TAC | total allowable catch (common fisheries policy) |
| TEU | Treaty on European Union |
| Treaty | European Economic Community Treaty (Treaty of Rome) |

# CHAPTER 1

# THE TREATIES AND THE INSTITUTIONS

## The three communities

Hitherto, as "the Common Market" or "the European Community" were normally spoken of as a single organisation, it was easy to lose sight of the fact that there were three distinct communities. First came the European Coal and Steel Community established in 1951 creating a common market in coal and steel, then in 1957 the European Economic Community and the European Atomic Energy Community were established to cover other areas of economic and industrial life. From the beginning these three bodies shared some common institutions, and since 1967 they have all been governed by the same institutions.[1] **1.01**

This organisational unity conceals the continuing consequences of separation. The treaties governing each community remain distinct, and so therefore do the rules by which activity in each is regulated; the powers given by the treaties for the communities to legislate are also different and, to some extent, so are the procedures and remedies. Because coal, steel and atomic energy are, however, of limited concern, they will not often be encountered in practice, and detailed reference to them will not normally therefore be made. Eventual fusion of the communities themselves may result, and meanwhile the Court has held in Case 328/85, *Deutsche Babcock Handel v. Hauptzollamt Lübeck-Ost*[2] that EEC regulations can apply to steel products where there is no corresponding ECSC provision applicable, an indication of the "catch-all" character of the provisions of the EEC treaty. **1.02**

[1] Treaty establishing a Single Council and a Single Commission of the European Communities, Brussels April 8, 1965, referred to as the Merger Treaty: [1967] O.J. L152.
[2] [1987] E.C.R. 5119.

1.03 As will become clear when the nature of the Community legal order is examined in Chapter 2, the European Communities are not a loose international organisation, nor yet a full confederation. They are in a constant process of evolution, and in this process the Treaty on European Union of 1993 (the Union Treaty) is the latest and most important landmark. The three base treaties are: the European Coal and Steel Community Treaty (Paris, April 18, 1951); the European Economic Community Treaty (Rome, March 25, 1957); and the European Atomic Energy Treaty (Rome, March 25, 1957).[3] Numerous changes and additions to these three base treaties were made, latterly by the Single European Act of 1986 and then by the Union Treaty. (Confusingly, the European Economic Community is now officially renamed "the European Community",[4] and the use of that latter term to describe the three communities is strictly incorrect; they remain "the European Communities".[5])

## The European Union Treaty

1.04 This treaty, concluded on February 7, 1992 and coming into force following ratification by all the Member States on November 1, 1993, establishes a European Union based on the European Communities and the inter-state co-operation it provides for. The two areas of inter-state co-operation are (i) foreign and security policy and (ii) justice and home affairs, dealt with in Titles V and VI of the Treaty respectively. In these two areas, the development of common policies and actions follows the classic pattern of international law, depending upon contractual relations being elaborated ad hoc. To underline this, Article L of the Union Treaty removes the interpretation of Titles V and VI from the jurisdiction of the European Court. The enforcement of the co-operation provisions thus depends upon political rather than legal sanctions. While the Union Treaty makes textual changes to the preceeding treaties, the main principles of legislation remain the same; most of the legislation now emerging being based on the treaties as they previously stood. References hereafter to "the Treaty" are, unless the contrary is stated, to the EEC Treaty as now amended.

## Inter-state Co-operation

1.05 The Union Treaty commits the Member States to define and implement a common foreign and security policy and to refrain from any action

[3] These treaties had previously been much amended by accession treaties, the Single European Act (Luxembourg, February 17, 1986 and The Hague, February 28, 1986: [1987] O.J. L169), the Merger Treaty of 1965: [1967] O.J. L152, and by two budgetary treaties, Luxembourg, April 22, 1970: [1971] O.J. L2, and Brussels, July 22, 1975: [1978] O.J. L91.

[4] Arts. G and A TEU.

[5] Art. A TEU.

likely to impair the Union's cohesive force in international relations.[6] The mechanism adopted is for the Council to decide unanimously that a matter should be the subject of joint action but that implementing measures should be decided by a qualified majority.[7] In regard to security policy, the Western European Union is declared to be an integral part of the European Union and it is requested to elaborate and implement decisions of the Union which have defence implications. In security matters, all decisions other than the purely procedural must be unanimous.[8]

In justice and home affairs, co-operation is pledged in relation to immigration, drugs, fraud, customs, terrorism and "judicial co-operation" in civil and criminal matters. The European Human Rights and Refugee Conventions are specifically required to be respected.[9] In principle, all action in these areas requires unanimity, though again implementation may be decided by a qualified majority.[10] A significant part of the action taken pursuant to these provisons is likely to consist of the making of conventions relating to areas not covered by Community law as such. The Commission (see paragraph 1.19 below) is to be fully associated with both foreign and security policy and justice and home affairs.[11] 1.06

## Citizenship

The Union Treaty establishes a citizenship of the Union, which brings with it the right to move freely between and to reside in any Member State, to vote in municipal and European Parliament elections, to consular protection in third countries from the diplomatic representation of any Member State which is available in the absence of his own and to petition the European Parliament or the European Ombudsman. 1.07

## The objectives of the Community

Articles 1–8c of the Treaty, as amended by the Single European Act of 1986 (the SEA) and the Union Treaty, make it clear that "an ever closer union among the peoples of Europe" is the ultimate goal, with the fundamental principle in Article 7 of non-discrimination between nationals of the Member States. This is to be achieved by measures in the following areas: freedom of movement of goods within a customs union, a common agricultural policy, the free movement of persons, services and capital, a 1.08

[6] Art. J.1 TEU.
[7] Arts. J.3 and J.8 TEU.
[8] Arts. J.4 and J.8 TEU.
[9] Arts. K.1, K.2 and F TEU.
[10] Arts. K.3 and K.4 TEU.
[11] Arts. J.9 and K.4 TEU.

common transport policy, a common trade and competition policy, economic and monetary union, a common social policy and a common environment policy.

## Subsidiarity

1.09 The subject of widespread debate when the Union Treaty was being negotiated and ratified, the principle of subsidiarity rests upon the following slender basis in the E.C. Treaty:

> "*Article 3b*
> The Community shall act within the limits of the powers conferred upon it by this Treaty and of the objectives assigned to it therein.
> In areas which do not fall within its exclusive competence, the Community shall take action, in accordance with the principle of subsidiarity, only if and in so far as the objectives of the proposed action cannot be sufficiently achieved by the Member States and can therefore, by reason of the scale or effects of the proposed action, be better achieved by the Community.
> Any action by the Community shall not go beyond what is necessary to achieve the objectives of this Treaty."[12]

In the absence of a federal constitution for the European Union, the demarcation between the competence of the States and that of the Community or the Union is governed by this vague formulation, which will need to be considered in the context of each set of provisions in the treaties. It remains to be seen what use the Court will make of the new doctrine.

## The Council

1.10 The Council of Ministers is the principal governing body where ultimate political power still resides. It passes all major legislation, and settles the policies which determine how the Community is run. Meeting often in closed session, it is composed of one representative from each Member State, who will be the minister of the national government most nearly concerned with the business under discussion. It functions both as the principal legislator for the Community and as the central organ of the Union in dealing with matters outside the scope of the Treaty. All draft legislation or other proposals coming before the Council are prepared by the Commission, either on its own initiative or at the Council's request. The Council is called the "European Council" when it is composed of

[12] Art. 3b of the Treaty, as amended.

the heads of government, especially when exercising its political role—see paragraph 1.05 above.

Since contentious political issues have often to be resolved, the system of voting which the Treaty provides for the Council is of importance. Under a political understanding known as the "Luxembourg compromise" reached in 1965, if a Member State considers an essential national interest to be at issue, the Council continues to discuss matter until unanimity is reached. This procedure is not recognised in the Treaty, which does however prescribe cases in which unanimity is required, as, for example, to adopt legislation under Article 235 for which there is no specific authority elsewhere in the Treaty, or to take further steps towards alignment of taxation in the Community under Article 100a. Whether the "Luxembourg compromise" will hold for the future remains to be seen. 1.11

For the most part, either simple majority voting is prescribed, or voting by what is known as a "qualified majority", when a system of weighting applies to give some Member States more votes than others. Thus, under Article 148, France, Germany, Italy and the United Kingdom have ten votes each, while Spain has eight, Belgium, the Netherlands, Greece and Portugal have five, Denmark and Ireland have three and Luxembourg has two. To determine which voting regime any matter falls within, reference must be made to the article of the Treaty under which it is proposed to act. It was held in Case 68/86, *United Kingdom v. Council*,[13] that failure on the part of the Council to adhere to essential procedural rules laid down for the adoption of legislation rendered the legislation adopted in violation of those rules invalid. More detailed reference is made to the legislative process if it has a particular bearing on specific areas of Community law in the chapter concerned. 1.12

## The Committee of Permanent Representatives

Officials with the rank of ambassador, known as Permanent Representatives, operate as each Member State's principal working link with the Commission, and at the same time they provide, through the Committee of Permanent Representatives, a kind of shadow Council with which the Commission prepares legislation or other proposals before they are considered by the Council itself. Also meeting behind closed doors, this body is staffed at working levels by the appropriate officials from each country depending on the matter under consideration, with the Permanent Representative themselves participating only to consider the most 1.13

[13] [1988] E.C.R. 855, [1988] 2 C.M.L.R. 543.

important or sensitive issue. "Coreper", as it is known after its French initials, is thus where legislation reaches its final form subject only to the settlement of policy questions in Council.

## Parliament

1.14 The functions of this institution are progressing slowly towards equivalence with those of national parliaments, which have been resistant to the transfer of their own functions, thereby producing the much-debated "democratic deficit" of the Community. Since 1978, it has been directly elected on a five-year basis as a result of elections held at the same time throughout the Community.[14] Political parties roughly corresponding to national political groupings are formed, but since membership of Parliament is incompatible with membership of a national government or of the Commission, no ministers sit as MEPs. Eighty-one MEPs are elected from United Kingdom constituencies. Parliament has three principal functions, the exercise of which has been considerably enhanced both by the Single European Act and the Union Treaty, but none yet includes actually enacting Community legislation which remains the prerogative of the Council and the Commission.

1.15 The first function is the scrutiny of draft legislation. All proposals for Community legislation are now in practice submitted to Parliament for an advisory opinion and, in those cases where the Treaty expressly provides for such consultation, failure to undertake it renders the legislation invalid: Case 138/79, *Roquette Frères v. Council*,[15] and there is a complex procedure for co-operation between Parliament, the Commission and the Council, designed to ensure Parliament's closer involvement in the legislative process.[16]

1.16 Secondly, Parliament enjoys a real degree of control over the budget pursuant to Article 203. The budget is prepared by the Commission and submitted to the Council, but Parliament has the right to approve or modify it, which, depending on the type of expenditure involved, may be subject to the Council's final decision. The procedure for settling the budget is again complex, making elaborate allowance for the interplay of Commission, Council and Parliament. It has more than once given rise to crises and even in one instance to litigation, when the 1986 budget was declared invalid. In Case 34/86, *Council v. Parliament*,[17] the Court

[14] Act concerning the election of the representatives of the European Parliament by direct universal suffrage, Brussels, September 20, 1976: [1976] O.J. L278/1.
[15] [1980] E.C.R. 3333.
[16] Art. 149.
[17] [1986] E.C.R. 2155, [1986] 3 C.M.L.R. 94.

held that an attempt by Parliament to cut short an unresolved disagreement with the Council over the level of expenditure failed because Parliament could not lawfully declare the budget to have been adopted without the full procedure prescribed having been followed through.

Thirdly, there is Parliament's overall role in surveillance of the Commission and also to an extent of the Council. The most drastic feature of this is found in the power in Article 144 to dismiss the Commission by passing (by a majority of two thirds of the votes cast) a vote of censure on it, a power which has never in fact been used, although it has been threatened. It was held in Case 302/87, *Parliament v. Council*,[18] that Parliament had no *locus standi* to challenge the legality of acts of either the Council or the Commission under Article 173, although it was competent to bring an action against them for failure to act in accordance with the Treaty, or to intervene in cases before the Court generally. The normal method of parliamentary control is provided by questions to the Commissioner and the Council, and through debates which are often attended by members of the Commission. 1.17

## The Ombudsman

Article 138e provides for Parliament to appoint an ombudsman to receive and investigate complaints of maladministration by any Community body, except for the Court of Justice or the Court of First Instance acting in their judicial roles. Complaints may be referred to the Ombudsman direct or by MEPs and he may decide to initiate investigations of his own motion. As in the case of the United Kingdom Parliamentary Ombudsman, the European Ombudsman will have no power to enforce the remedies he proposes where he finds maladministration but will report to Parliament on the outcome of his inquiries. 1.18

## The Commission

The Commission is the Community's administration, or civil service, but it plays an autonomous role in a number of respects which gives it a quasi-political character which has no real equivalent at the national level. The Commission has four main functions: 1.19

(a) it is responsible for promoting the interests of the Community as such;

[18] [1988] E.C.R. 5615.

(b) it administers the legislation contained in the Treaty and elsewhere, either directly or through the administrations of the Member States;
(c) it takes the initiative in making proposals to the Council for action or for legislation; and
(d) it enacts delegated legislation or adopts decisions which are legally binding on those to whom they are addressed.

**1.20** Promoting the interests of the Community includes acting for the Community in international matters within the Community's competence and taking action against Member States to enforce compliance with Community law. It is also apparent in the rule that Commission proposals for legislation can only be modified by the Council acting unanimously, the Commission's role being to assure respect for the interests of all the states and thus of the minority.[19] The Commission is answerable generally to Parliament for its guardianship of the Community interest.

**1.21** Administering the legislation includes such matters as maintaining in effect the Treaty provisions on competition, the common agricultural policy and the Customs Union. Usually, however, the bulk of the day-to-day administration remains at the national level under overall Commission supervision, a supervision which extends to ensuring that national legislation implementing Community provisions is adequate.

**1.22** Proposals for legislation in the form of draft texts for consideration by Parliament and the Council are initiated by the Commission, which also formulates general policy for consideration likewise. This function, as well as requiring a high degree of technical and legal expertise, involves the Commission in a political role as it pursues its duty of reconciling the interests of the Community as a whole with those of Member States.

**1.23** This task is accomplished, first, by the preparation of initial draft texts in working groups of experts in which national representatives help to thrash out what will be acceptable and workable in each Member State; then there is the examination of the draft formally proposed by the Commission, by the Council and by Parliament, in the course of which the Commission's job is to achieve unanimous agreement, or at least a qualified majority for the proposal. The procedure may also involve consultation with the Economic and Social Committee.

**1.24** The enactment of legislation by the Commission is usually pursuant to powers conferred by the Council in its own legislation, but the Commission is also specifically authorised to take binding decisions (*e.g.* in rela-

[19] Art. 149.

tion to competition by Article 90 and the legislation adopted under Article 87). Article 145 lays down rules governing the delegation of legislative powers by the Council to the Commission. Meanwhile, the Commission has on occasion adopted legislation without having any explicit authority to do so where the Council had failed to act, and it was a matter of necessity for action to be taken.

Under Article 157, the Commission itself consists of 17 members appointed unanimously by the Member States, and from 1995 they will hold office for terms of five years.[20] They must be approved by Parliament. All appointments are renewable. Each State must have at least one person of its nationality as a Commissioner, but no State may have more than two such persons. In accordance with the Commission's role as guardian of the interests of the whole Community, the commissioners undertake not to seek or accept instructions from any Member State in the discharge of their duties and their independence must be "beyond doubt".[21] 1.25

## The European Courts

Under Articles 164–188, the Court of Justice of the European Communities is established. Until 1988, it was the only Community court and it is still generally referred to as "the European Court". It has no connection with the European Court of Human Rights established under the auspices of the Council of Europe. The European Court consists of 13 judges appointed by unanimous decision of the Member States, and of six Advocates General similarly appointed. Both are appointed for six-year terms, which may be renewed. The President of the Court is elected by the judges from among their own number. Those eligible are persons satisfying the conditions necessary for appointment to the highest judicial offices in their respective countries, or who are "jurisconsults of recognised competence". Although there is no legal requirement to that effect, the judges are customarily representative of the Community's nationalities. 1.26

The Advocates General provide an impartial comment on each case, which in practice is of great influence, being delivered when the parties have closed their submissions and before the judges reach their decision. In 1992, the Court delivered 210 judgments in 345 cases,[22] taking an average of 18.8 months for Article 177 references, 25.8 months for direct 1.27

[20] Art. 158.
[21] Arts. 10 *et seq.* of the Merger Treaty; see n. 1 above.
[22] Many judgments cover several cases at once.

actions and 17.5 months for appeals. It would be impossible for all the cases emerging in a Community of 12 Member States to be considered in plenary session and, under Article 165 of the Treaty, only those where a Member State or an Institution is a party are required to be so heard if that party so requests. Important references from national courts may also be heard by the full court, but the majority are heard by chambers of three or five judges.

**1.28** Decision 88/591[23] provided for two classes of case involving direct actions to be heard by the Court of First Instance established pursuant to Article 168a of the Treaty; these are cases involving Community officials, and actions against the Community Institutions in the context of the competition policy. To that has now been added actions against the Institutions by parties other than the Member States except in matters relating to anti-dumping and subsidies.[24]

**1.29** The Court of First Instance, like the European Court, sits in chambers of three or five judges, but may also sit in plenary session. There is an appeal to the principal Court on a point of law, and the provisions regarding the appointment of judges mirror those for that Court. Article 168a allows the Council to redefine the jurisdiction of the new court from time to time, but not to include within it references under Article 177 by national courts. For simplicity, reference will be made hereafter simply to "the Court", but should be understood as including the Court of First Instance where appropriate.

**1.30** The jurisdictions of the Court are divided between the original and the consultative. In its *original jurisdiction*, the Court hears cases brought against any of the Institutions or by them, or between Member States.[25] Thus it deals with actions seeking the annulment of Commission decisions or the review of fines imposed under the competition policy, claims that legislation is invalid, and with staff cases against the Institutions. On the other side of the coin, are actions brought by the Commission against Member States (called "infringement proceedings"[26]) for declarations that they have failed to comply with Community law, for example in maintaining a restriction or in failing to implement a directive. The Court may now impose fines on Member States which do not comply with its judgments.[27] The states may also take proceedings against each other in reference to Treaty obligations.[28]

[23] [1988] O.J. L319/1 (corrected by [1989] O.J. C215/1).
[24] [1993] O.J. L144/21.
[25] Art. 173.
[26] Art. 169.
[27] Art. 171, as amended by Art. G.51 TEU.
[28] Arts. 169–179.

In its *consultative jurisdiction*, the Court gives rulings on the interpretation to be given to the treaties, Community legislation and to Community conventions. These rulings are given in the context of proceedings before national courts, and at their request, in order to enable them to reach a conclusion on issues of Community law arising before them.[29] The various judicial remedies available in Community law, both in the national courts and in the European Court, are examined in more detail in Chapter 2. A comparable, but sometimes more restricted, access to the Court may be provided for in conventions concluded by the Member States on matters of private law under Article 228 of the Treaty. 1.31

## The Court of Auditors

The use of the term "court" in the title of this institution does not mean that it is in any way a law court in which litigation is conducted. It is an audit body, composed of 12 members chosen from among persons who are or have belonged to external audit bodies or who are "especially qualified" for the office; Article 188b contains provisions similar to those which apply to the Court of Justice governing their appointment and tenure. The court is given full status as an Institution by the Maastricht Treaty.[30] 1.32

The Court of Auditors' function is to provide a complete and independent check on the financial activities of all the Community Institutions, including any organs established by them, and on the expenditure of Community money in the Member States—where it is to be accorded the collaboration of the national audit bodies. The Court's annual report, which is submitted to all the Institutions and published, contains the responses of the various administrations audited to the Court's comments on their affairs. There is an explicit obligation on the Court to assist Parliament in its duty of exercising control over the implementation of the budget, and the annual report guides the Council and Parliament in deciding on the discharge given to the Commission in respect of the implementation of each year's budget.[31] 1.33

## Other Institutions

The foregoing accounts for the principal bodies which govern the Community, but there is a constantly growing number of other organs which 1.34

[29] Art. 177.
[30] Art. 4, as amended by Art. G.6 TEU.
[31] Arts. 206a and 206b.

have a legally recognised role. They include organisations such as the European Investment Bank,[32] the European Monetary Institute,[33] the proposed European Central Bank,[34] the European Social Fund,[35] the Committee of the Regions[36] and the European Regional Development Fund.[37] These and others of the same kind have an operational function, while a further set of bodies led by the Economic and Social Committee[38] are consultative.

1.35 The Economic and Social Committee's role is to bring together representatives of all economic and social sectors to examine, at the request either of the Council or the Commission, proposals for legislation or other Community initiatives. The Committee may be consulted in any instance, and must be consulted where the Treaty article under which action is being taken so provides. Articles 49 on free movement of workers and Article 130a on the implementation of a Community environment policy are examples. A variety of more specialised consultative committees also exists, and provision for them will be found in the sectorial legislation concerned. Frequently, they have a particular role in approving delegated legislation by the Commission which, in the absence of their agreement, must be referred to the Council. Also established by the Union Treaty is, under new Article 198a of E.C. Treaty, a Committee of the Regions; it has a common organisational structure with the Economic and Social Committee.

## The Community's legal personality

1.36 Article 210 provides that the Community is to have legal personality, and Article 211 requires that it shall enjoy, in each Member State, the most extensive legal capacity accorded to legal persons by its law: the Community may acquire or dispose of all types of property, and be a party to legal proceedings. In *Maclaine Watson & Co. Ltd. v. Department of Trade and Industry*,[39] it was held that the Community was not within the scope of the general immunity from action conferred on sovereign states under the State Immunity Act 1978. The Commission represents the Community in proceedings within the Member States, and in international agreements its function is to negotiate on behalf of the Commun-

32 Art. 4b.
33 Art. 109f.
34 Art. 4a.
35 Arts. 123 *et seq.*
36 Art. 198a.
37 Art. 130c.
38 Art. 193.
39 [1990] 2 A.C. 418 (H.L.).

ity, but the agreements themselves are concluded by the Council: Article 228. Such agreements are binding upon both the Institutions of the Community and on the Member States.

## CHAPTER 2

# PRINCIPLES OF COMMUNITY LAW

## CHARACTERS AND SOURCES OF COMMUNITY LAW

### Character of Community Law

2.01 Community law is not conventional international law establishing a code of conduct between sovereign states, but a system of law which has essentially the same features as national systems, in that it creates enforceable rights and obligations which all may invoke in legal proceedings. That some matters may only be the subject of declarations by the European Court that a Member State has failed to give effect to a Community law obligation does not detract from the significance of the very large number of provisions which are as immediately binding on the individual as any provision of national law. Which Community provisions may be relied upon in national proceedings or impose obligations, and which may not, is discussed below under the heading "Direct applicability and direct effect" (paragraphs 2.13 *et seq.*)

2.02 The various Community treaties outline the principal objectives which inform the system of Community law, namely the creation of a single market for goods, services, workers and capital in which there are no impediments or discriminations related to nationality, and no internal frontiers. These concepts underlie the whole structure of the Treaty's provisions and constantly inform the way in which the Court addresses issues of interpretation of Community law coming before it.

### The sources of Community law

2.03 The principal sources of Community law are the treaties and conventions made between the Member States, legislation or other acts adopted by

Community Institutions by virtue of treaty provisions, the case law of the European Court, principles of law common to the Member States, and international agreements adhered to either by the Community itself or by the Member States generally, especially the European Human Rights Convention.[1]

The various Community treaties evidently form the basis from which all else proceeds, and they have been itemised in Chapter 1; as indicated there, reference will normally be made only to the E.C. Treaty and the treaties specifically amending it. The E.C. Treaty remains the continuing legal and policy base, and is constantly being supplemented by further treaties or conventions as new states join the Community or as new areas become the subject of Community-wide agreement; examples are the Accession treaties which have been made on the joining of each of the members since the original six and the Single European Act and the Treaty on European Union, which bring European political co-operation formally into the sphere of Community activity. **2.04**

The legislation adopted under the Treaty may take the form either of regulations or of directives. They are both published in the "L" series of the Official Journal of the European Communities. Regulations take effect from the date specified in them, or 20 days after publication, and directives upon notification to the Member States.[2] The presumption is that procedural legislation applies to proceedings pending when it enters into force but that substantive legislation does not apply to pre-existing situations.[3] **2.05**

Regulations may be made either by the Council or by the Commission, the former usually acting pursuant to a requirement in the Treaty and the latter under powers conferred by the Council. They take the form of detailed legislation which, in the majority of cases, stands on its own and needs no further legislation to make it immediately applicable. Article 189 states that regulations are to be binding in their entirety and "directly applicable" in all Member States. This means in effect that they are like legislation enacted by a national parliament and, subject to what appears below on the question of interpretation and annulment, they can be treated as such. Since matters of criminal and civil enforcement are normally left within the province of the Member States, regulations may need to be supplemented by national provisions for those purposes. **2.06**

Directives have, in principle, a different role. In Article 189 they are **2.07**

[1] Art. F TEU.

[2] Art. 191; the difference is due to the original concept of directives as affecting the States alone.

[3] Joined Cases C 121–122/91, *C.T. Control & Ors. v. Commission*: not yet reported.

described as binding on the Member States as to the result to be achieved, but leaving to the national authorities the choice of form and methods. It is therefore to be expected that implementing legislation or administrative action will follow at the national level (but see below under the heading "Direct Applicability and Direct Effect"). Although it was originally argued that the Treaty intended them normally to be treated as a blueprint for national legislation, it will be seen below that they have acquired a much wider role. Like regulations, they are either made by the Council acting under a provision in the Treaty, or by the Commission acting under powers conferred by the Council.

2.08 A third category of legal act is the decision. This is binding upon the person to whom it is addressed. Examples of decisions are those taken by the Commission addressed to undertakings under Articles 85 and 86 (competition policy), or to Member States under Article 90 (its application to public undertakings) or those which give effect to agreements with non-Community countries. Decisions which impose a pecuniary obligation, such as a fine, are enforced through the civil procedure in the relevant Member State.[4] Because they show the principles on which the competition policy is being applied, the Commission's decisions in that sphere are in practice treated as precedents and can, as such, be regarded as a subsidiary source of law.

2.09 There are other legally significant acts, for example opinions of Parliament or a declaration by it that the budget has been adopted, but these do not add to the corpus of Community law as such. Still less do the recommendations or opinions which the Commission is authorised to give, or the various programmes or resolutions adopted by the Council or Commission, which are of merely political significance. Nonetheless, it is possible that they may be taken into account by the Court as being of reference to the context of matters before it, and it has been held that a "communication" from the Commission to the Member States, though not in principle a legally binding act, was intended to have legal effect and could therefore be annulled.[5]

## Case law

2.10 The role of the European Court in interpreting the treaties and Community legislation, and in building up what might be termed the "common law" of the Community, has been very important. Strictly, there is no doctrine of binding precedent, but in practice the Court's concern for

[4] Art. 192.
[5] Case C–325/91, *France v. Commission*: not yet reported.

legal certainty has led it to follow precedent in much the same way as common law courts do. This trend has been encouraged by the fact that the Court's decisions consist of a single judgment, rather than a variety of judgments or speeches, with the result that clear judical doctrine is more easily established than it is in systems where decisions consist of a number of converging, though dissimilar, judgments.

It has been mentioned in Chapter 1 that the Court is assisted by Advocates General. In each case, the Advocate General assigned offers his reasoned submissions to the Court in addition to those of the parties, acting in the role similar to that of *amicus curiae*. These submissions may or may not be followed by the Court, but they will be regarded as authoritative where they are followed, when they often provide a helpful gloss on the rather terse language in which the Court's rulings are given. 2.11

The use of principles of law common to the Member States and of international agreements to which the States are parties, as sources of Community law, is illustrated below under the heading "Human rights".[6] 2.12

## Direct applicability and direct effect

These two concepts are frequently encountered in the Court's judgments and have sometimes caused confusion. Direct applicability is prescribed in Article 189 for regulations, though not for directives or decisions. It requires that the binding force of the regulation as it stands must be acknowledged in each Member State's legal system without the need for its individual "reception" or validation by national law. This concept is provided for in the United Kingdom by section 2 of the European Communities Act 1972, which states: 2.13

> "2.—(1) All such rights, powers, liabilities, obligations and restrictions from time to time created or arising by or under the Treaties, and all such remedies and procedures from time to time provided for by or under the Treaties, as in accordance with the Treaties are *without further enactment* to be given legal effect or used in the United Kingdom shall be recognised and available in law, and be enforced, allowed and followed accordingly; . . ." (emphasis added)

By this formula, the direct applicability of regulations is assured in United Kingdom law. Direct applicability can thus be summarised as meaning that, while on occasion supplementary measures may need to be taken with regard to directly applicable acts—as, for example, to pro- 2.14

[6] Paras. 2.40 *et seq.*

vide penalties for non-compliance—they need not, and indeed must not, be re-enacted in national legislation but must be taken as law as they are.[7]

2.15 By contrast, directives, decisions and articles of the Treaty are not designed to be directly applicable but to be the subject of national legislative action to implement them.[8] In a long sequence of judgments, however, the Court has held that both types of law may have direct effect. Direct effect means that a provision creates rights which may be relied upon by litigants in proceedings before national courts, and to which those courts must give effect. This is of course already the case with regulations which are designed to establish precise rules, but wherever the conditions requisite to enable any other text to have direct effect are present, the Court has held that it also will have such effect.

2.16 The development of this doctrine has owed much to the failure at various times either by Member States or by the Community Institutions to adopt measures in implementation of the Treaty, or of directives, by the required date. In such circumstances, the Court has held that it would be inconsistent with the binding effect of the Community legal system not to allow individuals to rely on provisions in so far as they establish clear, precise and legally complete obligations, leaving the judge no element of political evaluation or discretion beyond what is normal to the judicial process. This will not be the case where a time limit has been laid down for implementing action and it has not yet expired.

2.17 This principle may be illustrated by Case 9/70, *Grad v. Finanzamt Traunstein*.[9] In that case, the plaintiff had argued before a national court that he should not be subject to tax legislation which was inconsistent with both a decision of the Council, and a directive relating to turnover taxes; the European Court held that the provisions of both these acts could in principle be relied upon by the taxpayer in so far as they had not been incorporated into national legislation. The Court has reached similar conclusions in a wide variety of cases in relation to Treaty provisions or directives which have not been implemented correctly, or at all.

2.18 There is, however, an important restriction on this doctrine in consequence of which the possibility of unimplemented legislation being directly effective cannot be raised except against the state. This is the

[7] Case 34/73, *Variola*: [1973] E.C.R. 981; see also Case 50/76, *Amsterdam Bulb*: [1977] E.C.R. 137, [1977] 2 C.M.L.R. 218.

[8] Administrative action alone is not sufficient: see Case 169/87, *Commission v. France*: [1974] E.C.R. 359, [1974] 2 C.M.L.R. 216. See also para. 8.06 below.

[9] [1970] E.C.R. 825, [1971] C.M.L.R. 1.

so-called "vertical" direct effect which occurs when a provision is enforceable by a citizen in proceedings involving a Member State. It contrasts with the "horizontal" direct effect which a regulation has, by virtue of the fact that it is a fully developed legislative text, in establishing rights and liabilities between individuals, as well as in relation to national authorities.

Thus in Case 152/84, *Marshall v. Southampton Area Health Authority*[10] the Court held that Directive 76/207[11] could only be held to have direct effect as against the state, or a body to whom the state had delegated state functions; the health authority was a public body with such functions, and therefore fell within this definition. On the other hand, a wholly-owned state trading concern such as, at the time, Rolls-Royce or British Gas, was held not to.[12] It has been seen that in Case 9/70, *Grad v. Finanzamt Traunstein*, a decision was capable of having direct effect,[13] and in Joined Cases 21–24/72, *International Fruit Co. v. Produktschap*[14] it was held that international agreements concluded by the Community could also have such effect. In Case 80/86, *Kolpinghuis Nijmegen*[15] it was held that a directive cannot be invoked by the state against the subject.[16] 2.19

## Supremacy and effectiveness of Community law

Community law which has direct effect takes precedence over national law. An inconsistent national provision therefore is automatically overruled by a Community provision, and this is so whether the national provision is enacted before or after the Community one. Article 234 of the Treaty, however, gives precedence to prior obligations undertaken by Member States and in Case C–158/91, *Ministère Public v. Levy*[17] the Court held that if the obligations of France under an International Labour Organisation convention prior to the Treaty were inconsistent with a directive the implementation of the directive would, to that extent, have to be deferred. This rule, it may be objected, conflicts with the fundamental doctrine of United Kingdom constitutional law that no parlia- 2.20

[10] [1986] E.C.R. 723, [1986] 1 C.M.L.R. 688. See also *National Smokeless Fuels Ltd. v. IRC* [1986] S.T.C. 300.

[11] [1976] O.J. L39/40.

[12] *Doughty v. Rolls-Royce* [1988] C.M.L.R. 596 (E.A.T); *Foster v. British Gas* [1988] 2 C.M.L.R. 697 (C.A.).

[13] [1970] E.C.R. 825, [1971] C.M.L.R. 1.

[14] [1972] E.C.R. 1219, [1975] 2 C.M.L.R. 1.

[15] [1987] E.C.R. 3969, [1989] 2 C.M.L.R. 18.

[16] Followed in *Wychavon District Council v. Secretary of State for the Environment & Another: The Times*, January 7, 1994.

[17] Not yet reported.

ment can bind its successors, and that section 2 of the European Communities Act 1972, which accords precedence to Community law, may be repealed by any subsequent statute. While the possibility of the United Kingdom parliament deliberately legislating in opposition to Community law clearly exists, section 2(4) of the 1972 Act meanwhile suffices to incorporate in United Kingdom law the rule of supremacy, and it is presumed that the rule is not to be displaced except by a statute expressly repealing the section and making it clear that the obligations flowing from accession by the United Kingdom are abrogated.

**2.21** Reference to section 2(4) of the European Communities Act will not in fact disclose any mention of the doctrine of Community precedence; it refers simply to past or future enactments having effect subject to subsection (1), which provides for the rights and obligations arising under the treaties to have effect in the United Kingdom. The supremacy of Community law is one such feature, and was established by the European Court as the necessary corollary of the existence of the new legal order, which presupposes an equal and consistent application of Community law in all the Member States, and without which the Objectives of the Community cannot be achieved.

**2.22** The leading case, which has been followed on numerous occasions, is Case 6/64, *Costa v. E.N.E.L.*,[18] where it was claimed that the Italian legislature had, in the terms in which it had nationalised the electricity industry, acted in breach of the Treaty. Although the Italian government argued that such a breach could only be the subject of infringement proceedings leading to a formal declaration to that effect by the Court, it was held that as some of the provisions in question were capable of direct effect, they could override the national legislation and that, in such an eventuality, the national courts would be bound to give effect to the Community provisions, without more ado. As always in the case of references from a national court, it was a matter for that court to decide, in the light of the European Court's interpretation of the Community law, whether the national legislation in issue did indeed conflict with it.

**2.23** The rule of supremacy applies to all national law at odds with directly effective Community law, even if the national law is criminal in character. Thus in Case 8/74, *Procureur du Roi v. Dassonville*,[19] criminal proceedings against importers of Scotch whisky into Belgium, who had failed to satisfy a national requirement as to certificates of authenticity, had to be dismissed in the face of a ruling that the terms of the requirement were unnecessarily onerous, and amounted to a restriction in breach of Article

[18] [1964] E.C.R. 585, [1964] C.M.L.R. 425.
[19] [1974] E.C.R 837, [1974] 2 C.M.L.R. 436.

30. And in Joined Cases 266–267/87, *R. v. Royal Pharmaceutical Society of Great Britain, ex parte Secretary of State for Social Services*,[20] it was held that rules of a professional body, which by law controlled the exercise of a profession by its members, could amount to "measures" within the meaning of Article 30 of the Treaty.

Any national legislation which is in fact incompatible with Community law must be repealed for the sake of good legal order, even though it is automatically superseded.[21] Moreover, once an area of law has been made the subject of common Community legislation, the Member States may in general no longer legislate in respect of it, even if their legislation does not conflict with the Community provisions. Thus, in Case 60/86, *Commission v. United Kingdom*[22] the United Kingdom was held to be in breach of the Treaty in adopting national requirements on vehicle lights in addition to those laid down in the harmonisation directive. By contrast, where the Community legislation did no more than co-ordinate national social security schemes, its existence was held not to preclude Member States from adding to its provisions: see Case 21/87, *Borowitz v. Bundesversicherungsanstalt für Angestellte*.[23] 2.24

It follows from the principle of Community law supremacy that national courts are under an obligation to take steps to ensure its effectiveness in terms of the remedies and procedures open to the litigant. It is for the national legal system to determine the procedures to be used, provided that they are no less favourable to the litigant than those governing the equivalent right of action on an internal matter: see Case 158/80, *Rewe v. Hauptzollamt Kiel*.[24] The obligation to give effect to Community law in priority to national law, including Community law consisting of the directly effective provisions of a directive, was held in Case 103/88, *Costanzo*,[25] to extend to public authorities, and not to be confined to the courts. 2.25

The consequences of this approach have been spelled out in a number of detailed respects. Thus, in the absence of Community measures, national limitation periods are prima facie applicable to the enforcement of Com- 2.26

[20] [1989] E.C.R. 1295, [1989] 2 C.M.L.R. 751.

[21] Case 167/73, *Commission v. France*: [1974] E.C.R. 359, [1974] 2 C.M.L.R. 216.

[22] [1988] E.C.R. 3921, [1988] 3 C.M.L.R. 437. See also Case C–222/91, *Philip Morris Belguim SA*: not yet reported. If a directive requires one health warning on tobacco products, a Member State may not then require two.

[23] [1988] E.C.R. 3715, [1990] 1 C.M.L.R. 34. See also Cases C–222/91, *Philip Morris Belgium SA* and C–11/92, *R. v. Secretary of State for Health*: not yet reported, on the same distinction within the scope of a single directive.

[24] [1981] E.C.R. 1805, [1982] 1 C.M.L.R. 449.

[25] [1989] E.C.R. 1839, [1990] 3 C.M.L.R. 239.

munity rights, so long as it is not impossible in practice to exercise them;[26] a ruling by the European Court that a provision is contrary to Community law does not reopen the limitation period, if it had already expired when the proceedings were commenced;[27] interest and rights of counter-claim and set-off are likewise governed by the relevant national provisions;[28] remedies must be real and of value (*e.g.* not confined to nominal damages or subject to fixed limits);[29] and there must be no ouster clauses whose effect is to prevent the national court evaluating whether or not the Community right has been respected.[30]

**2.27** Regulations must be published in the Official Journal and will come into force on the date specified in them, or on the 20th day following publication.[31] In practice directives and decisions, since they have also been recognised by the Court as being capable of legal effect are also published in the Official Journal. The Court has held in Joined Cases C 121–122/91, *C.T. Control v. Commission,*[32] that procedural rules usually apply to all proceedings pending at the time they come into force but that substantive rules are usually to be interpreted as not applying to situations existing before their entry into force. Retrospection is possible only on condition that (a) the object to be achieved requires it and (b) legitimate expectations are duly respected; the instrument must recite the reasons which justify retrospective effect.[33]

## INTERPRETATION AND GENERAL PRINCIPLES

### Interpretation

**2.28** Article 190 requires that regulations, directives and decisions "shall state the reasons on which they are based". Thus, each piece of Community legislation is preceded by recitals, of the kind found in some commercial documents and in old English statutes. Their purpose is to enable the

[26] Case 45/76, *Comet v. Produktschap*: [1976] E.C.R. 2043, [1977] 1 C.M.L.R. 533.
[27] Case 33/76, *Rewe v. Landwirtschaftskammer*: [1976] E.C.R. 1989, [1977] 1 C.M.L.R. 533.
[28] Case 130/79, *Express Dairy v. IBAP*: [1980] E.C.R. 1887, [1981] 1 C.M.L.R. 451, and Case 177/78, *Pigs and Bacon Commission v. McCarren*: [1979] E.C.R. 2161, [1979] 3 C.M.L.R. 389.
[29] Case 14/83, *von Colson v. Land Nordrhein-Westfalen*: [1984] E.C.R. 1891, [1986] 2 C.M.L.R. 430; Case C–271/91, *Marshall v. Southampton Area Health Authority (No. 2)*: [1993] 3 C.M.L.R. 293.
[30] Case 222/84, *Johnston v. Chief Constable of the RUC*: [1986] E.C.R. 1651, [1986] 3 C.M.L.R. 240; Case C–97/91, *Borelli v. Commission*: not yet reported.
[31] Art. 191(2).
[32] Not yet reported.
[33] Joined Cases C 260–261/91, *Diversinte SA*: not yet reported.

user to construe the text in accordance with the legislator's intentions. This approach to interpretation, sometimes referred to as the "teleological approach", is designed to be flexible and purpose-orientated, and generally avoids literal analysis. The context of the legislation and its purpose must be considered, and the meaning given to it which is in line with them.[34] This is limited, however, by the need to ensure legal certainty: see, for example, Case 122/80, *Analog Devices*,[35] where the Court would not adapt the interpretation of the Common Customs Tariff to take account of technological change, but left it to legislative action to provide for unforeseen cases, citing the need to ensure legal certainty for traders.

Following these principles through into the construction of United Kingdom legislation section 2(4) of the European Communities Act 1972 requires United Kingdom statutes to be so interpreted as to be consonant with governing Community legislation. The European Court has, moreover, now held in Case C–106/89, *Marleasing*,[36] that national legislation should be interpreted in the light of the wording and purpose of a directive, even if the national law ante-dates the Community legislation and even though the state was not a party to the action (so that the traditional doctrine of vertical direct effect did not come into play). The implications of this decision for the development of a horizontal direct effect, *i.e.* in cases where the state is not a party to the proceedings, have yet to be fully worked out. 2.29

The House of Lords, in *Duke v. GEC Reliance*,[37] has held that national legislation pre-dating a directive (and therefore not presumed to be passed to give effect to it), should not be strained so as to be consistent with the directive, and that the obvious meaning should be adopted; in that case, the result was that, since the defendant was not a public authority, the directive (though capable of direct effect) could not be relied upon and the inconsistent national law prevailed. In *Pickstone v. Freemans plc*,[38] however, the House construed statutory provisions purposively in order to give effect to the Community law they were intended to implement; and the court was willing, to achieve this objective, to take into account the statement in parliament of the minister who had moved the regulations inserting the provisions in the statute concerned. 2.30

[34] Case 292/82, *Merck v. Hauptzollamt Hamburg-Jonas*: [1983] E.C.R. 3781.
[35] [1981] E.C.R. 2781.
[36] [1990] I E.C.R. 3313, [1992] 1 C.M.L.R. 305.
[37] [1988] 2 W.L.R. 359.
[38] [1988] 3 W.L.R. 265.

## Languages

2.31 In the context of a Community with 12 Member States, with a rather greater number of legal systems, and in the light of the Community's overall objectives, it is evident that there is a need to ensure that the law is interpreted uniformly throughout. This task is undertaken by the European Court through the mechanism of preliminary rulings given in response to requests by national courts under Article 177 of the Treaty. This jurisdiction ensures that national litigants can always seek to have questions of Community law resolved outside the sometimes distorting confines of the national legal system. In Directive 77/388,[39] on the harmonisation of value added tax, the expression "consideration" is used, and the Court has held in Case 102/86, *Apple and Pear Development Council v. Customs and Excise,*[40] that, even though it is well known in English law, its use in the directive requires that its interpretation should be established on a Community basis.

2.32 Community legislation is published in the nine official working languages in the Official Journal of the European Communities. All texts are equally authentic, and in the event of divergence between them (or, strictly speaking, in every case), each must be interpreted in the light of all the others. Thus, in Case 122/87, *Commission v. Italy,*[41] Italy had implemented Directive 77/388[42] on value added tax by exempting veterinary services pursuant to a provision exempting the services provided by "medical and paramedical professions as defined by the Member State". This could arguably have included the case of veterinary services; every language version except the English and Italian, however, stated that the services in question were those provided "to persons", making the construction contended for by Italy implausible, and the Court therefore found against Italy.[43] Applying United Kingdom legislation implementing the same Directive, the Court of Appeal has referred to the French text in order to resolve an ambiguity in the English version: see *Bell Concord Educational Trust v. Customs and Excise.*[44]

## Passing on

2.33 In the sphere of taxation (which includes customs duties and other levies), the Court has evolved a doctrine specifically to deal with claims

[39] [1977] O.J. L145/1, [1978] 1 *Commercial Laws of Europe* 115.
[40] [1988] E.C.R. 1443, [1988] 2 C.M.L.R. 394.
[41] [1988] E.C.R. 2685, [1989] 3 C.M.L.R. 844.
[42] [1977] O.J. L145/1, [1978] 1 *Commercial Laws of Europe* 115.
[43] See, however, Case C–34/92, *Grusa Fleisch*: not yet reported, for a case where the Court accepted that the German version could validly differ from the others.
[44] [1987] 3 C.M.L.R. 424.

for repayment of dues levied contrary to Community law in circumstances where a ruling to that effect may serve only to provide the taxpayer with a windfall. The principle, known as "passing on", provides that where the burden of a tax or levy which has been charged illegally has been passed on to the taxpayer's customers, Member States may deny him the right to repayment, notwithstanding a declaration by the European Court of its unlawfulness. This exception may not, however, be hedged about with rules of procedure or evidence which make it virtually impossible for the taxpayer to show that the charge was not passed on, even if the same rules apply to purely national claims: see Case 199/82, *San Giorgio*.[45] The relevant United Kingdom provision in relation to value-added tax is now contained in section 24 of the Finance Act 1989.

## Nationality discrimination

The fundamental prohibition of discrimination on grounds of nationality, enunciated in Article 7 of the Treaty, applies to all areas of Community law. Its scope may be illustrated by Case 186/87, *Cowan v. French Treasury*,[46] where a British tourist, who had been mugged in Paris, was denied a payment in respect of his injuries by the French Criminal Injuries Compensation Board on the ground that he was neither a French national nor from a State which had a reciprocal arrangement with France in the matter. It was held that the tourist must be considered for compensation on the same basis as a French national, because he was entitled under Community law to go to another Member State to receive the (tourist) services supplied there.[47] The corollary of that entitlement was the right to protection against the risk of assault, and to compensation in default, on the basis provided by the law of the State where the services were rendered. 2.34

In general, it may be said that any nationality discrimination will be contrary to Community law unless a specific authorisation for it can be found, as where Article 48(4) of the Treaty excludes employment in the public service from the provisions on free movement of workers. Discrimination which is the result of Community legislation may render the legislation liable to annulment, as in Case 305/85, *United Kingdom v. Commission*,[48] where the Court declared invalid regulations on the calcu- 2.35

[45] [1983] E.C.R. 3595, [1985] 2 C.M.L.R. 658.
[46] [1989] E.C.R. 195, [1990] 2 C.M.L.R. 613.
[47] Joined Cases 286/82 & 26/83, *Luisi and Carbone v. Ministero del Tesoro*: [1984] E.C.R. 377, [1985] 3 C.M.L.R. 52.
[48] [1988] E.C.R. 467, [1988] 2 C.M.L.R. 169.

lation of sheep premiums which uniquely prejudiced United Kingdom producers, or in Case C–279/89, *Commission v. United Kingdom*,[49] which concerned a requirement that a certain proportion of a British ship's crew should reside ashore in the United Kingdom.

## Prospective overruling

**2.36** The Court has recognised that, both in the tax sphere and elsewhere, the effect of declaring a measure to be contrary to Community law may be to upset retrospectively a large number of transactions which the parties to them had good reason to suppose were lawful. Article 174 states that if a regulation is annulled, the Court may decide which elements of it are nonetheless to be regarded as definitive. It has been held that this enables the Court to overrule the disputed act, while maintaining its effect in relation to past transactions. In the wider context of findings pursuant to an Article 177 reference that a national measure is unlawful, the decision may have effect only for the future, or in cases where a claim had already been brought at the date of the ruling.[50] If such a limitation is to be adopted, however, it must be provided by the Court in its ruling on the case, and may not be sought subsequently.[51]

## Legitimate expectations

**2.37** A doctrine similar to that known in English administrative law is recognised by the European Court. In Case 120/86, *Mulder v. Minister van Landbouw*,[52] the plaintiff had gone out of milk production for a limited period pursuant to a Community scheme under which he had received compensation for doing so. A subsequent regulation introducing milk quotas failed to make any provision for persons in his position, as a result of which, after the period for which he had agreed to leave production had expired, he was unable to obtain any quota allocation at all, and was forced out of the business permanently.

**2.38** The Court held that the farmer had had a legitimate expectation that at the end of the period during which he had ceased production at the Community's instance, he would be in a position no less favourable than that he would have enjoyed had he not acceded to the scheme. The quota

[49] [1993] 1 C.M.L.R. 564.
[50] Case 24/86, *Blaizot v. University of Liège*: [1988] E.C.R. 379, [1989] 1 C.M.L.R. 57; Case C–163/90, *Legros*: not yet reported.
[51] Case 24/86, see above.
[52] [1988] E.C.R. 2321, [1989] 2 C.M.L.R. 1.

regulation was therefore held *pro tanto* invalid. But in Joined Cases C 143/88 & 92/89, *Zuckerfabrik*,[53] the Court held that sugar producers who were aware before the end of a marketing season that an equalisation was likely to be introduced in respect of it had no legitimate expectation that the legislation adopted after the end of that period would not be effectively retrospective to it.

A number of recent decisions suggest that the Court will be reluctant to extend this doctrine very far. Thus in Joined Cases C 258–259/90, *Pesquerias v. Commission*[54] the Court held that a trader had no legitimate expectation that legislation would not be changed. And in Joined Cases C 31–44/91, *Lageder & Ors*,[55] it was held that a mistaken interpretation of E.C. legislation by national authorities could not give rise to a legitimate expectation that it would be applied consistently with that interpretation; nor in Joined Cases C 13–16/92, *Driessen en Zonen V.o.f.*,[56] was there a legitimate expectation that proposed legislation would be enacted. **2.39**

## Proportionality

The doctrine of proportionality is an example of the non-literal and purpose-orientated way in which Community law is interpreted. It requires that an action which is brought within the scope of a legal concept should be proportionate to its avowed objective. Frequent illustrations of this principle at work may be seem in the context of Articles 30 and 36. Article 30 prohibits, in trade between Member States, "quantitative restrictions" or measures having equivalent effect, but Article 36 allows exceptions from this rule where the restriction is, *inter alia*, justified on grounds of public health and is not a disguised restriction on trade. **2.40**

Restrictions prima facie within Article 30 are often encountered in the absence of Community-wide health standards. In Case 216/84, *Commission v. France*,[57] France had imposed an absolute ban on the import and sale of milk substitute products on the ground that they were less healthy than real milk products, and that consumer protection justified their prohibition. The Court held that, although consumer protection was a proper objective for a Member State to pursue for the purpose of the exceptions in Article 36, it could adequately be attained by means of less drastic measures, such as sufficient labelling of products, leaving it open **2.41**

[53] [1991] I E.C.R. 415, [1993] 3 C.M.L.R. 1.
[54] Not yet reported.
[55] Not yet reported.
[56] [1994] 2 C.M.L.R. 141.
[57] [1988] E.C.R. 793.

to consumers to make an informed choice. The absolute ban was out of proportion to the permitted objective, and declared illegal. Likewise, in Case 319/90, *Otto Pressler,*[58] it was held that excessively and unreasonably tight time limits imposed in a Commission regulation were invalid.

## Human Rights

2.42 Although the European Convention for the Protection of Human Rights is not a Community treaty (it is a convention of the Council of Europe), it is regarded by the Court as important persuasive authority on the general principles of law which are accepted by all the Member States, and thus as a source of Community law itself.[59] In a number of decisions this Convention has been influential, as has the general adherence of Member States' legal systems to particular principles of law. Thus in Case 374/87, *Orkem* and Case 27/88, *Solvay*[60] the Court annulled Commission decisions, requiring undertakings to answer questions in the course of investigation into anti-competitive practices, on the ground that they sought to induce answers as to the intention of certain activities which would have been self-incriminatory. The Court has also recognised that rights to privacy and to medical secrecy are fundamental rights protected by Community law.[61]

2.43 In Case 222/84, *Johnston v. Royal Ulster Constabulary,*[62] the plaintiff was denied continued full-time employment as a police reservist in consequence of a policy decision that women should not carry firearms. This decision was protected from challenge on the ground of sex discrimination by a provision in the Sex Discrimination (Northern Ireland) Order[63] covering any act done for the purpose of safeguarding national security, and providing that a certificate from the Secretary of State that an act was so done should be conclusive of the fact. Relying on the general principle stated in Articles 6 and 13 of the Convention, that the rule of law requires that all persons must be entitled to test the lawfulness of any action in a competent court, the European Court went on to hold that the provisions of the relevant directive[64] should be interpreted in the light of those principles, and that the purported ouster of judicial control was contrary to Community law.[65]

[58] Not yet reported.
[59] See also now Art. F TEU.
[60] Case 374/87: [1989] E.C.R. 3283, [1991] 4 C.M.L.R. 502; Case 27/88: [1989] E.C.R. 3355, [1991] 4 C.M.L.R. 502.
[61] Case C–62/90, *Commission v. Germany*: not yet reported.
[62] [1986] E.C.R. 1651, [1986] 3 C.M.L.R. 240.
[63] S.I. 1976 No. 1042 (N.I. 15).
[64] Directive 76/207, [1976] O.J. L39/40.
[65] See also Case C–97/91, *Borelli v. Commission*: not yet reported.

### ..jeure

2.44 This concept, little known in English law outside the commercial sphere, is widely used in Community legislation but its precise meaning may differ according to the context. Two recent cases illustrate this. In Case C–50/92, *Mölkerei-Zentrale v. BLM*[66] the Court repeated the definition of *force majeure* as unusual or unforseeable circumstances beyond a trader's control, the consequences of which could not have been avoided even if all due care had been exercised, and held that unexpected delay by the administration of a Member State could qualify. But in Case C–124/92, *An Bord Bainne v. IBAP*[67] the Court employed a slightly different formulation, referring to abnormal and unforeseeable circumstances outside the trader's control, whose consequences—even with the exercise of all due care—could not be avoided except at the cost of excessive sacrifice; in that case, the Court held that a last minute unforseen change in the legislation of a third country to which an intervention export had been arranged, making it impossible for the trader to complete the transaction for which it had given a deposit to the authorities, was not *force majeure*.

## ENFORCEMENT OF COMMUNITY LAW

### Enforcement in the English courts

2.45 It has already been emphasised that it is an essential characteristic of Community law that directly effective provisions may be relied upon in national courts in the same way as national statutes can. The corollary of this, and of the facility for any court or tribunal to make a reference to the European Court, is that all courts have a duty to apply Community law themselves, even if it means recognising that a provision of national law is invalid—and there must be no rule or practice reserving such a decision to a particular court or courts.[68]

2.46 In principle, therefore, issues of Community law may be raised in the course of any proceedings before an English court or tribunal, whether they involve the state or are between private parties. Community law creates no new remedies for use in national courts, and no special procedural steps are necessary in order to raise a Community law matter. The normal English law remedies are available, though to a limited extent they may be modified by substantive Community law, *e.g.* by the

[66] Not yet reported.
[67] Not yet reported.
[68] Case 106/77, *Simmenthal*: [1978] E.C.R. 629, [1978] 3 C.M.L.R. 263.

rule against ouster provisions discussed under the previous heading, or the Court's doctrine of "passing on" in claims for recovery of sums wrongfully charged by the state. Attention may be drawn, however, to two classes of remedy, and their interaction with Community rights.

*(i) Judicial review*

2.47 Judicial review will be granted for any breach by a public authority of Community law as for national law.[69] In *R. v. Inland Revenue Commissioners, ex parte Imperial Chemical Industries,*[70] the plaintiff successfully sought judicial review of an arrangement between the Inland Revenue and one of its competitors, in relation to the taxation of oil exploration activities, on the ground that the arrangement was unduly favourable and amounted to an illegal state aid.

*(ii) English Torts*

2.48 Actions in tort based upon or related to a breach of Community law may also be available, and two possibilities in particular exist for proceedings in tort: for the tort of breach of statutory duty (to give effect to Community law under section 2 of the European Communities Act 1972, or treating a duty imposed by Community legislation as analogous to one imposed by a United Kingdom statute), or for the little-used tort of misfeasance in a public office.

2.49 The House of Lords has recognised that a contravention of Article 86 (on abuse of a dominant position in the market) may give rise to a cause of action for breach of statutory duty, and to a right to damages and/or an injunction; see *Garden Cottage Foods v. Milk Marketing Board.*[71] Likewise, it was held in *Cutsforth v. Mansfield Inns Ltd.*[72] that an injunction could be obtained to restrain a breach of Article 85. The state will be a prospective defendant where national legislation is passed or government action is taken in contravention of Community law. In *An Bord Bainne v. Milk Marketing Board,*[73] the Court of Appeal held that the Crown was not liable in damages for a breach of Community law occasioned by legislative or quasi-legislative acts, or administrative action involving the exercise of discretion.

2.50 The situation where the private law regime of damages may also apply to government action, however, was illustrated in *Bourgoin v. Ministry of*

[69] *Bourgoin v. Ministry of Agriculture* [1985] 3 W.L.R. 1027 (C.A.).
[70] [1987] 1 C.M.L.R. 72.
[71] [1984] A.C. 130.
[72] [1986] 1 All E.R. 577.
[73] [1984] 2 C.M.L.R. 584 (C.A.).

*Agriculture*. In that case, the Minister of Agriculture withdrew a general import licence permitting the importation of turkeys just before the 1981 Christmas season on the pretext of stopping the spread of Newcastle disease. The European Court subsequently held that the ban was more severe than was genuinely necessary to check the disease and was contrary to Article 30. Although the judgment was delivered in July 1982, the Minister did not reissue the licence until November 1982, too late for the 1982 Christmas season's business.

The plaintiffs, French turkey producers, and importers in the United Kingdom, sought damages for the tort of misfeasance in a public office, alleging that the Minister's act was knowingly illegal and calculated to inflict economic damage on them by giving an unfair advantage at a crucial time to United Kingdom producers. On trial of the preliminary question of law, the Court of Appeal held that if the allegations were proved, then liability in damages would result, even though the acts complained of were public law governmental actions in the classic sense of the term. But it should be noted that for such liability to exist, there will need to have been a deliberate and conscious violation of Community law calculated to cause loss or damage. 2.51

A further limitation on state liability in national actions for damages was laid down by the Court in Joined Cases 106–127/87, *Asteris v. Hellenic Republic*.[74] The plaintiffs were producers of tomato concentrate who claimed to have suffered loss as a result of the annulment of Regulation 1615/83[75] by the Court,[76] and had failed in an action against the Commission[77] to recover damages under Article 215 of the Treaty (see below). The Court held that actions against national authorities for damages in respect of acts done in the application of Community law could be maintained without conflict with Community law, but could not be brought on the same grounds as an action brought against the Community itself under Article 215 of the Treaty, which the European Court alone would have jurisdiction to entertain. 2.52

*(iii) Community Tort*

A development of the widest importance in the enforcement of Community law appears to have taken place in the ruling of the Court in Joined Cases C 6 & 9/90, *Francovich v. Italy*.[78] There, the plaintiff in Italian 2.53

[74] [1988] E.C.R. 5515, [1990] 1 C.M.L.R. 575.
[75] [1983] O.J. L159/48.
[76] Case 192/83, *Greece v. Commission*: [1985] E.C.R. 2791.
[77] Joined Cases 194–206/83, *Asteris v. Commission*: [1985] E.C.R. 2851.
[78] [1991] I E.C.R. 5357, [1993] 2 C.M.L.R. 66.

proceedings was an employee whose employers had become insolvent, in consequence of which he had been unable to enforce a judgment against them for arrears of wages. He then sued the Italian State for the money on the ground that his inability to recover it stemmed from the latter's failure to implement Directive 80/987 on the protection of employees' rights in the event of their employer's insolvency,[79] a matter which had already been the subject of an adverse finding by the European Court in Case C–22/87, *Commission v. Italy.*

2.54 The Court held (a) that most, but not all, of the relevant provisions of the directive were directly applicable but that (b) Community law, especially in such a case, laid down the principle under which a Member State was bound to compensate an individual for damage caused to him by infringements of Community law imputable to that State. The right of action thus established is subject to three conditions: first, that the result intended by the directive involved the attribution of rights attaching to individuals; secondly, that the subject matter of those rights could be identified by reference to the directive; and thirdly that there should be a causal link between the infringement of its obligations by the Member State and the loss suffered by the plaintiff.

2.55 Where those conditions are satisfied the entitlement of individuals to compensation is based directly upon Community law, though national procedures must be used to enforce it. As to that, the substantive and formal conditions laid down by national law must not be less favourable in regard to the application of such a remedy than they are for similar claims of an internal nature and they must, in any event, not make it excessively difficult or virtually impossible to obtain the compensation.

## Enforcement and penal sanctions

2.56 With few exceptions (principally in relation to the competition policy),[80] Community law does not prescribe criminal-type sanctions for its non-observance. Article 5 requires Member States to "take all appropriate measures, whether general or particular, to ensure fulfilment of the obligations arising out of this Treaty. . ." It is therefore for national legislation to give criminal "teeth" to Community provisions, and this is provided for on a general basis by section 2 of the European Communities Act 1972 which permits ministers to make delegated legislation to give

[79] [1980] O.J. L283/23.

[80] See also Case C–240/90, *Germany v. Commission* for penalties imposed under Article 40 in relation to the CAP.

effect to Community obligations generally. This includes a power to create criminal offences, as well as a general power to enact implementing or amending legislation.

This provision may be used where the enactment of specific primary legislation to implement a Community measure would be unduly cumbersome; but does not of course preclude such legislation, which may indeed be necessitated by the restrictions in Schedule 2 on the section 2 powers. The restrictions involve a prohibition on (a) imposing or increasing taxation, (b) retrospective legislation, (c) subdelegation, *i.e.* authorising another minister or body to enact delegated legislation, and (d) creating new criminal offences punishable by more than two years' imprisonment. It should be noted, however, that the Court has held in Case 63/83, *R. v. Kirk*,[81] that Community legislation entailing a retrospective criminal liability is contrary to the general principles of Community law. National criminal provisions undergirding such legislation are therefore likely themselves to be unenforceable. **2.57**

## Proceedings before the European Court

The European Court's jurisdictions, which are both original and consultative, fall under five distinct headings. First, in relation to the enforcement of Treaty obligations by the Commission or by Member States (Articles 169 and 170), secondly, for annulment of a Community act (Article 173), thirdly, for failure by the Commission or the Council to adopt a measure required by Community law (Article 175), fourthly, in relation to the non-contractual liability of the Institutions (Articles 178 and 215) and, fifthly, for preliminary rulings on questions of Community law at the instance of national courts (Article 177). The position of the Court of First Instance is referred to in Chapter 1. **2.58**

In its *original jurisdiction*, the Court hears cases brought against any of the Institutions or by them, or between Member States. Thus it deals with actions seeking the annulment of Commission decisions or the review of fines imposed under the competition policy, claims that legislation is invalid, and with staff cases against the Institutions. On the other side of the coin are actions brought by the Commission against Member States (called "infringement proceedings") for declarations that they have failed to comply with Community law, for example in maintaining a restriction, or in failing to implement a directive. Member States may also **2.59**

[81] [1984] E.C.R. 2689, [1984] 3 C.M.L.R. 522. In Case 68/88, *Commission v. Hellenic Republic*: [1989] E.C.R. 2965, [1991] 1 C.M.L.R. 31, Greece was held to be in breach of Article 5 for not having prosecuted frauds against Community agricultural levies.

take proceedings against each other in reference to Treaty obligations.[82]

2.60 Parties other than Member States and Community Institutions have very limited rights before the Court in its original jurisdiction. First, an individual or a corporation may bring proceedings under Article 173 against the Commission or the Council claiming that a decision of direct concern to them (or a regulation if it satisfies the same condition) should be annulled.[83] Challenges under this heading are often attempted in connection with anti-dumping regulations, but are seldom successful: for example, in Case 260/85, *Tokyo Electric Company Ltd. v. Council*,[84] a Japanese company sought the annulment of such a regulation which, it claimed, discriminated in favour of a competitor who was not affected by it, but it was held that, even if this could be shown to be the case, it would not be a ground for annulment of legislation validly adopted in so far as the plaintiff was concerned. No compensation may be awarded under Article 173, even if the act is annulled,[85] and when the time for challenging a decision under the article has expired it can no longer be called in question.[86] If an act other than a decision or regulation purports to produce legal effects, it too may be the subject of proceedings under Article 173.[87]

2.61 The action must be brought within two months of publication or notification and may only succeed on grounds of (a) lack of competence; (b) infringement of an essential procedural requirement; (c) infringement of the Treaty or any rule of law relating to its application, or (d) misuse of powers. In Case 294/83, *Parti Ecologiste 'Les Verts' v. European Parliament*,[88] the Court held that action under Article 173 could also be taken for annulment of acts of the Parliament, even though Parliament is not mentioned as a possible defendant in the article. In Joined Cases C 181 & 248/91, *Parliament v. Council*,[89] the Court declined to extend the scope of the article to collective action taken by the Member States, even though the machinery of the Community institutions had been used for the purpose.

2.62 There is no right on the part of an individual to challenge the validity of

[82] Arts. 169–179.

[83] See Joined Cases 16–17/62, *Confédération Nationale des Fruits et Légumes v. Council*: [1962] E.C.R. 471, [1963] C.M.L.R. 160. But the European Parliament may not do so: Case 302/87, *Parliament v. Council*: [1988] E.C.R. 5615.

[84] [1988] E.C.R. 5855, [1989] 1 C.M.L.R. 169.

[85] Nor the basis for compensation: Case C–199/91, *Foyer Culturel de Sart-Tilman v. Commission*: not yet reported.

[86] Case C–183/91, *Commission v. Hellenic Republic*: not yet reported.

[87] Case C–325/91, *French Republic v. Commission*: not yet reported.

[88] [1986] E.C.R. 1339, [1987] 2 C.M.L.R. 343.

[89] Not yet reported.

general legislation by direct action under Article 173, and in any proceedings under that article an individual plaintiff must show that the decision or regulation is "of direct and individual concern" to him.[90] Article 184 by contrast entitles any party to plead the general invalidity of a regulation[91] in proceedings before the Court, notwithstanding the two-month time limit under Article 173 having elapsed, by invoking any of the four grounds mentioned in that article. There is, therefore, in effect a separate and much wider ground of challenge to Community legislation always open to the litigant in any proceedings before the European Court, either in its original jurisdiction or on a reference for a preliminary ruling.

Under Article 175, there is a right for anyone to take action against an Institution for failure, contrary to the Treaty, to address to that person "any act other than a recommendation or an opinion". This could be the case for example in connection with the Commission's powers in relation to the competition policy, or to approve a project for Community aid. No compensation may be ordered in the context of proceedings under Article 175.[92] **2.63**

Articles 178 and 215(2) confer jurisdiction on the Court to deal with actions against the Community for non-contractual liability for damage caused by the Institutions or their servants "in accordance with the general principles common to the laws of the Member States". This jurisdiction may not be replicated at the national level by means of actions against national authorities in national courts.[93] Contractual liability is governed by the proper law of the contract, and is within the jurisdiction of the appropriate national court. Exceptionally, where the Community legislature has been held to have manifestly and gravely disregarded the limits of its discretionary power, damages may be awarded to a person prejudiced thereby.[94] **2.64**

A little-used jurisdiction under Article 228 permits the Council, the Commission or a Member State to seek a ruling from the Court on the compatibility with the Treaty of a proposed agreement between the Community and third countries or international organisations.[95] **2.65**

[90] See, *e.g.* Case 25/62, *Plaumann v. Commission*: [1963] E.C.R. 95, [1964] C.M.L.R. 29.

[91] Or certain other legal acts: see Case 92/78, *Simmenthal v. Commission*: [1978] E.C.R. 1129, [1980] 1 C.M.L.R. 25.

[92] Case C–25/91, *Pesqueras Echebastar SA v. Commission*: not yet reported.

[93] Cases 106–120/87, *Asteris v. Greece*: [1988] E.C.R. 5515, [1990] 1 C.M.L.R. 575, but see also Case 187/91, *Belgium v. Société Coopérative Beloro*: not yet reported, allowing a distinct national right of action for national errors.

[94] Joined Cases C 104/89 & 37/90, *Mulder & Ors. v. Council and Commission*: [1992] I E.C.R. 3062.

[95] Recent examples are the Court's opinions on the European Economic Area Agreements.

2.66 The Court's *consultative jurisdiction* is of the widest practical importance from the point of view of the individual affected by Community law. It arises under Article 177, and exists to enable the uniform application of Community law by providing national courts with the means of clarifying points which emerge in proceedings before them in relation to: (a) the interpretation of the treaties; (b) the validity and interpretation of acts of the institutions (such as legislation); and (c) the interpretation of the statutes of bodies established by the Council. In a number of other cases, a similar jurisdiction has been conferred on the Court, for example by the 1968 Civil and Commercial Judgments Convention and by the European Patent Convention.

2.67 Proceedings involving the European Court, whether in its original jurisdiction or on a reference, are governed by the Court's consolidated rules of procedure.[96] They contain an outline of the stages of the procedure, time limits for service of documents and details of parties to be served, provisions with regard to witnesses and taking evidence on commission, interim measures, costs and enforcement. In general it may be said that much more emphasis is placed upon the written stage than in the United Kingdom, and that it is at this stage that the main presentation of the case normally occurs.

2.68 The rules provide a wide degree of privilege for the papers and persons of lawyers acting in proceedings. The Institutions and the Member States may be represented by an "agent" appointed for the purpose (in practice usually a legally-qualified person) and other parties by a lawyer admitted to practise before the courts of a Member State. In so far as England and Wales are concerned, this means a barrister, or a solicitor if he could have appeared in the national proceedings or there are no national proceedings involved.

## References under Article 177

2.69 Preliminary rulings by the European Court *may* be sought by "any court or tribunal" (which does not include an arbitrator or the head of a tax administration)[97] in a Member State which considers a reference necessary to enable it to give judgment. A reference *must* be made by any court or tribunal against whose decisions there is no judicial remedy, *i.e.* in most cases in the United Kingdom, the House of Lords, but the Court

[96] [1991] O.J. L176/7; corrected at [1992] O.J. L383/117.

[97] Case 102/81, *Nordsee v. Reederei Mond*: [1982] E.C.R. 1095; Case C–24/92, *Corbiau*: not yet reported.

of Appeal if leave to appeal to the House of Lords is refused.[98] A ruling may cover any issue of Community law which the Court judges relevant, even if it has not been raised by the national court,[99] but the Court will not rule on hypothetical questions.[1]

Weighing up whether the expense and delay involved in seeking a preliminary ruling would be justified may often be difficult, especially where relevant issues of fact are to be contested. Save where the reference is obligatory, this is a matter for the national court's discretion: see Joined Cases 98, 162 & 258/85, *Bertini.*[2] Guidance on the exercise of this discretion has been given by the Court of Appeal in *H. P. Bulmer Ltd. v. J. Bollinger SA,*[3] where the principles to be followed were laid down. They include that no reference should normally be made unless the facts have been ascertained or agreed, or if the point raised is clear and free from doubt, whether or not the European Court has previously ruled on it. It has subsequently been held, however, that courts should be hesitant in reaching the conclusion that there is no doubt[4] and that, in an appropriate case, magistrates may refer at the close of the prosecution case, if a submission of no case to answer based on an issue of Community law necessitates it.[5] 2.70

Ultimately, the European Court has jurisdiction to decide when, as a matter of overriding Community law, a reference under Article 177 should be made, and it has given guidance itself from time to time emphasising the wide measure of freedom which national courts have to make use of the procedure. In Case 283/81, *CILFIT v. Ministry of Health,*[6] the Court has, in the context of the situation in which reference is prima facie obligatory (because proceedings are before a court of final resort), indicated those cases in which a reference is not called for: where the Community issue is irrelevant; where it has already been the subject of a ruling, and where there is no room for reasonable doubt about its meaning—the so-called doctrine of the *acte clair*. It should be noted, however, that only the European Court may declare a Community act invalid: see Case 314/85, *Foto-Frost v. Hauptzollamt Lübeck-Ost.*[7] 2.71

The provisions of R.S.C. Order 114 deal with references from the High Court and the Court of Appeal to the European Court, while references 2.72

[98] *Hagen v. Fratelli*: [1980] C.M.L.R. 253.
[99] Case C–280/91, *Finanzamt Kassel v. Viessmann KG*: [1993] 3 C.M.L.R. 153.
[1] Case C–83/91, *Meilicke v. F. A. Meyer AG*: [1992] I E.C.R. 4871.
[2] [1986] E.C.R. 1893, [1987] 1 C.M.L.R. 774.
[3] [1974] Ch. 401.
[4] *R. v. Pharmaceutical Society of Great Britain* [1987] 2 C.M.L.R. 769.
[5] *R. v. Plymouth Justices, ex parte Rogers* [1982] Q.B. 863.
[6] [1982] E.C.R. 3415, [1983] 1 C.M.L.R. 472.
[7] [1987] E.C.R. 4199, [1988] 3 C.M.L.R. 57.

from other courts or tribunals will be governed in procedural terms by such courts' own rules. While a reference is made by the national court or tribunal (not by the parties) and is in its discretion, it will be normal for the terms of the reference to be settled by agreement between counsel and the court. No reference can be made after a court has given judgment, even though the order of the court has not yet been drawn up, nor if the possibility of an appeal no longer exists.[8] The effect of a reference is to stay the national proceedings, unless the court otherwise orders.[9]

## Interim Relief

2.73 In principle, a challenge to national legislation on the ground of incompatibility with Community law does not itself suspend the appplication of the national law while the reference under Article 177 proceeds.[10] Thus, in *Portsmouth City Council v. Richards* an injunction restraining breaches of the criminal law was upheld, even though a reference to the European Court was pending to test the legality of the offence provisions. But it was held in Case C–213/89, *R. v. Secretary of State for Transport, ex parte Factortame Ltd.*[11] that national courts must be able to provide interim relief against the enforcement of provisions about which there is serious doubt concerning their compatibility with Community law where it can be shown that their enforcement will lead to serious and irreparable damage. The same is true if there are serious doubts as to the legality of Community legislation itself, and the matter has to be referred to the European Court.[12]

8 *Magnavision v. General Optical Council* [1987] C.M.L.R. 262.

9 R.S.C. Ord. 114, r. 4.

10 *R. v. Secretary of State for Transport, ex parte Factortame* [1990] 2 A.C. 85, and [1991] 1 A.C. 603.

11 [1990] I E.C.R. 2433, [1990] 3 C.M.L.R. 1.

12 Joined Cases C 143/88 & 92/89, *Zuckerfabrik*: [1991] I E.C.R. 415, [1993] 3 C.M.L.R. 1.

CHAPTER 3

# FREE MOVEMENT OF GOODS WITHIN THE COMMUNITY

## Objectives

Article 2 of the Treaty states briefly the objectives of the Community, which are set out at greater length in the preamble to the Treaty, and specifies two courses of action for the attainment of these objectives: by establishing a common market and by progressively approximating the economic policies of Member States. It is clear that the Treaty considers the establishment of the Common Market as the more urgent of the two, while in Case 167/73, *Commission v. France*[1] the Court held that the establishment of the Common Market refers to all the economic activities of the Community, and that the basis of the Common Market was the free movement of goods, persons, services and capital. **3.01**

Article 3 states that for the purposes set out in Article 2 the activities of the Community shall include, *inter alia,* the elimination as between Member States of customs duties and of quantitative restrictions on the import and export of goods, and of all other measures having equivalent effect; and the establishment of a common customs tariff and of a common commercial policy towards third countries (see Chapters 4 and 5). It is thus apparent that the free movement of goods is the basic part of a real common market. The part of the Treaty dealing with free movement of goods contains detailed and specific rules, while other parts often go no further than to supply guidelines. **3.02**

The two chapters of the Treaty dealing with free movement of goods are headed "Customs Union" and "Elimination of Quantitative Restrictions Between Member States". Article 9 provides that the Community shall **3.03**

[1] [1974] E.C.R. 359, [1974] 2 C.M.L.R. 216.

be based on a customs union which shall cover all trade in goods, and which shall involve the prohibition between Member States of customs duties on imports and exports and of all charges having equivalent effect and the adoption of a common cus[illegible] countries. This distinguishes [illegible] that a free trade area h[illegible] rules of customs adm[illegible]

## Free circulation

**3.04** The provisions relating to elimination of customs duties and the elimination of quantitative restrictions between Member States apply both to products originating in Member States and to products coming from third countries which are in free circulation in Member States. The term "goods" has been defined by the Court in Case 7/68, *Commission v. Italy*[2] as meaning products which can be valued in money, and which are capable of forming the subject of commercial transactions. Coins which are in the form of legal tender do not fall within the definition: see Case 7/78, *R. v. Thompson.*[3]

**3.05** Article 10 enlarges Article 9 by saying that products coming from a third country shall be considered to be in free circulation in a Member State if the import formalities have been complied with and any customs duties or charges having equivalent effect which are payable have been levied in that Member State, and if they have not benefited from a total or partial drawback of such duties or charges. This definition enabled the Court to hold in Case 119/78, *SA des Grandes Distilleries Peureux v. Directeur des Services Fiscaux,*[4] that the provisions of Article 30 relate not only to goods from other Member States, but also to goods of third country origin but in free circulation in a Member State. No import licence may be required for the importation into one Member State of goods of third country origin which are in free circulation in another Member State. But the country of final destination of the goods may require an indication of the country of origin of the goods: see Case 41/76, *Donckerwolcke.*[5]

**3.06** Article 10(2) required the Commission to determine the methods of administrative co-operation to be adopted for the purposes of applying Article 9(2), taking into account the need to reduce as much as possible

[2] [1968] E.C.R. 423, [1969] C.M.L.R. 1.
[3] [1978] E.C.R. 2247, [1979] 1 C.M.L.R. 47.
[4] [1979] E.C.R. 975, [1980] 3 C.M.L.R. 337.
[5] [1975] E.C.R. 1921, [1977] 2 C.M.L.R. 535.

the formal ties imposed upon trade. Directive 83/643[6] provided for the reduction of formalities and inspections at internal borders and for the mutual recognition of inspections in other Member States. The single market adaptations now aim to eliminate border controls altogether.

## Customs duties and equivalent charges

Article 12 plays an essential part in the creation of the Customs Union since it prohibits Member States from introducing between themselves any new customs duties on imports or exports or any charges having equivalent effect, and from increasing those which they already apply in their trade with each other. The article introduces the concept of "charges having equivalent effect". This concept has been given a wide interpretation by the Court which, in an early development of the law, held in Joined Cases 2 & 3/62, *Commission v. Luxembourg and Belgium,*[7] that a charge falls within the definition if, whatever its name, it amounts to a charge imposed unilaterally, either at the time goods are imported or at a later time, which directly affects goods imported from a Member State but not similar domestic goods, so that it increases the price of the goods and has thus the same consequences on the free movement of goods as a customs duty. 3.07

As a general rule a charge imposed on goods at the time they cross the border, and not authorised by the Treaty, amounts to a charge having equivalent effect: see Joined Cases 2 & 3/69, *Social Fonds voor de Diamantarbeiders v. Brachfeld et al.*[8] Statistical fees levied at the time imported goods were declared for statistical purposes have been held to be such a charge: see Case 24/68, *Commission v. Italian Republic.*[9] Likewise, charges for customs administration within the obligatory opening hours laid down by Directive 83/643[10] are forbidden: See Case 340/87, *Commission v. Italy.*[11] The same principle is applied to charges levied on exports, where the prohibition is contained in Article 16. 3.08

The prohibition of such charges applies even if the charge is imposed as payment for a service actually rendered, such as a sanitary inspection of animal products, when no charge or a smaller charge is imposed for the inspection of products not imported or destined for export: see Case 87/ 3.09

6 [1983] O.J. L359/8, as last amended by Dir. 91/342, [1991] O.J. L187/47. See also Reg. 3925/91, [1991] O.J. L374/4, on controls and formalities relating to passengers' luggage.
7 [1962] E.C.R. 425, [1963] C.M.L.R. 199.
8 [1969] E.C.R. 211, [1969] C.M.L.R. 336.
9 [1969] E.C.R. 193, [1971] C.M.L.R. 611.
10 [1983] O.J. L359/8, as last amended by Directive 87/53, [1987] O.J. L24/33.
11 [1989] E.C.R. 1483, [1990] 2 C.M.L.R. 492.

75, *Bresciani v. Amministrazione Italiana delle Finanze.*[12] In Case 26/62, *Van Gend en Loos v. Nederlandse Administratie der Belastigen,*[13] it was held that

Member States abolished all duties on industrial goods (Decision 66/532[14]). This has now been accomplished for all the subsequent Member States. Article 16 called for the abolition of customs duties on exports and charges having equivalent effect by the first stage envisaged by Article 14. Article 17 applied Articles 9 to 15 to customs duties of a fiscal nature. These customs duties were intended not to protect domestic producers but had a revenue gathering object; they have now been converted in the United Kingdom to excise duties prima facie compatible with the internal taxation requirements of Article 95—see Chapter 11.

## Quantitative restrictions on intra-community trade

3.11 The objective of free movement of goods in the Community involves, in addition to the abolition of customs duties, the abolition of all other impediments to imports and exports within the Community. This objective is given effect in Articles 30 to 37 of the Treaty, which provide that quantitative restrictions on imports or exports, and all measures having equivalent effect, shall be prohibited between Member States. Community law envisages a broad meaning for the term "measure", to include any instruments issuing from a public authority which, even though not legally binding on the addressees, cause them to pursue a certain conduct. In Case 249/81, *Commission v. Ireland,*[15] a "Buy Irish" campaign funded by the Government was held to be capable of infringing Article 30. These articles have direct effect (since the end of the transitional period): see Case 74/76, *Ianelli & Volpi v. Meroni.*[16]

3.12 The jurisprudence of the Court has established very wide parameters in interpreting the concept of measures having equivalent effect to quantitative restrictions, and directives which were enacted under Article 33(7)

[12] [1976] E.C.R. 129, [1976] 2 C.M.L.R. 62.

[13] [1963] E.C.R. 1, [1963] C.M.L.R. 105.

[14] J.O. 2971/66.

[15] [1982] E.C.R. 4005, [1983] 2 C.M.L.R. 104; contrast *Apple and Pear Development Council v. Lewis*: [1983] E.C.R. 4083, [1984] 3 C.M.L.R. 733.

[16] [1977] E.C.R. 557, [1977] 2 C.M.L.R. 688.

to give effect to Article 30 have been overtaken by the Court's decisions. In Case 8/74, *Procureur du Roi v. Dassonville*,[17] the Court stated that "All trading rules enacted by Member States which are capable of hindering, directly or indirectly, actually or potentially intra-Community trade are to be considered as measures having equivalent effect to quantitative restrictions." In that case the Belgian rule requiring a British Customs certificate of origin for Scotch whisky imported into Belgium after being in free circulation in France was found to be such a measure. A requirement by Belgium allowing for certified copies of the certificate of origin was, however, lawful: see Case 2/78, *Commission v. Belgium*.[18]

As a general principle, all rules that hinder trade between the Member States are prohibited by Article 30: see Case 119/78, *SA des Grandes Distilleries Peureux v. Directeur des Services Fiscaux*.[19] Thus the Court starts with the presumption that health checks are contrary to the prohibition: see Case 4/75, *Rewe v. Zentralfinanz*.[20] Case 155/73, *Sacchi*,[21] indicated that even measures not directly connected with the import or export of goods may violate Article 30; there, the Court considered the practice by Italian radio and television authorities of choosing advertisements which would hinder the promotion of non-Italian goods. And in Joined Cases C 46/90 & 93/91, *Lagauche*,[22] the Court held that Belgian legislation which gave a public undertaking power to approve the use of telephone equipment which it had not supplied was contrary to Article 30 if the decisions of the undertaking were not appealable to the courts. 3.13

The Court also held that a restriction on the total production of goods could fall within the prohibition of Article 30 where the country imposing the restriction was the only producer of any consequence: see Case 190/73, *Officier van Justitie v. van Haaster*.[23] And in Case 56/87, *Commission v. Italy*,[24] it was held that rules fixing the prices of pharmaceutical products which were likely to favour domestic products to the detriment of imported ones were contrary to Article 36. Article 31 prohibits all new quantitative restrictions and equivalent measures. This article has direct effect: see Case 13/68, *Salgoil v. Ministry of Foreign Trade*.[25] All these prohibitions apply to intra-Community trade. It was held in Case 225/78, *Procureur v. Bouhelier*,[26] that they did not apply in trade with third coun- 3.14

[17] [1974] E.C.R. 837, [1974] 2 C.M.L.R. 436.
[18] [1979] E.C.R. 1761, [1980] 1 C.M.L.R. 216.
[19] [1979] E.C.R. 975, [1980] 3 C.M.L.R. 337.
[20] [1975] E.C.R. 843, [1977] 1 C.M.L.R. 599.
[21] [1974] E.C.R. 409, [1974] 2 C.M.L.R. 177.
[22] Not yet reported.
[23] [1974] E.C.R. 1123, [1974] 2 C.M.L.R. 521.
[24] [1988] E.C.R. 2919, [1989] 3 C.M.L.R. 707.
[25] [1968] E.C.R. 453, [1969] C.M.L.R. 181.
[26] [1979] E.C.R. 3151, [1980] 2 C.M.L.R. 541.

tries, to the extent not inconsistent with the Community commercial

Ltd., or where there are licensing requirements, even where the licensing is automatic, because the inconvenience and delay of the licence requirements is itself a restraint on trade: see Case 68/76, *Commission v. France.*[29]

3.16 The Court of Justice took the *Dassonville* principle further in the *Cassis de Dijon* case,[30] in which it held that Germany was not entitled to prohibit the import of the drink, lawfully marketed in France, on the grounds that its alcoholic content was less than 25 per cent. The Court recognised that non-discriminatory measures taken to satisfy mandatory requirements such as "the effectiveness of fiscal supervision, the protection of public health, the fairness of commercial transactions and the defence of the consumers" may be acceptable. These measures must of course apply to both imported and domestic products. In this particular case, the Court replied that the measures in question were not necessary to attain these objectives and that consumer protection could have been adequately achieved by other means such as labelling. If such measures breach Article 30, they may nevertheless be authorised as exceptions under Article 36 if the appropriate conditions are met.

## The permitted restrictions—Article 36

3.17 Article 36 lays down exceptions to the requirement for the abolition of quantitative restrictions and measures having equivalent effect between Member States. The task of particularising the scope of the exceptions to Articles 30 to 34, which Article 36 allows, falls largely to the Court to undertake on a case by case basis. The article provides that the provisions of Articles 30 to 34 do not preclude prohibitions or restrictions on imports, exports or goods in transit justified on the grounds of:

[27] [1978] E.C.R. 2347, [1979] 1 C.M.L.R. 177.
[28] [1979] E.C.R. 2161, [1979] 3 C.M.L.R. 389.
[29] [1977] E.C.R. 515, [1977] 2 C.M.L.R. 161.
[30] Case 120/78, *Rewe-Zentrale AG v. Bundesmonopolverwaltung für Branntwein*: [1979] E.C.R. 649, [1979] 3 C.M.L.R. 494.

(a) public morality, public policy or public security;
(b) the protection of health and life to humans, animals and plants;
(c) the protection of national treasures possessing artistic, historic or archeological value; or
(d) the protection of industrial and commercial property.

Such prohibitions or restrictions must not, however, constitute a means of arbitrary discrimination or a distinguished restriction on trade between Member States. The article has to be interpreted strictly: see Case 29/72, *Marimex v. Ministry of Finance*,[31] and may not be used to by-pass specific provisions in Articles 30 to 34. The last sentence of the article makes it clear that every prohibition has to be reasonable and justified, and much use is made by the Court in applying this provision of the principle of proportionality referred to in Chapter 2. Article 36 cannot be used in relation to subjects not specified in the article itself: see Case 113/80, *Commission v. Ireland*.[32] The Court has had to apply the principles of Article 36 in a large number of cases which, following the four main categories in the article, may be illustrated as follows. **3.18**

(a) *Public morality, public policy and public security*

Case 34/79, *R. v. Henn and Darby*[33] upheld a prohibition on the importation of obscene articles on the basis of the reference to public morality, affirming that the content of this concept is for each Member State to determine. The Court appears to have left significant discretion to Member States when it comes to restrictions on trade due to the concept of public policy and the protection of domestic products is not in issue. Restrictions on export and import protecting coinage are valid: see Case 7/78, *R. v. Thompson*.[34] **3.19**

There are, however, indications that the Court's decisions move in response to general changes of climate, as where the maintenance of essential supplies was considered a matter of public security in Case 72/83, *Campus Oil Ltd. v. Minister for Industry*.[35] In Cases C–304/90, *Reading Borough Council v. Payless DIY*[36] and C–169/91, *Stoke-on-Trent City Council v. B&Q*,[37] the Court considered the relationship between the United Kingdom's Sunday trading laws and Article 30, holding that such restrictions were not intended to regulate the flow of goods and that, since they **3.20**

[31] [1972] E.C.R. 1309, [1973] C.M.L.R. 486.
[32] [1981] E.C.R. 1625, [1982] 1 C.M.L.R. 706.
[33] [1979] E.C.R. 3795, [1980] 1 C.M.L.R. 246.
[34] [1978] E.C.R. 2247, [1979] 1 C.M.L.R. 47.
[35] [1984] E.C.R. 2727, [1984] 3 C.M.L.R. 544.
[36] [1993] 1 C.M.L.R. 426.
[37] *Ibid.*

affected imported and nationally produced goods indifferently, they did

104/75, *De Peijper*. Case 788/79, *Gilli and Andres* and Case 193/80, *Commission v. Italy*,[40] illustrate the Court's attitude; in these cases, the Court considered contrary to Article 30 Italian legislation requiring that only vinegar made from wine should be sold as "vinegar", reasoning that since vinegars made from other agricultural products were not harmful to health, consumers' interest could be protected by the listing of ingredients.

**3.22** To avoid the prohibition of the article, a national measure alleged to protect health must constitute a "seriously-considered health policy": see Case 40/82, *Commission v. United Kingdom*,[41] and the burden of showing that the measure is necessary for the protection of health, and goes no further than is needed for that purpose, lies on the Member State: see Case 227/82, *van Bennekom*.[42] A minor burden or a rule aimed at prevention of alcoholism is not considered unlawful: see Case 75/81, *Blesgen v. Belgium*.[43] Where Community measures to harmonise provisions on health protection have been adopted, recourse to Article 36 is no longer possible: see Case 190/87, *Handelsonderneming Moormann BV*.[44]

**3.23** Where a product is lawfully marketed in a Member State there is a presumption that there is an adequate guarantee of its quality and safety, especially where the exercise of the profession concerned in its marketing is already governed by Community legislation. Thus a ban on private import from France to Germany of a medicinal product lawfully purchased in France (for a quarter of the German price), and available at pharmacies without prescription in Germany, was held not to be justified on public health grounds in Case 215/87, *Schumacher*.[45] Likewise, it was

38 [1976] E.C.R 613, [1976] 2 C.M.L.R. 271.
39 [1980] E.C.R. 2071, [1981] 1 C.M.L.R. 146.
40 [1981] E.C.R. 3019.
41 [1982] E.C.R. 2793, [1982] 3 C.M.L.R. 497.
42 [1983] E.C.R. 3883, [1985] 2 C.M.L.R. 692.
43 [1982] E.C.R. 2111, [1983] 1 C.M.L.R. 431.
44 [1988] E.C.R. 4689, [1990] 1 C.M.L.R. 656.
45 [1989] E.C.R. 638, [1990] 2 C.M.L.R. 465.

held in Case C–369/89, *Piageme v. Peeters Pvba,*[46] that national legislation requiring food labelling to be exclusively in the local language infringed Article 30 and Directive 79/112,[47] which provided that a language easily understood by consumers, or that "other measures" to ensure that the purchaser was informed, would suffice.

3.24 Fees may be charged to reflect the actual cost of carrying out such checks as are provided for in Community legislation: see Case 18/87, *Commission v. Germany.*[48]

(c) *Protection of national heritage*

3.25 Case 7/68, *Commission v. Italy,*[49] shows that concern for the protection of national treasures of historic, artistic or archeological value does not enable a Member State to impose a tax on the export of such objects.

(d) *Protection of intellectual property*

3.26 The interrelation between national intellectual property law and the principles of Article 36 has been considered by the Court on many occasions. In this area, the Court has tended to be readier to accept the need for national restrictions to be maintained pending harmonisation of legislation at Community level. Various Community measures such as the Community Patent Convention[50] will override the general prohibitions on restrictions on trade in the Treaty. So far, there has also been Directive 89/104[51] on trade marks and Directive 91/250[52] introducing a harmonised copyright protection for computer programs, both taking effect from January 1, 1993. In addition, Directive 92/100[53] on rental and lending rights provides a right to authorise and prohibit the use of copyright material; it will require extensive national implementing legislation and may not be given full effect until as late as 1997. Regulation 3842/86[54] prohibits the release into free circulation of counterfeit goods from third countries.

3.27 Meanwhile, in Case 119/75, *Terrapin v. Terranova*[55] the Court laid down

[46] [1993] 3 C.M.L.R. 725.
[47] [1979] O.J. L33/1.
[48] [1988] E.C.R. 5427, [1990] 1 C.M.L.R. 561.
[49] [1968] E.C.R. 423, [1969] C.M.L.R. 1.
[50] See [1976] O.J. L17/1572, and [1989] O.J. L401/1.
[51] [1989] O.J. L40/1.
[52] [1991] O.J. L122/42.
[53] [1992] O.J. L346/61.
[54] [1986] O.J. L357/1.
[55] [1976] E.C.R. 1039, [1976] 2 C.M.L.R. 482.

30 for United Kingdom law to treat a case where demand for a patented product was satisfied on the domestic market by imports from other Member States as one in which a compulsory licence might be granted on the ground of insufficient exploitation of the patent, because the effect was to discriminate against imports and to favour national production.

## State monopolies

**3.28** Concluding the section of the Treaty on free movement of goods is Article 37 with its requirement that commercial state monopolies must not operate to discriminate between nationals of different Member States in regard to the conditions under which goods are procured and marketed. This has particular relevance to restrictions on importation, whether they take the form of exclusive rights to import certain products or of charges or levies on such goods. The article applies not only to state undertakings as such, but also to any body through which a State "supervises, determines or appreciably influences" imports or exports, or any body to which a monopoly is delegated by the State. It does not apply to monopolies of services maintained by States: see Case 30/87, *Bodson v. Pompes Funèbres*.[59]

**3.29** Monopolies themselves are not affected and may continue, but any form of intra-State impediment to trade associated with them has been illegal since the end of the transitional period in 1970 and liable to be set aside in litigation before national courts: see Case 59/75, *Pubblico Ministero v. Manghera*.[60] Thus quotas or duties (however described) are prohibited, and products of the kind in question coming from another Member State must be capable of both importation and marketing on the same com-

[56] [1990] I E.C.R. 3711, [1990] 3 C.M.L.R. 571.
[57] [1988] E.C.R. 6211, [1989] 4 C.M.L.R. 122.
[58] [1992] I E.C.R. 829, [1992] 2 C.M.L.R. 709.
[59] [1988] E.C.R. 2479, [1989] 4 C.M.L.R. 984.
[60] [1976] E.C.R. 91, [1976] 1 C.M.L.R. 557

mercial terms as the products dealt in by the state monopoly. Inconsistent with these requirements are: an exclusive right to import a particular product, Case 59/75, *Manghera*;[61] a price adjustment designed to place the imported product on the market at the same price as those marketed by the monopoly, Case 91/75, *Hauptzollamt Göttingen v. Miritz*;[62] and marketing a product with the assistance of public funds so as to undercut comparable imported products, Case 91/78, *Hansen v. Flensburg Customs Office*.[63]

The only exceptions now permitted to the right to free movement of goods are those specified in Article 36—public morality, public policy, or public security, etc. Article 37(4) does, however, provide that in the case of agricultural products measures may be taken to ensure equivalent safeguards for the employment and standard of living of producers affected, though this does not justify any measure which would infringe the article's policy. It should be noted, however, that Article 37 does not apply in the case of imports from outside the Community, but only to trade between Member States: see Case 91/78, *Hansen v. Flensburg Customs Office*.[64] 3.30

## Community transit

The Community transit systems exist in order to facilitate the passage of goods through two or more Community States without Customs formalities. The basic legislation is now contained in the Customs Code[65] and its implementing regulation.[66] The scheme operates in two parts. 3.31

First comes internal Community transit to allow goods either made in the Community, or imported and now in free circulation within the Community, to pass from one point to another within the Customs Union *via* a third country without changing their customs status. A parallel result may be obtained under cover of a TIR convention carnet, an ATA convention carnet, the Rhine Manifest or by using the post.[67] The external transit system allows the movement within the Community of uncustomed third country goods and Community goods which have already been cleared for export; the same alternatives are allowed as 3.32

[61] *Ibid.*
[62] [1976] E.C.R. 217.
[63] [1979] E.C.R. 935, [1981] 1 C.M.L.R. 331.
[64] *Ibid.*
[65] Reg. 2913/92, [1992] O.J. L302/1, Arts. 91–97 and 163–165.
[66] Reg. 2454/93, [1993] O.J. L253/1, Arts. 341–381.
[67] Reg. 2913/92, Art. 163, above.

person established there and approved by the customs administration of a Member State; detailed requirements have been enacted with regard to the form and scope of the guarantees and the situations in which the need for them may be waived.[70]

3.34 Of great practical importance are the transit provisions of the European Economic Area Agreement[71] which, covering Austria, Finland, Iceland, Norway and Sweden, accounts for a very important number of all journeys using the transit regimes.

[68] Reg. 2913/92, Art. 91, above.
[69] Arts. 92 and 94–97 of Reg. 2913/92 apply to internal and external transit, see above.
[70] Reg. 2454/93, Arts. 359–377; Reg. 2913/92, Arts. 94–95, above.
[71] [1994] O.J. L1/1.

CHAPTER 4

# THE CUSTOMS UNION

## Role and Purpose

4.01 Article 9 prescribes that the Community is to be based on a customs union covering all trade in goods. It has been seen in Chapter 3 that the existence of a customs union makes possible the establishment of an internal free trade area, developing into a single market. Looking outwards, the Customs Union makes possible the Community's common commercial policy towards third countries, developed in the context of action under Articles 113 and 238. The external Community Customs Union is now complete, and operating through the customs administrations of the Member States who (save in so far as they are concerned with matters such as prohibited imports, or with internal taxes) act as the Community's agents in applying the Common Customs Tariff and Community customs law.

4.02 The area of customs law has accordingly had to be the subject of much Community activity and almost all the existing legislation now in force in the Community consists of Community legislation with national legislation playing a purely ancillary role in enforcement. Over the life of the Customs Union, there was a steady trend towards the use of regulations instead of directives, and the process has now culminated in the enactment of a Community Customs Code.[1]

4.03 The Code is effective from January 1, 1994 and is accompanied by an extensive subsidiary regulation effective from the same date.[2] In this chapter they will be referred to respectively as the Code and the Implementing Regulation. The Code establishes a Code Committee with per-

[1] Reg. 2913/92, [1992] O.J. L302. It must, by Art. 253, be reviewed before January 1, 1998.
[2] Reg. 2454/93, [1993] O.J. L253.

operate, is defined in Article 3 of the Code to include the territories of all the Member States *plus*: the Austrian territories of Jungholz and Mittelberg (with Germany), Monaco, Guadeloupe, French Guyana, Martinique and Réunion (with France), San Marino (with Italy), the Channel Islands and the Isle of Man (with the United Kingdom), and the territorial sea and airspace of each Member State; but *minus* Heligoland and Busingen (from Germany), the non-European territories of the Netherlands and France, the Faeroe Islands and Greenland (from Denmark), Livigno, Campione d'Italia and part of Lake Lugano (from Italy), Ceuta and Melilla (from Spain).[4] The territorial waters and airspace of each Member State, but not of these additional territories are included in the customs territory.[5]

4.05 Special customs arrangements exist for certain territories which are not within the Community's customs territory. They are Andorra, the Faeroe Islands, Greenland, Heligoland, Busingen, Livigno and Campione d'Italia, Ceuta and Melilla, Gibraltar, the Vatican and various colonial or former colonial territories outside Europe. Although they are within the customs territory, the full range of Community customs legislation is not applied to the Pays de Gex, the Haute Savoie, the Alto Adige, the Valle d'Aosta, Gorizia and Mount Athos.[6]

## The Common Customs Tariff

4.06 The Common Customs Tariff (CCT) has replaced national customs tariffs, and contains a comprehensive categorisation of goods together with the rates of duty and an indication of whether or not agricultural levies are chargeable. The tariff is subject to amendment throughout the year, but is consolidated and reissued annually. In the case of goods covered

[3] Art. 247.

[4] For the position of Gibraltar see Art. 28 of the Act of Accession of the United Kingdom.

[5] Art. 3(3) of the Code.

[6] See the Report of the Court of Auditors, [1993] O.J. C347.

by the treaties governing the European Coal and Steel Community, the national tariffs remain in force, albeit on a harmonised basis, but details of the position in relation to coal and steel are given in the CCT for ease of reference.

The CCT in its present form was first laid down in Council Regulation 2658/87[7] and based on the Combined Nomenclature adopted in an international convention sponsored by the Customs Co-operation Council (CCC), signed in June 1983. Regulation 2551/93[8] amends the Combined Nomenclature classifications and the CCT with effect from January 1, 1994. The Community is a party to the convention, which is expected in due course to be adopted by the great majority of countries. The CCC has a Nomenclature Committee which offers classification opinions in cases of doubt, and prepares explanatory notes on the nomenclature. Neither of these has binding force in the Community, but the Court will treat them as persuasive authority in the absence of any relevant Community material. 4.07

At Community level, there also existed a Nomenclature Committee whose functions were to approve delegated legislation proposed by the Commission on classification matters, to give classification opinions in cases referred to it and to prepare explanatory notes on the nomenclature; its functions are now undertaken by the Code Committee.[9] Regulation 2658/87[10] provides general rules for the interpretation of the Combined Nomenclature and for the Commission, after consulting the Code Committee, to adopt clarification regulations where necessary. Generally, the Committee's opinions and explanatory notes, even where they are strictly non-binding, are respected in practice and are published in the "C" (information) series of the Official Journal. 4.08

In many instances, the Court has been asked for an advisory opinion under Article 177 EEC (see Chapter 2) on the interpretation of the tariff and the European Court Reports should therefore always be checked when questions arise. Meanwhile, the Code now allows traders to require the customs administration to issue binding tariff opinions.[11] When such an opinion is given, it stands for six years and the holder of it may rely on it before any Community customs administration, but a ruling may not be sought *ex post facto* and ceases to be valid if overruled by legislation or by reason of a judgment of the Court or of a decision 4.09

[7] [1987] O.J. L256.
[8] [1993] O.J. L241.
[9] Art. 252 of the Code.
[10] [1987] O.J. L256.
[11] Art. 12, and Implementing Regulation Title II.

policy and the common agricultural policy, and throughout the year in numerous detailed regulations. In general, the duties on agricultural products are higher than those on industrial products. The duties may be *ad valorem*, as a percentage of the value of the goods, or specific, *i.e.* a sum fixed by reference to the weight, volume or number of the goods, or a combination of the two. The amount payable is indicated opposite each subdivision in the tariff.

**4.11** Within the framework of the duties laid down in the tariff, the common commercial policy requires the application of a variety of quotas designed to meet particular sectoral or, in a few remaining instances, even national needs. Thus a tariff quota opened for specific goods enables a limited quantity of goods to be imported at reduced or nil rates of duty; an unlimited quantity of the same goods may be imported at the normal rate of duty. In a less rigid version of that regime, tariff ceilings allow import at reduced or nil rates of a fixed quantity of goods, but remain in force until revoked or the expiry of the period of the concession rather than, as in the case of tariff quotas, until the strict limit has been reached.[13]

**4.12** Quotas are centrally managed by the Commission and drawn down by the Member States, which administer their allocations, with a reserve sometimes being held by the Community. The opening, conditions and termination of quotas are the subject of Council or Commission regulations. In Case 51/87, *Commission v. Council*,[14] the Court annulled a regulation dividing quotas into national shares on the ground that the Council had not been justified in rejecting Commission proposals for Community management of the quotas.

[12] There is a transitional provision for cases in which an advance fixing certificate has been issued or a binding contract has been entered into: Art. 12 of the Code.
[13] Art. 20 of the Code.
[14] [1988] E.C.R. 5459.

## Reliefs

A number of reliefs from duty on a standard basis are available on the conditions laid down in Regulation 918/83.[15] Under this regulation, customs duty and agricultural levies on import or export are relieved, but not value added tax or excise duty which are the subject of separate provisions. Those internal taxes, though levied on import into the United Kingdom from outside the Community as customs duties, are subject to Community control only through the directives and Treaty provisions on taxation. The provisions of Regulation 918/83 are lengthy, detailed and have been much amended, with the individual reliefs provided for being subject to a variety of limitations. 4.13

Among the headings under which relief is available are: small non-commercial consignments not exceeding given value limits, with quantity limits for tobacco, alcohol and perfume; goods in passengers' personal baggage of a non-commercial character not exceeding specified value limits, again with quantity limits for tobacco, alcohol and perfume; scientific, educational or cultural items, in some cases only where not obtainable within the Community; goods imported for charities, handicapped persons or catastrophe victims; the household goods of persons transferring their normal residence to the Community from a third country either generally or, subject to slightly different conditions, on marriage or establishing a secondary residence in the Community; students' personal belongings; inherited goods; plant and equipment transferred by a business migrating into the Community; samples, publicity material, goods for exhibitions or for examination, analysis or tests. 4.14

There are a number of further reliefs relating to medical, agricultural and other purposes to which space precludes reference. It should be noted that Article 131 of Regulation 918/83 provides for the drawback of the relief if conditions to which it is subject are not complied with, and places the burden of proof on the importer. Member States' freedom to allow further reliefs in certain areas, notably in relation to medical research and diplomatic imports, is preserved, and a Reliefs Committee, similar to the Nomenclature Committee, was established to approve legislation by the Commission resolving difficulties of application which arise; its functions are now fulfilled by the Code Committee (see paragraph 4.03 above). 4.15

Other reliefs may be authorised pursuant to Article 184 of the Code. In particular, relief from duty is available for goods which are exported 4.16

[15] [1983] O.J. L105, as last amended by Reg. 2913/92, [1992] O.J. L302.

4.17 A wide range of reliefs is available to avoid payment of duty in the event of importation being followed by re-export.[17] In these circumstances, the duty payable on import into the Community is relieved, either in total or in part, subject only to becoming payable in the event of the conditions attaching to it not being complied with. In general, the permitted period of temporary import may not exceed 24 months, but in a number of cases will be much shorter. A bond or guarantee for the payment of the duty relieved is usually required against the eventuality of its becoming payable due to failure to comply with conditions.

**4.18** The temporary import is concluded by export within the permitted period, by the goods being placed in an approved warehouse or a free zone with a view to export, by destruction of the goods under customs control or by their being placed under one of the various customs regimes discussed later. Alternatively, the goods may be allowed to be released into free circulation on payment of the duty. If duty becomes payable, it is based on that normally payable on the goods at the time of actual import, plus interest.

**4.19** The legislation allows for either part or total relief. Part relief is available for any goods not allowed full relief, and is on the basis that 3 per cent. of the duty will be payable for every month, or part of a month, during which the goods are inside the Community; certain goods specified in the regulation are excluded altogether. Total relief is available, subject to conditions, in respect of a wide variety of goods listed, of which the following are the main examples:[18]

(a) certain business or professional equipment belonging to an individual or company operating temporarily within the Community;
(b) materials for demonstration or use at an exhibition or fair;
(c) certain teaching and scientific materials;
(d) medical and laboratory materials for hospitals;

16 Reg. 2551/93, [1993] O.J. L241, Annex 1.
17 Arts. 137–144 of the Code.
18 See Implementing Regulation, Arts. 671–689.

(e) materials for the relief of catastrophes;
(f) packaging of containers;
(g) the personal belongings of travellers;
(h) goods for testing, experiment or demonstration;
(i) at a Member State's discretion in individual cases, any import with no economic significance.

## Origin of goods

In order to apply the terms of the common commercial policy with regard to preferences for goods from certain countries, or restrictions on goods from other countries, the concept of origin is laid down in Community legislation. It is designed to establish the country (or customs territory) in which goods originated, rather than where they were sent from. In the application of the Common Customs Tariff, this notion is essential in enabling Community industries to be protected, or overseas industries to be assisted. Following from the 1973 CCC Kyoto Convention on Simplification, the Community legislation is now to be found in the Code and the Implementing Regulation, which contain general provisions often given further precision by regulations applicable in particular sectors or in trade with particular countries. 4.20

The basic concept[19] is applicable alike both to exports from the Community and imports to it. It treats as originating in a customs territory goods which are either wholly obtained or produced there, or goods which are derived from materials whose last economically justified and substantial processing took place in it. The concept of goods being wholly obtained in an area is for the most part self-explanatory, but it includes: products mined or grown in the territory; products obtained from living animals born or reared in the territory; products of hunting or fishing; sea products from boats (including factory ships) registered in and flying the flag of a country; and products from the sea or its subsoil over which the country has exclusive rights of exploitation. 4.21

Also treated as originating in a country are goods derived from materials substantially processed there. This refers to the last substantial processing which is economically justified, by a business equipped for the purpose, resulting in a new product or constituting a major stage of manufacture. The position with regard to oil products has not yet been the subject of legislation. It will be seen that the approach is to identify the place of origin by reference to an economic reality test, and it is specifically provided, in an anti-avoidance clause, that origin status is to be 4.22

[19] Arts. 22–27 of the Code.

denied where processing or manufacture has been carried out in a particular place solely to take advantage of the Community origin provisions.[20]

**4.23** There are numerous deeming regulations to provide certainty in particular areas of trade which are adopted by the Commission, or by the Council in the context of third country preferences. The Court has not always upheld the terms of these regulations, requiring that the criterion of objectivity should be strictly adhered to. In Case 385/85, *SR Industries v. Administration des Douanes*,[21] however, it was held that a stricter concept of origin might be adopted in the context of generalised trade preferences.

**4.24** Certificates of origin are prescribed generally in the Implementing Regulation,[22] and given on export from the Community by authorities authorised for the purpose (frequently chambers of commerce). In the case of imports, the Community cannot, save where so provided in Community agreements with third countries, insist on the exporting state using the prescribed forms, but the regulation remains applicable in regard to the information which must be furnished on import, and which the importer must therefore procure from the exporting authorities. In Case 218/83, *Les Rapides Savoyards*[23] it was held that there is a co-responsibility between the authorities of the exporting state and those of the Community in relation to certificates given pursuant to a preference agreement with the Community.

**4.25** Where, under the safeguard for national interests provisions of Article 115 of the Treaty, a Member State is authorised to take restrictive measures against certain imports, the same concepts of origin are applied; it should be noted, however, that the Court has held that in intra-Community trade, a state may not demand of an importer more information with regard to the origin of goods already in free circulation in the Community than he could reasonably be expected to know: see Case 41/76, *Donckerwolcke v. Procureur de la République*.[24]

**4.26** The Community has concluded a wide network of trade agreements with third countries which carry with them refinements of the general origin rules. The relevant legislation is extensive and complex, being contained in regulations based on the various agreements or conventions and the

[20] Art. 25 of the Code.
[21] [1986] E.C.R. 2929, [1988] 1 C.M.L.R. 378.
[22] Arts. 78–97.
[23] [1984] E.C.R. 3116, [1985] 3 C.M.L.R. 116.
[24] [1976] E.C.R. 1921, [1977] 2 C.M.L.R. 535.

decisions of the committees established under them. The groupings include the EFTA countries (almost all of which are now covered by the European Economic Area Agreement), the countries with which there are special trade or association agreements, developing countries benefiting from the generalised system of preferences and the African, Caribean and Pacific countries covered by the current Lome convention (see Chapter 5). The agreements may provide for reciprocal acceptance of certificates of origin and for simplified procedure in certain circumstances, and make provision for mutual assistance between customs administrations in verifying claims of origin. The other groupings are also subject to detailed modifications of the general rules.

## Valuation

In order to establish the amount of customs duty to be paid on goods, it is necessary to have rules to establish their dutiable value. These, based on the provisions of Article VII of the GATT, are now contained in Articles 28 to 36 of the Code and Part I, Title V, of the Implementing Regulation, which apply to all customs duties (including those payable on coal and steel products and Euratom goods) and to value-added tax on import to the Community. The fundamental concept of the legislation is that goods should be given their actual commercial value, at the place of introduction into the Community, by reference to the price paid for them on an arm's length sale on export. **4.27**

(a) *Arm's length sales*

Where a sale on export to the Community does take place, and the parties are unconnected (as defined), the way is open for the sale price to be taken as the value for customs purposes. This is the basic method of valuation, referred to as the transaction value. A number of further requirements have, however, to be satisfied: (a) the buyer must be free to use or dispose of the goods without restrictions save those imposed by law, those relating to the area in which the buyer may operate or any which have no substantial effect on value; (b) no further payment must be due to the seller with reference to the subsequent resale or hire of the goods; and (c) no part of the consideration may be unquantifiable—in this connection, expenditure by the buyer on his own account, *e.g.* on advertising, is disregarded, even though it may be of indirect benefit to the seller. To the sale price, there are additions and subtractions which, if applicable, must then be made. **4.28**

If borne by the buyer, there must be added: if not included in the sale price, sale commission or brokerage and the cost of packaging; the cost **4.29** of certain free or reduced price goods or services provided by the buyer and used for the goods; royalties or licence fees payable on sale of the goods (reproduction or distribution fees are not added, and may be subtracted if included in the invoice); the value of any payments to the seller from resale or hiring of the goods; the cost of transport and insurance up to the Community frontier, and loading and handling charges to the same point.

4.30 To be subtracted from the sale price if included in it are: customs duties, taxes and customs clearance charges; transport following import; the cost of installation or maintenance following import; reproduction fees; purchase commissions; interest payments, and price reductions allowed by the seller. All other costs are disregarded, including unloading and storage (including the cost of warehousing where the goods are warehoused under a special scheme for that purpose—see below). There are special provisions relating to computer software.

(b) *No arms' length sale*

4.31 Where the parties to the export sale are connected, the transaction value may still be used as the base for valuation if the importer can prove that the connection has had no influence on it. If he cannot do this, or if there was no sale, *e.g.* the goods were leased or gifted, or if they are released after a period in warehouse, various alternative methods of valuation are used in the order in which they must be resorted to; they constitute in effect, a "best evidence" rule under which in order to rely on any one method, the importer has to show that the evidence to operate any of those earlier in the order of preference cannot be had. The alternatives may themselves of course only be used where it is shown that the basic method described above is not possible. The order of preference is as follows:

4.32 (1) Sale price of identical goods. The circumstances must be as near as possible to those in the basic method, especially in regard to the timing of the export sale to the Community, the type, quantity and quality of the goods, and must have been accepted by customs in a case which has actually occurred.

(2) Sale price of similar goods. The goods must have been produced in the same country as the goods to be valued, have the same use and be in commercial terms interchangeable with them.

(3) Deductive method. This proceeds on the basis of working backwards from the unit resale price of the goods in the importing country (or of identical or similar goods). Thus an appropriate

profit margin is deducted, together with all other admissable taxes or costs on import.

(4) Constructed value. This method may, at the importer's option, be reversed with the previous method in order of preference. It consists of building up the value of the goods from their constituent elements of cost, plus a margin for profit. It involves the production of the manufacturer's accounts, and agreement to checking of the information by the customs authorities of the exporting State.

(5) Default method. This is a last resort using reasonable accounting practices on the basis of the principles contained in Article VII of the GATT. In practice it usually involves a large element of negotiation with Customs, but the importer has a right to a written statement of the basis of the valuation which, at the end of the process, Customs adopt.

It was held in Case 357/87, *Schmid v. Hauptzollamt Stuttgart-West*,[25] that, since packagings are chargeable to duty at the rates applicable to the goods they contain, where returnable packings are not returned and compensation is paid to the sender, the compensation is part of the cost of the goods for the purposes of customs valuation. In that case, the packagings consisted of beer barrels, bottles and crates, payment for the non-return of which was assessable to duty, and made the subject of a post-clearance recovery. **4.33**

Articles 169 to 172 of the Implementing Regulation provide for the rate of exchange to be used in evaluating in the importing Member State's currency the price of goods denominated in the currency of a third country. The Code Committee approves detailed regulations made by the Commission to clarify particular matters arising in the course of applying the principal legislation. Pursuant to this, the Implementing Regulation[26] prescribes the form for declaring particulars relating to customs value. A declaration is not necessary for imports whose value is below 5,000 European currency units (ECU) or which are non-commercial in character, unless required by the Customs authorities. The point in time by reference to which valuation takes place is that prescribed in the rules of any special customs procedure applicable, or on the entry of the goods for free circulation. **4.34**

A large number of detailed provisions in the Implementing Regulation supplements the main principles. Thus, there are definitions of "control", **4.35**

[25] [1988] E.C.R. 6239, [1989] 1 C.M.L.R. 605.
[26] Arts. 178 *et seq.*

relevant to cases in which the importer and exporter are related, rules on royalties and licence fees, the place of introduction to the Community, the valuation of perishable goods, transport costs, carrier media for use in ADP equipment, notes interpreting the provisions of the Code and notes on the accounting principles to be used for the default method of valuation (see paragraph 4.32).

## Warehousing and free zones

**4.36** The system for customs warehousing of goods is designed to allow goods to be imported into the Community customs territory, and yet for many of the consequences of importation, notably the obligation to pay duty and levies, to be held in suspense. There is now in principle no upper time limit for warehousing,[27] but the goods must be entered in the normal way; they may not be processed and will be subject to various checks by Customs to ensure that there is no abuse. Warehouses may be owned by the Customs administration itself, but are normally privately owned and subject to Customs approval before they can be used for this purpose.[28]

**4.37** Detailed legislation governing the warehousing scheme is now contained in the Implementing Regulation.[29] After warehousing, goods may be released for free circulation in the Community, placed under a specific customs regime (such as inward processing) or be re-exported. In the first case, they will be liable to duty at the date of their release at the rates then prevailing, with rules to ascertain the value to be taken into account in the various situations which may obtain. While in the warehouse, goods may be subject to normal handling operations. Alternatively, they may be sold while remaining in the warehouse without incurring liability to duty. If the goods are removed illicitly, duty is payable, but no duty is payable if they are lost by reason of *force majeure*, accident or deterioration.

**4.38** Under Article 49 of the Code, customs entry procedures may permit the temporary warehousing of goods in approved premises before they are finally cleared for release or entry to a particular customs scheme. In the case of imports arriving by sea, this may last up to 45 days from first entry being made; where the goods arrive by land or air, the maximum delay is 20 days. In either case, a longer period may be permitted by Customs which "shall not however exceed genuine needs which are jus-

[27] Art. 108 of the Code.
[28] Arts. 99 & 100 of the Code.
[29] Title III, Chapter 2.

tified by the circumstances". Only normal handling to maintain the condition of the goods is allowed. Goods which are not, within the time limits, definitively entered for free circulation, placed under a customs procedure or re-exported, may be sold or stored at the importer's expense.[30]

Similar in concept to customs warehouses are free zones as they are called in some States, free ports.[31] They consist of small enclaves in the Community's customs territory inside which goods are treated as not having entered the Community, at least for the purpose of payment of duties and agricultural levies, or of any quantitative restrictions applicable. Goods may thus be imported to them without regard to the Community tariff regimes normally applicable, and normally without entry and for an indefinite period. The goods may be the subject of normal handling, be destroyed, be entered for inward processing or may be subject to certain other actions. They may not, however, be consumed within the free zone, and when they are released into free circulation they are dutiable as at that date and in the condition in which they then are, the costs of storage being disregarded.[32] **4.39**

## Inward processing

The inward processing scheme established under Articles 114 to 129 of the Code allows the import free of duty of goods from third countries in order to be processed within the Community and subsequently re-exported outside it in the form of compensating products; provision is also made for the remission or repayment of duties on goods which have been released into free circulation but which undergo processing and re-export in the same way. The goods covered by the scheme may include those which are necessary or useful for the processing operation, but which themselves cease to exist in the course of it. The operation must be approved by Customs if the goods are above a certain value limit per importer per annum, when it must be shown that the processing will create the best conditions for the export of the compensating products and that the essential interests of Community producers will not be prejudiced. **4.40**

The scheme therefore has an important discretionary element and is intended to serve the Community economy's needs; it is accordingly restricted to persons established within the Community. Part II, Title III, **4.41**

[30] Art. 53 of the Code.
[31] Arts. 166–181 of the Code.
[32] See also the Implementing Regulation, Title V.

Chapter 3, of the Implementing Regulation lays down a large number of criteria on the basis of which the economic judgment is made whether the use of the scheme is justified. The goods exported will be compensating products, which are defined as products incorporating the imported item, either in the same State or after processing, or incorporating similar products obtained in the Community and equivalent to the imported ones. Where equivalent products are used in exported compensating products, the import of the goods to replace the equivalent goods may be subsequent; thus, the use of immediately available Community goods, rather than waiting for goods to be imported under relief, is not penalised and exports are facilitated.

**4.42** The importer must furnish all relevant information and, if requested, give security for the duty which will become payable if the terms of the scheme are not complied with. The national authorities will determine the period within which the operation must be completed and the compensating products exported (or in some cases they may instead be placed in a warehouse, in a free zone or destroyed, etc.); permission can be given for the goods to be released into free circulation, though normally only on payment of the duty which has been suspended. Any duty thus payable (or payable if the conditions of the scheme are not complied with) is normally based on the liability as at the date of entry for inward processing, but in some cases the compensating products may be dutiable.

## Outward processing

**4.43** This is the converse of inward processing, and provides the means by which goods in free circulation within the Community can be exported to be processed, adapted or repaired outside the Community, and re-imported wholly or partly free of duty. It applies equally to goods originating in the Community and to those which have previously been imported (but not those which have attracted an export refund or remission of import duty), and it may also be applied to goods which have undergone inward processing. Like inward processing, the import to and export from the Community may take place in different Member States. In this scheme, it is also necessary for it to be established that its use will not seriously prejudice the essential interests of Community undertakings in the same field; it is only open to businesses established within the Community, and security for the duty may be required.

**4.44** Where it is proved that goods have been repaired in a third country free of charge pursuant to a contractual guarantee, or on account of a fault in manufacture, there is total exemption from duties on re-import. In other cases, the relief is calculated by crediting against the duty payable on the import of the compensating products from the country where processing has taken place, the duty which would be payable on the import of the goods themselves from the same country. For this purpose, the duty is based on the quantity and classification of the goods at the point at which they are accepted for outward processing, while the rate and valuation to be taken into account are those applicable when the goods are reimported in the form of compensating products.

The principal legislation is now contained in Articles 145–160 of the Code and Part II, Title III, Chapter 6, of the Implementing Regulation, which also covers the temporary export of goods for repair or replacement. The imported product may enter free of charge as a replacement under a contract guarantee or on account of a defect in manufacture. In other cases, in order to qualify for this relief, the imported item must be classed under the same tariff subheading as that which is exported in exchange, be of the same quality and have the same technical characteristics. The import must normally be within the time limits laid down by the customs administration. Permission may be given for the import to precede the export of the faulty item, so long as the latter goes out within 12 months of the import. 4.45

## Processing before release for free circulation

Articles 130 to 136 of the Code allow for the processing of goods under customs control before assessment to and payment of duty on import. This facility is limited to certain processes and to persons established within the Community, offering such security for duty as the customs administration may require, and to other detailed conditions prescribed in Part II, Title III, Chapter 4, of the Implementing Regulation. It is subject to it being economically impossible to reverse the process, to the effect not being to circumvent the origin rules and quantitative restrictions applicable to the goods before transformation and—as in the inward processing regime—to the operation being conducive to establishing or maintaining a Community industry undertaking such work without prejudicing the interest of Community producers of similar goods. The goods resulting are dutiable on their release into free circulation at the rates then appropriate to them as processed. 4.46

## Returned goods

Under Articles 185–187 of the Code, goods which have been exported and are returned to the Community may be readmitted free of duty, if 4.47

they were in free circulation before export. The normal time limit for this is three years. Agricultural products will not be eligible if agricultural export subsidies have been paid, unless they are repaid; proof must be furnished that the goods could not be used in the third country for reasons outside the exporter's control, or that they could not be entered for home use in the third country or were returned as defective. The relief does not apply to goods exported under outward processing. The person reimporting need not be the same as the exporter. The Implementing Regulation, Part III, governs the scheme and prescribes in detail the reasons for which a return of goods may be recognised.

## Dumping and export subsidies

**4.48** Dumping is the practice by which goods are imported at a price lower than their price on the domestic market of the exporting country. It must be distinguished from the import of goods at a price lower than that at which they are or can be produced within the Community, *e.g.* because the exporting country enjoys lower production costs or a higher degree of efficiency in its industry. Dumping may be the object of anti-dumping duties if it is considered that it gives rise to significant prejudice to an existing or possible Community-based industry.

**4.49** The general legislation is contained in Regulation 2423/88,[33] although there are often specific anti-dumping clauses in third country trade agreements, which will take precedence over the general rules. Following a complaint of dumping practices and a preliminary investigation, a provisional duty may be imposed by the Commission, while a definitive duty will susbequently be imposed by the Council if the Commission's investigation justifies it; the Commission may accept undertakings from exporters in lieu of imposing duties.

**4.50** The regulation makes provision for the ascertainment of the domestic selling price where there are no domestic sales of the goods, or where the domestic sales do not take place on a normal commercial basis, as where domestic sales are to a captive market or consistently at less than cost. Also covered are cases where the dumped product is routed through a third country, and cases in which the price differential is concealed until an arm's length sale within the Community takes place, for example by reason of arrangements between the exporter and the importer. Formulae for calculating the dumping margin are laid down, with special provisions in the case of state trading countries where there is no market economy.

[33] [1988] O.J. L209.

The same regulation provides for the imposition of countervailing duties on entry to the Community in the case of products the subject of aids or subsidies in the exporting country. There must, in this case also, be significant prejudice to a Community industry before the powers can be invoked. An illustrative (but not exhaustive) list of subsidies is given, including favourable transport charges, remission or repayment of direct taxes or social security contributions related to exports, remission or repayment of indirect taxes on exported goods of an amount greater than that charged on the same goods internally, and preferential export credit guarantees or loans. 4.51

A special case of dumping is encountered when, in order to circumvent the legislation, goods are imported in parts and then assembled or otherwise subjected to manufacturing processes within the Community and sold at prices which would have attracted the anti-dumping provisions had the finished goods been imported. Anti-dumping duty may be imposed on the finished product leaving the factory in the Community, at the anti-dumping rate applicable to the finished product but by reference to the c.i.f. value of the parts imported for assembly in this way. 4.52

Three conditions must also be satisfied: 4.53

(a) that the assembly is carried out by a person connected with an exporter of like products subject to a definitive anti-dumping duty;
(b) that the assembly has started or substantially increased after the anti-dumping investigation leading to the duty in (a) had commenced; and
(c) that the value of the parts or materials used in the finished product which have come from the country concerned is at least 50 per cent. of that of all the parts and materials used.

It will be seen that this is essentially a supplementary provision which will only be of significance in the context of anti-dumping measures of the normal kind.

## Co-operation between customs authorities

Virtually all legislation relating to customs, while previously contained in Community directives and national legislation, is now in the form of regulations, which need little in the way of national provisions to supplement them. This is part of an explicit policy to give as close a degree of uniformity to customs law throughout the Community as possible, in view of the fact that the Customs Union is one of the Community's foundations and needs to function in the same way throughout, in 4.54

order to avoid distortions to trade and business patterns. Although it is too soon for a Community customs administration to have emerged,[34] particularly in view of the number of non-Community matters still the responsibility of the national administrations, there is now close collaboration between the 12 Member States.

4.55 The first form this takes is prescribed by Part IV, Title IV, Chapter 4, of the Implementing Regulation which, following a number of earlier provisions, provides for officials of each State to liaise, and to offer assistance to each other in investigating fraud, including the creation ad hoc of Community-wide enquiry teams which may also conduct investigations in third countries. It covers customs duties and agricultural levies.

4.56 Directive 76/308[35] provides, in contrast to the traditional rule of law to the contrary, that any Member State must, on request by another, take legal action to recover payment of duties, agricultural levies and debts due in the context of the common agricultural policy, together with related costs and interest. In the United Kingdom, therefore, customs, etc., debts due in any other Member State are recoverable by action taken by Customs and Excise against any debtor within the jurisdiction. There are safeguards to ensure that the defendant has had an opportunity to contest liability, and to prevent the recovery machinery being used if he can show that he has not. This directive also applies to value-added tax and is discussed further in Chapter 11.

## Payment of duty

4.57 It is necessary to ascertain the point in time at which duties are chargeable in order to deal with such questions as tariff rates, reliefs, valuation and the like. Likewise, it is necessary to ascertain the identity of the person or persons liable to make payment and the circumstances in which payments may be refunded or remitted. These topics are now covered under the overall heading of "customs debt" by Articles 189 to 242 of the Code and Part IV of the Implementing Regulation.

4.58 The customs debt is of course primarily discharged by payment of the duty, but may also be discharged in a number of other circumstances detailed in the legislation but notably by limitation, cancellation of an entry by Customs or on remission. Confiscation of the goods also oper-

[34] Since 1991 there has been a Community-wide training scheme for customs officials: see [1991] O.J. L187/41 (the Matthaeus Programme).

[35] [1976] O.J. L73/18, as last amended by Directive 79/1071, [1979] O.J. L331/10.

ates to extinguish duty liability, but criminal penalties related to duty payable on forfeited goods are unaffected, and there is a saving regarding national provisions on seizure and forfeiture of goods. Exceptions are also made for cases of *force majeure*, authorised destruction of goods re-exported from the Community.

Detailed rules apply to specific situations such as inward processing and certain preferential trade regimes, and there is a saving for national rules which impose liability on other persons than those listed in the Community legislation. In general, the combined effect of the regulations in relation to duty points on importation and liable persons may be summarised in the table following. 4.59

| *Circumstances in which duty is payable* | *Person liable for payment* |
|---|---|
| (a) The acceptance of an entry where the goods are put into free circulation | The person in whose name the entry is made and any principal |
| (b) The physical entry of goods into the customs territory of the Community in violation of customs procedure | The persons bringing the goods into the territory and any person acquiring them or associated with the offence |
| (c) The time at which goods under customs control are removed therefrom | The person removing the goods from control and any person acquiring them or associated with the offence |
| (d) The time at which a condition to which goods are subject is breached, or they are admitted to a customs regime subject to conditions which they did not satisfy | The person liable to carry out the conditions or to satisfy them initially |
| (e) The point at which goods are used for a purpose other than that for which an end-use relief has been given, or at which they are put into free circulation without satisfying a condition subject to which such relief was given | The person responsible for compliance with the end-use obligations or conditions |
| (f) The movement at which goods are destroyed with a replayment or remission of duty if the waste or scrap remaining from them is retained with the Community | The person in whose name the goods are entered and any principal |

**4.60** The post-clearance recovery of duties is regulated by Articles 220 to 221 of the Code and by Part IV, Title III, of the Implementating Regulation. Duties not paid at the normal time (or not fully paid) may be recovered from the person liable for their payment at any time within three years from the date of the original duty assessment or, if none, the date of the duty point. This time limit does not apply if the initial non-recovery was due to action liable to penalty, in which case national time limits apply. Various provisions safeguard the debtor, no recovery may take place if the underpayment was due to incorrect information given by the administration, or was made under provisions later quashed or annulled by a court; likewise, a mistake by the administration which could not reasonably have been detected by the person liable to pay duty, acting in good faith and in compliance with the law, will prevent recovery action.

**4.61** Case 161/88, *Binder v. Hauptzollamt Bad Reichenall,*[36] demonstrated, however, the limitations of these provisions. In that case, the official German Customs manual showed the duty on certain goods at 10.4 per cent. on the basis of a Commission proposal to reduce the duty to that level; the proposal, however, was not adopted by the Council, and the duty remained at 13 per cent. The importer, who had imported goods in reliance on the information contained in the manual and had been charged duty at 10.4 per cent., claimed to be entitled to the benefit of the regulation. The Court held that, since the correct position had been apparent from the *Official Journal,* the full duty must be recovered. But in Case C–250/91, *Hewlett Packard,*[37] the Court held that, when an error by the customs administration of a second Member State had led to the importer making an error he could plead good faith if the matter was complex and he could not reasonably be expected to have spotted the error. Article 871 of the Implementing Regulation provides for doubtful cases of this kind to be referred to the Commission for consideration by the Code Committee.

**4.62** Under Articles 217 to 221 of the Code, rules are established governing the assessment of duty and the time limits within which it must be done. Following determination of the duty, the amount payable must be communicated to the person liable to pay, unless the amount is the same as that shown in the import entry, in which case the release of the goods may be taken to be the requisite communication. If security is given, there may be composite assessments to duty where goods are allowed to be removed from charge over a period not exceeding 31 days, the assessments being made within five days there-

[36] [1989] E.C.R. 2415.
[37] Not yet reported.

after. Otherwise, duty should be entered in the accounts within two days after the release of the goods from customs charge, or the happening of events which crystallise a liability. Subject to any rights of appeal, payment is then due within a maximum of 10 days[38] (or less in the case of composite assessments, if the result would be to give the importer longer than he would be entitled to under deferment). There is a normal overall time limit of three years for assessment of duty.[39]

## Deferment of duty

Deferred payment of duty, interest free, for up to 30 days from the date the duty is assessed is also provided for by Articles 225 to 228 of the Code. Deferment may be given by reference to all the amounts assessed over a period not exceeding 31 days, or by reference to composite assessments in respect of clearances during a similar period—in which case the deferment period is reduced by half the number of days in the assessment periods—or by reference to individual assessments. Any delay in assessment beyond the permitted time limit is deducted from the deferment period. Any further period of credit may only be granted on commercial terms. Member States must require bonds or guarantees for the duty thus deferred. The means of payment acceptable are for Member States to determine. **4.63**

## Remission or repayment of duty

Lastly, a variety of circumstances, laid down in Articles 235 to 242 of the Code and Part IV, Title IV, of the Implementing Regulation 1430/79, may entitle the importer to remission or repayment of duty subject to the time limits indicated, and subject to conditions to prevent abuse. Applications for relief are decided upon in the Member State where duty was assessed, even if the goods have since passed elsewhere in the Community. The cases include: error in assessment (three years); entry in error for free circulation instead of for a customs regime (three months); and goods rejected by an importer because of failure to comply with the requirements of the contract under which they were imported, or which were damaged in transport to the customs post where they were entered or while in customs charge (12 months). **4.64**

[38] Art. 222 of the Code.
[39] Art. 221 of the Code.

4.65 Remission, etc., is also given for goods which are dispatched in error, unsuitable for use by reason of a mistake in the order for them, are discovered after release not to comply with the legal requirements relating to their use (or where such requirements are changed after release), delivered later than a strict contractual time limit, or given to charities where the charity sends them overseas or could have imported them itself with relief from duty; likewise relief is available in cases in which duties may be relieved under Article 220 of the Code by reason, *inter alia,* of an error made in good faith. It is generally necessary for the goods either to be re-exported, destroyed under customs control or, exceptionally, to be warehoused, placed in a free zone, or in certain cases given to charity. Cases of particular difficulty are referred to the Commission, who consult the Code Committee.[40]

## Customs control

4.66 Provisions about customs control are frequently found in Community legislation dealing with individual customs regimes or reliefs and in considerable detail in the Code and the Implementing Regulation. In so far as it is not superseded by the Community legislation, national machinery provisions are also applicable; since some national customs business, such as legislation on drugs, arms control and pornography, is largely outside Community competence the local law applicable to it remains unaffected.[41]

4.67 The Code and the Implementing Regulation deal in detail with the procedures to be adopted by importers and Customs on the arrival of goods in the Community Customs territory, the movement of goods into Customs charge, their handling, the making of entries or customs declarations and the point at which goods under the external Community transit procedure (see Chapter 3) become subject to the normal customs regime. Liability for compliance with the obligations prescribed is placed on any person who assumes responsibility for the carriage of the goods after they have entered the customs territory of the Community (unless they are simply crossing that territory without having a destination within it), or any person who holds goods after they have been unloaded. Provision is made for simplified procedures, but Customs authorities are given full powers of control over the

[40] Implementing Regulation, Art. 905.

[41] Because of this phenomenon, there can be the appearance of national machinery legislation remaining extant over the whole area of customs law when the E.C. legislation alone will be applicable to the greater part of it.

movement of goods before clearance, including powers of destruction and extensive information powers.

## United Kingdom legislation

As has been seen, Community customs law is now in the form of directly applicable regulations, requiring little or no supplementary national legislation. In general, the administrative and procedural provisions will be found in the Customs and Excise Management Act 1979, as amended, and in regulations and orders made thereunder. The general law on the direct applicability of Community regulations is sufficient to ensure that no implementing legislation is needed in the United Kingdom for the charging of Community customs duties. Section 5 of the European Communities Act 1972, nonetheless, specifically authorises the charge of such duties and treats them as duties due to the Crown. Section 6, similarly, treats agricultural levies as Community customs duties, and provides for the Commissioners of Customs and Excise to collect them on behalf of the Intervention Board for Agricultural Produce (now called the Intervention Board Executive Agency). **4.68**

## Appeals

Apart from cases in which a preliminary reference to the Commission in connection with relief from or remission of duty is sought (see paragraphs 4.61 and 4.65 above) Articles 243 to 246 of the Code provide for all appeals to be made to the national customs administration or to an independent body, which may be a judicial body or an equivalent specialised jurisdiction. An appeal may be made on any matter concerning the application of Community customs legislation (which includes agricultural levies but not value-added tax) but it does not lead to the suspension of the customs decision. The Code requires that in cases of special hardship the appeal may be brought without deposit of the duty. **4.69**

These requirements have been implemented in the United Kingdom by sections 14 to 16 of the Finance Act 1994, which interpret the Code as making the possible administrative appeal it mentions a precondition for the exercise of the right of appeal to the independent judicial body, namely the VAT and Duties Tribunal. Included in the right of appeal provided by the British legislation is the right to appeal against the conditions upon which goods have been restored following forfeiture. Decisions in criminal matters are not within the **4.70** scope of the right of appeal and prosecutions for offences thus remain unaffected. Also unaffected is the right to give notice of claim against seizure, with the concomitant obligation of Customs to initiate condemnation proceedings to establish the legality of the seizure.

# CHAPTER 5

# TRADE WITH NON-COMMUNITY COUNTRIES

The Treaty envisages the Community being a party to foreign trade agreements and conventions, entering negotiations and forming association agreements with third countries. Article 210 provides that the Community shall have legal personality. This gives the Community the capacity to establish links with third countries in varying areas of activity which form the subject-matter of the Treaty and enable the Community to enjoy the capacity to establish contractual links with non-Member States over the whole field of objectives defined in Part I of the Treaty: see Case 22/70, *Commission v. Council (AERTA)*.[1] Another important step was the decision of the Court of Justice, in Joined Cases 21–24/72, *NV International Fruit Company v. Produktschap*,[2] that the GATT rules bind the Community, because the Member States were originally parties to GATT and the commercial policy powers of the Member States were taken over by the Community. **5.01**

As and when a new state becomes a party to the GATT Agreement the E.C. issues decisions incorporating the accession of such a state to its agreement with the USA to the GATT Agreement.

## The common commercial policy

Article 113 of the Treaty provides that the common commercial policy shall be based on uniform principles, particularly in regard to changes in tariff rates, the conclusion of tariff and trade agreements, the achievement of uniformity in measures of liberalisation, export policy and measures to protect trade such as those to be taken in cases of dumping or **5.02**

[1] [1971] E.C.R. 263, [1971] C.M.L.R 335.
[2] [1972] E.C.R. 1219, [1975] 2 C.M.L.R. 1.

subsidies. Where agreements with third countries need to be negotiated, the Commission must make recommendations to the Council, which authorises the Commission to open the necessary negotiations. The Community has adopted measures under Article 113 in connection with the administration of the Common Customs Tariff in the field of valuation of goods or rules of origin of goods. It has adopted means of protection against unfair trade practices by third countries. Regulation 2176/84[3] provides for an anti-dumping duty on any product which causes injury to a Community industry if it is dumped. Special anti-dumping agreements have been drawn up; Commission Decision 90/378[4] as amended by a Commission Notice[5] with Brazil, Regulation 541/91[6] with China, and Regulation 993/93[7] with Japan. Regulation 2641/84[8] provides remedies against improper commercial practices. Pursuant to Article 113 the Community has entered into a large number of agreements, and is now a party to all GATT agreements (including the original one by virtue of the decision in *NV International Fruit Company*).

5.03 Other multinational agreements have been drawn up by the Community to establish an International Science and Technology Centre with the United States, Japan and Russia (Regulation 3955/92),[9] emphasising the objective to redirect the skills and knowledge of scientists and engineers in the field of weaponry from mass destruction to peaceful purposes. Commission Decision 92/439[10] provides for co-operation between the E.C. Japan, Russia and the United States in the field of engineering design activities for the International Thermonuclear Experimental Reactor (ITER) to demonstrate the scientific and technological feasibility of fusion energy for peaceful purposes. Decision 90/170[11] provides for control of trans-frontier movements of hazardous wastes between the E.C. and OECD members. Decision 93/98[12] deals with the Basle Convention for control of transboundary movement of hazardous wastes.

## Relations with the EFTA States

5.04 An important set of agreements is those that are with the EFTA countries which have not joined the Community (Austria, Finland, Iceland,

[3] [1984] O.J. L201/1.
[4] [1990] O.J. L184/16.
[5] [1990] O.J. L218/62.
[6] [1991] O.J. L60/1.
[7] [1993] O.J. L104/4.
[8] [1984] O.J. L252/1.
[9] [1992] O.J. L409/1.
[10] [1992] O.J. L244/13.
[11] [1990] O.J. L92/52.
[12] [1993] O.J. L39/1.

Norway and Sweden). In the case of the agreements between the EEC and Austria,[13] Iceland,[14] Norway,[15] Sweden[16] and Switzerland,[17] the primary reason for the agreements was to consolidate and to extend, upon the enlargement of the Community in 1972, the economic relations between the Community and the EFTA States (see the preambles to the agreements), whilst the agreement with Finland[18] expresses a desire to contribute appropriate solutions to the economic problems facing Finland as a result of the enlargement (see preamble). The aim of all the agreements is the harmonious development of economic relations leading to an improvement in living and employment conditions in both the EEC and its treaty partners, fair conditions of competition between the contracting parties, and liberalisation of world trade. The main instrument in achieving this is the creation of a free trade zone between the parties to each agreement through the removal of tariff barriers in relation to certain industrial products originating in either the Community or the contracting States. Rules governing the free movement of goods constitute an important part of the agreements. Arrangements for the dismantling of customs duties prohibit the introduction of any new customs duties or of charges having the equivalent effect to customs duties and charges and equivalent measures on exports between the parties, and lay down timetables for the progressive abolition of existing duties (now completed). (See Articles 9–12).

To determine whether or not products are covered by the provisions of the main agreements, Protocol 3 to all the agreements sets out the detailed rules for determining their origin. The rules of origin have been amended several times since the original agreements were signed. Modifications and derogations were codified in 1984, replacing and repealing the original Protocol 3 by an exchange of letters, now published in the *Official Journal*.[19] Further adjustments appear later.[20] The last agreement dealing with Protocol 3 concerning the definition of the concept of "originating product" and methods of administrative co-operation was concluded in 1988,[21] and amended by regulations applicable to individual EFTA States: Regulation 2144/90 with Austria,[22] Regulation 2145/90 with Finland,[23] Regulation 2146/90 with Iceland,[24] Regulation 2147/90 5.05

13 [1972] O.J. L300/2.
14 [1972] O.J. L301/2.
15 [1973] O.J. L171/2.
16 [1972] O.J. L300/97.
17 [1972] O.J. L300/189.
18 [1973] O.J. L328/2.
19 [1984] O.J. L323.
20 [1986] O.J. L134 and L47.
21 [1988] O.J. L149/75.
22 [1990] O.J. L199/1.
23 [1990] O.J. L199/3.
24 [1990] O.J. L199/5.

with Norway,[25] 2148/90 with Sweden[26] and Regulation 2149/90 with Switzerland.[27] These regulations deal with Article 28 of Protocol 3 and in particular with Note 7 in Annex III to the protocol dealing with textile products. Article 13 prohibits the introduction of quantitative restrictions on imports or measures having equivalent effect between the Community and the EFTA States with provision for the abolition of existing ones. The agreements do not apply to agricultural products, but the contracting parties have granted each other a number of agricultural and fishery concessions, particularly in the case of Iceland, one half of whose exports to the Community were fisheries. Internal fiscal measures which may directly or indirectly discriminate between products of one party and like products originating in the territory of the other are proscribed (Article 18), as are restrictions on payments relating to trade in goods and on commercial credit in which an EEC/EFTA resident participated (Article 19). Derogations from the free movement of goods provisions, if permitted, must not amount to "means of arbitrary discrimination or a disguised restriction on trade".

**5.06** The agreements contain a number of safeguard clauses concerned with security interests or defence. There are also safeguard provisions relating to competition, dumping or serious deterioration in a regional economy, to be invoked in accordance with the procedure prescribed in Article 27. The agreements establish a joint committee responsible for the administration of the agreement, to be convened at least once a year. All the agreements contain a "denunciation clause". With the exception of the Finnish one, the agreements can be terminated on 12 months' notice, while the agreement with Finland provides for termination three months after notification has been given. Additional protocols to the agreements were concluded on the accession of Spain and Portugal.[28] As we have seen, the agreements contain rules approximating to those of the Treaty concerning the free movement of goods and free competition. However, the interpretation of the terms of the agreements does not always have to follow the rules of the EEC Treaty, since their basis is not the Treaty itself with its principles and objectives: see Case 270/80, *Polydor Ltd. v. Harlequin Record Shops Ltd.*,[29] dealing with important restrictions based on domestic copyright laws.

**5.07** Pursuant to Article 113 of the EEC Treaty, EFTA and the E.C. entered into an agreement on common transit procedures, Decision 93/69,[30]

25 [1990] O.J. L199/7.
26 [1990] O.J. L199/9.
27 [1990] O.J. L199/11.
28 [1986] O.J. L321 and L337.
29 [1982] E.C.R. 329, [1982] 1 C.M.L.R. 677.
30 [1993] O.J. L25/26.

agreeing to the amendment of the EEC/EFTA Convention of May 20, 1987, now incorporated into the European Economic Area Agreement.[31] Decision 90/518[32] provides for the establishing of procedures, mutually agreed, for the exchange of information in the field of technical regulation, with the aim of avoiding the creation of technical barriers to trade. In addition to multilateral agreements, bilateral agreements have been agreed between the E.C. and individual EFTA members such as Decision 91/122,[33] a co-operation agreement between the E.C. and Finland on a programme for research and development in the field of applied metrology and chemical analysis. Similar agreements have been drawn up with Sweden (Decision 91/123)[34] and Switzerland (Decision 91/124).[35]

## The European Economic Area

On May 2, 1991, seven of the EFTA countries, the EEC and its 12 Member States signed the Agreement on the European Economic Area (EEA), later amended to take into account an opinion of the European Court on its compatibility with the EEC Treaty. Following a Swiss referendum an adjusting protocol was negotiated to proceed without Switzerland. The agreement[36] became effective from January 1994. The aim of the EEA Agreement is to strengthen trade and economic relations between the Community and the six EFTA signatories. One such feature is known as the "four freedoms" of the E.C., which are extended to the EEA: free movement of goods, services, capital and persons (Articles 8 to 52). 5.08

The basic principles for the free movement of goods, (Part II, Articles 8 to 27), are to prohibit customs duties on imports and exports, (Article 10, Protocol 5), and any other charges having an equivalent effect, although the agreement does not extend to agriculture or remove border controls. Special arrangements for agriculture, fisheries and transport are laid down in bilateral agreements which enter into force simultaneously with the EEA Agreement. Restrictions both on imports and exports are also prohibited, (Articles 11 and 12), except for goods in transit and except on grounds of public morality, public policy or public security, protection of health and life, (not only of humans but of animals and plants), protection of national treasures and industrial and commercial property, (Article 13). Two areas of the provision for the movement of goods are agricultural and fishery products, (Articles 17 to 20, Protocol 9 Annex I), 5.09

[31] [1994] O.J. L1.
[32] [1990] O.J. L291/1.
[33] [1991] O.J. L61/31.
[34] [1991] O.J. L61/37.
[35] [1991] O.J. L61/43.
[36] [1994] O.J. L1.

and coal and steel products, (Article 27, Protocols 14 and 25). The Rules of Origin (Protocol 4) have been simplified and improved. Here the value of any processing carried out in the EEA can now be added to the value of materials originating in the EEA for the purpose of determining whether a product qualifies for EEA preferential treatment. The agreement provides that agreements reached between one of the contracting parties and third countries must be equivalent to those reached with the Community. It provides for the technical requirements, standards, testing and certification applicable to products such as motor vehicles, agricultural and forestry tractors, household appliances, gas appliances, construction plant and equipment (Article 23, Protocol 12, Annex II). Annex III implements Article 23(c) which provides for product liability. Amending Directive 85/374,[37] it defines the party liable for imported products. Article 24 and Annex IV contain specific provisions and arrangements concerning energy.

5.10 The other "three freedoms", free movement of persons, services and capital are provided for in Part III, Articles 28 to 52 of the agreement. The aims are to achieve freedom of movement for workers and self-employed persons (Articles 28 to 30), allowing them the freedom to accept employment and thereby establish themselves in any one State of the contracting parties (Articles 31 to 35). Such rights are limited only on the grounds of public policy, public security or public health. Annexes V, VI, and VII make specific provisions for the free movement of workers, social security (and the payment of benefits), and the mutual recognition of professional qualifications achieved by individuals in their own State. Annexes VIII to XI contain specific provisions on the right of establishment. Provisions relating to the free movement of services (Articles 36 to 39) allow E.C. and EFTA nationals the freedom to provide services within the territory of one of the contracting parties. In particular, such services include activities of an industrial or commercial character, and those of craftsmen and professionals. Specific provisions for this freedom are provided for within Annexes IX to XI of the Agreement. The free movement of capital (Articles 40 to 45) emphasises that there should be no restriction or discrimination between the contracting parties based on nationality or residence of the parties or on the place where the capital is invested. Annex XII provides specific provisions for the implementation of this objective. Article 41 makes specific provisions to allow the relevant contracting party to take protective measures in the event of capital fluctuations or disturbances arising as a result of this freedom or because of an imbalance of payments or alteration of exchange rates at national level.

[37] [1989] O.J. L210/29.

Transport by rail, road and inland waterways is provided for in Articles 47 to 52 with specific provisions relating to all modes of transport laid down in Annex XIII. The agreement prohibits any discrimination which takes the form of different rates charged by reference to the country of origin or destination of the goods in question. It further prohibits support or protectionist measures aimed at assisting particular undertakings or industries. Charges or dues over and above transport rates should not exceed reasonable levels and the contracting parties undertake to reduce them progressively. 5.11

The introduction of common rules on competition and state aids is another major achievement of the agreement. The main aim in this area is to achieve parity of rules between the E.C. and EFTA countries. Its main objectives are the prohibition of restrictive agreements, undertakings or decisions which may adversely affect trade between the contracting parties, the object or effect of which may be to prevent, restrict or distort competition within the territories covered by the agreement. Such agreements may concern price fixing, the limitation or control of markets, production or market share. Such agreements are void. However, if agreement or undertakings have a positive effect such as improving production, distribution or promotion of goods, promoting technical and economic progress, they will be valid subject to certain restrictions (Article 53). Any abuse by one or more undertakings in a dominant position is also forbidden (Article 54). To ensure that these provisions are strictly adhered to, the agreement provides for appropriate authorities to be established by the contracting parties jointly (Article 105), and separately (Article 108). Such authorities will co-operate in accordance with the provisions of Protocols 23 and 24. Annex XIV further sets out specific provisions for the enforcement of the competition rules, the E.C. Commission and the EFTA Surveillance Authority monitoring and enforcing these rules. 5.12

In providing for the "four freedoms" the contracting parties have further agreed on a social policy improving the working conditions of the labour force with particular attention drawn to health and safety, the elimination of sex discrimination at work and the promotion of labour/management co-operation (Articles 66 to 71, Annex XVIII). Consumer protection is provided for by Annex XIX and company law by Annex XXII. This annex provides for uniformity to be adopted between the contracting parties in the manner in which companies are established, operated and managed. State aid is dealt with in Articles 61 to 64 which provide that any aid which distorts or threatens to distort competition by favouring certain undertakings or the production of certain goods, will be incompatible with the agreement. However, aid which has a social character, makes good damage caused by natural disaster or is granted to certain 5.13

areas of the Federal Republic of Germany will be valid. Other state aid which may be included in this area may be that given to implement an important project to the common benefit of Europe or for the development of certain economic areas (Article 61). Each contracting party will be responsible for enforcing the state aid provisions. Uniformity must, however, be maintained and such enforcement is strictly provided (Article 62 to 64, Protocols 26 and 27 and Annex XV). Other common rules have been provided for in Annex XVI concerning procurement of products and services covered by the agreement (Article 65.1 and Annex XVI). Also provided for are rules relating to intellectual, industrial and commercial property (Article 65.2) which apply to all products and services, unless otherwise stated (Protocol 28 and Annex XVII). Protocol 28 incorporates international agreements such as the Paris Convention for the Protection of Industrial Property, the Berne Convention for the Protection of Literary and Artistic Works, the Madrid Agreement for the International Registration of Marks and the Patent Co-operation Treaty. It further provides for the improvement of the provisions in Article 65.2 in the light of the GATT Uruguay Round negotiations. Other areas of co-operation agreed upon, outside the "four freedoms", are research and development, information services, environment, education, training and youth, social policy, consumer protection, small and medium-sized enterprises, tourism, audiovisual sector and civil protection (Part VI Article 78), though there is no protocol on civil liberties or human rights. The aim is to achieve closer co-operation which could contribute to the attainment of common objectives. The procedures for developing co-operation in these fields are provided in Articles 79 to 88, Part VII and Protocol 31.

**5.14** The control and enforcement of the agreement will rest in the hands of a number of institutions provided for in the agreement so as to ensure proper implementation and smooth functioning of its provisions. The EEA Council, comprising members of the European Community, members of the E.C. Commission and one member of the government of each EFTA country shall be responsible for giving the political impetus in the implementationt of the agreement. The office of the president of the EEA council is to be held alternately, for a period of six months, by a member of the Council of European Communities and a member of the government of an EFTA State (Articles 89 to 91). An EEA Joint Committee responsible for the effective implementation and operation of the agreement will consist of representatives of the contracting parties and will take decisions speaking with one voice. The office of the President of the EEA Joint Committee will be held as in the EEA Council (Articles 92 to 94). The EEA Joint Parliamentary Committee will have equal numbers of parliamentary representatives from the European Parliament and the parliaments of the EFTA States. While this Committee is intended to promote mutual understanding, it will not enjoy any legislative powers (Article 95). The EEA Consultative Committee with members from the E.C. Economic and Social Committee and EFTA's corresponding bodies will be responsible for examining economic and social issues and promote increased co-operation in this area between the E.C. and EFTA States (Article 96). The decision-making procedures between the contracting parties and the Committees are provided for in Articles 97 to 104 and Protocol 37. To ensure uniformity of interpretation of the agreement a system of case law is to be established by the EEA Joint Committee in full deference to the independence of the various courts of the contracting parties (Article 105 to 107). In addition an EFTA Surveillance Authority will be established responsible for proper compliance with the agreement within the EFTA States (Articles 108 to 110). Further, an EFTA Court will be established competent to settle disputes between EFTA States on EEA matters, take actions concerning EFTA Surveillance procedures and hear appeals from the EFTA Surveillance Authority (Article 108). In the event of disputes arising, Article 111 and Protocol 33 provide procedures to receive them. Measures to safeguard against serious economic, social or environmental difficulties are provided for in Article 112 and 113.

Various protocols allow for special provisions for the participation by Switzerland and Liechtenstein in certain areas of the agreement without full participation in the agreement. Since Austria, Sweden, Finland and Norway have applied to join the Community, the life of the agreement is uncertain. Switzerland, in spite of the negative referendum on the EEA Agreement, has also decided to leave its application to join the Community open. 5.15

## Trade with less developed countries

Agreements with the less developed countries are numerous, often granting preferential tariff treatment and dealing with individual products (*e.g.* textiles). Commodity agreements relate to coffee, cocoa, jute, rubber, tin and wheat. They are intended to stabilise prices and supplies. Decisions 91/179[38] 91/178[39] and 91/537[40] implement the terms of reference for the international study groups for copper, tin and nickel. An agreement establishing a Common Fund for Commodities was introduced by Decision 90/373[41] between the E.C. and all members of the 5.16

[38] [1991] O.J. L89/39.
[39] [1991] O.J. L89/33.
[40] [1991] O.J. L293/23.
[41] [1990] O.J. L182/1.

United Nations or specialised agencies or of the International Atomic Agency. Its main objectives is to serve as a key instrument in attaining the agreed objectives of the integrated programme for commodities as embodied by resolutions of Unctad. The Multi-Fibre Arrangement is designed to prevent the decline of traditional textile industries by stabilising imports and has been implemented by bilateral agreements. These agreements were signed between 1987 and 1988 with 22 countries, in the form of actual agreements or of an exchange of letters. However, in 1992, in accordance with Article 113 of the Treaty, all previous agreements and exchanges of letters were implemented in one Decision 92/625[42] with all countries listed in Annex I. Additional protocols provide for the incorporation of Poland, Hungary, the Czech Republic and Slovakia into this agreement.

## Agreements with Central and East European countries

5.17 There are only limited agreements with state trading countries. The agreement with Yugoslavia contained aid features akin to agreements with the Maghreb countries under Article 238 amended by Regulation 3073/90.[43] However, this agreement was suspended by Decision 91/586[44] and denounced by Decision 91/602.[45] Regulations 1432/92[46] and 2656/92[47] provided for an embargo on Serbia and Montenegro. These have been strengthened by Regulation 990/93.[48] Past agreements with Romania, Hungary and Poland were limited in their scope and nature, and since then bilateral trade and co-operation agreements have been signed between the Community and Hungary, Czechoslovakia and Poland. Decisions 92/611,[49] 92/612[50] and 92/613[51] extend, by way of exchange of letters, the duration of the agreement on trade and co-operation between the E.C., the Czech Republic and Slovakia, Poland and Hungary respectively by deleting the termination date of the agreement and leaving it open. A Europe agreement between between the E.C., and Poland,[52] Hungary[53] and interim agreements with Bulgaria

[42] [1992] O.J. L410/1.
[43] [1990] O.J. L295/6.
[44] [1991] O.J. L315/47.
[45] [1991] O.J. L325/23.
[46] [1992] O.J. L151/3.
[47] [1992] O.J. L266/12.
[48] [1993] O.J. L102/14.
[49] [1992] O.J. L408/1.
[50] [1992] O.J. L408/2.
[51] [1992] O.J. L408/4.
[52] [1993] O.J. L348.
[53] [1993] O.J. L347.

(Decision 93/690)[54] and Czechoslovakia[55] have now been adopted, and when in force will override previous agreements. Decision 89/593[56] concluded an agreement between the E.C. and Poland on trade, commercial and economic co-operation, with Decision 90/115[57] varying the obligations dealing with agricultural trade concessions. Decision 91/159[58] concluded an agreement with Romania on trade, commercial and economic co-operation. The Agreement on Trade and Commercial Economic Co-operation with the USSR, signed on December 18, 1989, covers a wide area of co-operation, but apparently does not affect the level of customs duties. Joint Committees have been set up to discuss and co-ordinate future developments. A further agreement was concluded between E.C. and the USSR (Decision 90/116)[59] allowing for relief for duties, taxes and other charges, with the parties undertaking to abolish most of the quantitative restrictions by the end of 1995. Regulation 2150/91,[60] amended by Regulations 3363/91[61] and 3426/91,[62] provides for a credit agreement and guarantees relating to the export of agricultural products to the USSR. Since the dissolution of the USSR, bilateral trade, commercial and economic agreements have been concluded between the E.C. and most of the former eastern block countries. Each party accords the other most favoured nation treatment, Decision 90/519,[63] concerning Bulgaria, undertakes to abolish quantitative restrictions on imports and exports by the end of 1995. Decisions 92/601[64] with Estonia, 92/602[65] with Latvia and 92/603[66] with Lithuania are very similar in nature and provide for trade, commercial, and economic co-operation, and most favoured nation status, recognising the democratic principles and human rights established by the Helsinki Final Act. The agreements do not preclude the prohibition on imports on the grounds specified in Article 36 of the Treaty.

## Association Agreements

Article 238 of the Treaty forms the basis for a vital part of the commercial policy of the E.C. by providing authority for the Community to enter 5.18

54 [1993] O.J. L323/1.
55 [1993] O.J. L345.
56 [1989] O.J. L339/1.
57 [1990] O.J. L69/69.
58 [1991] O.J. L79/12.
59 [1990] O.J. L68/1.
60 [1991] O.J. L200/12.
61 [1991] O.J. L318/31.
62 [1991] O.J. L325/7.
63 [1990] O.J. L291/8.
64 [1992] O.J. L403/1.
65 [1992] O.J. L403/10.
66 [1992] O.J. L403/19.

into association agreements with a third country or a group of third countries. These agreements now replace many provisions originally included in Part Four of the Treaty dealing with special relations which the original Member States had with former colonial territories either dependent or newly independent. The Community itself is a customs union with a common commercial policy towards third countries and the concept of association involves the extension of the mechanisms of the Customs Union to the associated state. Association does not transfer sovereign powers to common institutions, but the principle of association extending the Customs Union to the associated states avoids the contravention of the General Agreement on Tariffs and Trade. Article 238 provides that the Community may conclude with a third state, a union of states or an international organisation agreements establishing an association involving reciprocal rights and obligations, common action and special procedures. These agreements are to be concluded by the Council acting unanimously after having received the assent of the European Parliament, which must achieve an absolute majority of all its members. The long-term objective of association agreements is the raising of living standards and economic levels of the associated parties, the system of "reciprocal rights and obligations" being aimed at promoting the political and social development of the third state rather than creating strict equality of obligations between the contracting parties: see Case 87/75, *Bresciani*.[67]

5.19 Article 238 also states that an association is to involve its partners in common action and special procedures, and so association agreements establish an institutional framework along the lines of the Community model itself. A Council of Ministers, parliamentary bodies composed of parliamentary delegates and adjudicative institutions (an arbitration tribunal or the European Court of Justice) are responsible for the management and development of the association. As part of Community law association agreements take precedence over conflicting provisions of domestic law: see Case 17/81, *Pabst*.[68] The Community is competent to enter into any association agreement whose subject-matter falls within the scope of the Treaty, although Article 238 envisages agreements falling outside this scope by referring to a procedure laid down in Article 236. Where the division of competence between Member States on the one hand and the Community on the other is not clearly demarcated, the Member States and the Community have concluded what are known as mixed agreements, agreements to which Member States and the Community are signatories, so that they are valid in relation to one group if not the other. In order to safeguard national competence, yet still to pro-

[67] [1976] E.C.R. 129, [1976] 2 C.M.L.R. 62.
[68] [1982] E.C.R. 1331, [1983] 3 C.M.L.R. 11.

duce a common Community position, the Member States have entered into *Internal implementation agreements, e.g.* Internal Implementation Agreement 86/127[69] in relation to the Third Lomé Convention which provides for the common position to be supported by the representatives of the Community in the Council of Ministers under the Convention. The establishment of the European Development Fund called for an internal agreement where financial assistance agreed upon is borne by the Member States. The Community is competent to agree upon financial assistance in its own right if it forms part of the Community budget. In Case 1/76, *Stillegungsfonds,*[70] the Court held that mixed agreements were only authorised so long as they did not infringe the allocation of competence between the Community and the Member States, and Member States' participation was necessary for the realisation of the agreement. The Court will only apply those provisions of mixed agreements which fall within the Community's competence.

Article 238 has been used to conclude a number of association agree- **5.20**
ments which fall into three general categories. Agreements with Greece, Turkey and Malta contemplated eventual membership of the E.C. (The association agreement with Greece lapsed on January 1, 1981 when Greece became a full member of the EEC.) The same also applies to Cyprus. The second group of agreements is with countries in the Mediterranean, as part of a unified and global approach by the Community. The Community has concluded co-operation agreements with Maghreb countries (Algeria, Morocco and Tunisia) and Mashrek countries (Egypt, Lebanon, Jordan and Syria). These agreements are strictly speaking association agreements entered into under Article 238, although they are known as co-operation agreements. Similar provisions exist in the protocols supplementing a trade agreement with Israel, the protocols being based on Article 238. A third group of agreements is represented by the Conventions between the Community and a number of African, Caribbean and Pacific (ACP) states (see paras. 5.25–5.30). Article 131 envisaged these agreements in their original form. The association agreements represent in most cases several agreements, permanent or interim, which reflect changes in the economic climate. Agreements may also take the form of an exchange of letters in the field of trade in specific groups of products.

The association agreement with Turkey, which was entered into in **5.21**
1963,[71] contemplated three stages for achieving a customs union and the harmonisation of measures in various fields. During the first stage, tradi-

[69] [1986] O.J. L86/221.
[70] [1977] E.C.R. 741, [1977] 2 C.M.L.R. 279.
[71] [1964] O.J. 217 3687

tional preferential duties were applied by the Community to specified Turkish exports. The Community also provided loans through the European Investment Bank. During the second stage, which began in 1973, reciprocal trade concessions covered industrial and agricultural products. Regulation 562/81,[72] amended by Regulation 3825/81,[73] provided for the reduction or elimination of customs duties on agricultural products imported by the Community. The third stage has not yet been reached as originally contemplated for a variety of reasons of a political and economic nature. The original agreement was supplemented by Agreement 88/227.[74] Decisions of the Association Council set up under the Association Agreement were held by the Court of Justice to fall within the scope of Article 177 of the Treaty and to have direct effect in the Member States of the Community: see Case C–192/89, *S. Z. Sevince v. Staatssecretarie van Justitie.*[75]

5.22 The association agreement with Malta provides for two stages of five years with the object of attaining a customs union. The agreement provides for a reduction of duties in the industrial sector of 70 per cent. by the Community and 35 per cent. by Malta, and in the agricultural sector of 35 per cent. by Malta only. The original agreement was implemented by Regulation 492/71.[76] It was extended as to the validity of arrangements by Regulation 3670/81[77] and in respect of trade arrangements by Regulation 3508/80[78] and Regulation 3681/85.[79] Financial and technical co-operation was further dealt with by a protocol in 1986 (Decision 87/177).[80]

5.23 The agreements, known as co-operation agreements, with the three Maghreb countries, Algeria, Morocco and Tunisia, are similar. They replace agreements based on Article 113 and are based on Article 238, and came into effect on November 1, 1978. Regulation 2212/78[81] implements the agreement with Tunisia, Regulation 2211/78[82] that with Morocco and Regulation 2210/78[83] that with Algeria. These agreements are supplemented by various protocols, particularly on financial and

[72] [1981] O.J. L65/1.
[73] [1981] O.J. L388/3.
[74] [1988] O.J. L53/91.
[75] [1992] I E.C.R. 3461, [1992] 2 C.M.L.R. 57.
[76] [1971] O.J. L61/2.
[77] [1981] O.J. L367/2.
[78] [1980] O.J. L367/86.
[79] [1985] O.J. L351/87.
[80] [1987] O.J. L71/29.
[81] [1978] O.J. L265/1.
[82] [1978] O.J. L264/1.
[83] [1978] O.J. L263/7.

technical co-operation, the latest being implemented by Decision 88/34[84] in the case of Tunisia, Decision 88/30[85] in the case of Algeria and Decisions 88/452[86] and 88/453[87] in the case of Morocco. Regulation 2211/78 with Morocco is amended by Regulation 3072/90[88] which amends Article 6 and 17 of the protocol concerning the concept of "originating products". Decision 92/548,[89] based on Article 238 of the Treaty, implements the protocol on financial and technical co-operation with Morocco stipulating 220 million ECUs of financial assistance. The trade provisions of each agreement allow for free access to the Community from the respective country except for certain agricultural products listed in Annex II of the EEC Treaty. These products can receive access in certain circumstances but subject to restrictions. There are also provisions relating to social security and family allowances of workers from Maghreb countries working in the Community but the agreements do not guarantee freer access to the Community. In Case C–18/90, *ONEN v. Bahia Kziber*[90] the Court of Justice ruled that the Co-operation Agreement with Morocco precludes a Member State from refusing to grant an unemployment benefit to a member of the family of a worker of Moroccan nationality residing with him on the ground that the person seeking work is a Moroccan national. The concept of social security in the agreement was to be interpreted by analogy with the same concept in Regulation 1408/71.[91] Attached to the agreements are financial protocols granting development aid.

There are similar agreements with the Mashrek countries. Co-operation agreements which were based on Article 238 were concluded with Egypt, Jordan, Lebanon and Syria. They were implemented by Regulation 2213/78[92] with Egypt, Regulation 2214/78[93] with Lebanon, Regulation 2215/78[94] with Jordan and Regulation 2216/78[95] with Syria. Additional protocols to these co-operation agreements were implemented by Decision 88/31[96] in the case of Egypt, Decision 88/33[97] in the case of Lebanon, 5.24

[84] [1988] O.J. L22/33, 34.
[85] [1988] O.J. L22/1, 2.
[86] [1988] O.J. L452/17, 18.
[87] [1988] O.J. L452/32, 33.
[88] [1990] O.J. L295/5.
[89] [1992] O.J. L352/13.
[90] [1991] I E.C.R. 199.
[91] [1971] O.J. Spec. Ed. 416.
[92] [1978] O.J. L266/1.
[93] [1978] O.J. L267/1.
[94] [1978] O.J. L268/1.
[95] [1978] O.J. L269/1.
[96] [1988] O.J. L22/9.
[97] [1988] O.J. L22/25.

Decision 88/32[98] in the case of Jordan and Decision 88/598[99] in the case of Syria. These agreements resemble the agreements with Maghreb countries as to trade arrangements and machinery, although there are no provisions relating to social security. Maghreb and Mashrek agreements also focus on economic and social development co-operation, diversification of the economic structure and promotion of investment. Regulation 3973/86[1] deals with the application of the protocols on financial and technical co-operation concluded between the Community and Maghreb and Mashrek countries, Malta and Cyprus. Additional regulations have been concluded to amend the protocols concerning the concept of "originating products": see Regulation 3069/90[2] with Egypt, Regulation 3071/90[3] with Lebanon, Regulation 3070/90[4] with Jordan.

**5.25** Israel is another Mediterranean country where agreements under Article 238 provide for a Co-operation Council (Additional Protocol) and development aid in form of regular European Investment Bank loans (Financial Protocol). These protocols are implemented by Regulation 2217/78[5] and they form a supplement to a trade agreement with Israel concluded in 1975 under Article 113 and providing for free trade (Regulation 1274/75).[6] These instruments taken together represent an association agreement as usually effected. The Third Protocol of December 18, 1984, entered into under Article 113, provided for the abolition of customs duties by January 1, 1989 (Regulation 3565/84).[7] The definition of "originating products" was further dealt with in Regulation 4163/87[8] in the light of the co-operation agreement. Important protocols were concluded in 1988: the Fourth Additional Protocol to the agreement between the Community and Israel, implemented by Decision 88/596[9] and a protocol relating to financial co-operation, implemented by Decision 88/597.[10] Decision 91/408[11] provides for financial aid for Israel and the Palestinian population of the occupied territories. The agreement of 1975 was interpreted by the Court of Justice in Case 174/84, *Bulk Oil (Zug) AG v. Sun International Ltd.*,[12] where a prohibition of export of oil

[98] [1988] O.J. L22/17.
[99] [1988] O.J. L327/57.
[1] [1986] O.J. L370/5.
[2] [1990] O.J. L295/2.
[3] [1990] O.J. L295/3.
[4] [1990] O.J. L295/4.
[5] [1978] O.J. L270/1.
[6] [1975] O.J. L136/1.
[7] [1984] O.J. L332/1.
[8] [1987] O.J. L397/1.
[9] [1988] O.J. L327/35.
[10] [1988] O.J. L327/51.
[11] [1991] O.J. L227/33.
[12] [1986] E.C.R. 599, [1986] 2 C.M.L.R. 732.

from a Member State (in this case the United Kingdom) to Israel was held to be outside the terms of the agreement.

The association of Cyprus with the Community is now governed by Decision 87/607 of December 21, 1987[13] laying down the conditions and procedures for the implementation of the second stages of the original agreement further amended by Regulation 3914/91.[14] Decision 87/608[15] deals with the conclusion of the protocol to the association agreement consequent upon the accession of Spain and Portugal. The provisions of the original agreement were laid down in a protocol, implemented by Regulation 1247/73,[16] which introduced a mutual reduction of import duties by 35 per cent. over five years, but this has been overtaken by the second stages mentioned above. Decision 90/153[17] concludes the agreement on the protocol for financial and technical co-operation. Its aim is to participate in the financing of projects intended to contribute to the economic and social development of Cyprus. 5.26

Decision 91/114[18] repeals Decision 86/517[19] imposing sanctions on South Africa. Regulation 2340/90[20] prevents trade between the E.C. Member States and Iraq and Kuwait, amended by Regulation 3155/90.[21] Regulation 542/91[22] lifted the embargo against Kuwait, Regulation 811/91[23] amended the list of products to which the embargo applies and Regulation 1194/91[24] amended both Regulations 2340/90 and 3155/90.

## African, Caribbean and Pacific Countries

An association between the Community and dependent territories outside Europe was originally provided for by Articles 131–136 of the Treaty. After these territories (mainly Francophone) obtained independence, they joined in a formal agreement which is represented by the Yaoundé Convention of 1964, replaced by the Second Yaoundé Convention of 1969. Other (Anglophone) African countries (Kenya, Uganda and Tanzania) sought a comparable agreement, resulting in the Arusha Convention of 1968, renewed in 1969. The second Arusha Agreement of 1969 5.27

13 [1987] O.J. L393/1.
14 [1991] O.J. L372/26.
15 [1987] O.J. L393/36.
16 [1973] O.J. L133/87.
17 [1990] O.J. L82/32.
18 [1991] O.J. L59/18.
19 [1986] O.J. L305/45.
20 [1990] O.J. L213/1.
21 [1990] O.J. L304/1.
22 [1991] O.J. L60/5.
23 [1991] O.J. L82/50.
24 [1991] O.J. L115/37.

was essentially limited to trade matters (the second Yaoundé Convention had provided for Community assistance as well) and was based on Article 238. After the accession of the United Kingdom in 1972, independent Commonwealth countries took up the option of joining a comprehensive agreement replacing the Yaoundé Convention. The parties to the Yaoundé Convention with Mauritius and the Arusha Agreement, independent Commonwealth countries and African countries unconnected with the Member States, collectively known as African, Caribbean and Pacific (ACP) countries, all joined, after long negotiations, a comprehensive convention signed at Lomé on February 28, 1975. The extent and nature of the convention is best illustrated by the two lists annexed at the end of this chapter.

5.28 The Lomé Convention continues the principles of free trade and development assistance. It does not refer to "association" but in fact it is such an agreement. Regulation 199/76,[25] which is the legal instrument of the Community in concluding the convention, refers to Article 238. The Lomé Convention covers trade and commercial co-operation, stabilisation of export revenues, financial and technical co-operation and industrial co-operation. The provisions of trade arrangements are non-reciprocal and exports from ACP states are admitted to the Community free of import duties and quantitative restrictions. A small proportion of agricultural exports is subject to certain restrictions. An important part of the convention is a system for the stabilisation of export earnings (Stabex) with a separate protocol on sugar. Under the Stabex system payments are made to ACP economies to compensate for falls in export earnings which normally would have come from the market, but which have been prevented by production or other economic difficulties. The Sugar Protocol is contractual in nature, involving a commitment on the part of the Community to purchase annually at a guaranteed price agreed quantities of cane sugar from ACP producer countries, and a reciprocal commitment on the part of the ACP countries to supply the Community with those quantities. The protocol was concluded for an indefinite period and although it has been annexed to successive conventions, it exists independently. There is a clause providing for termination at the end of five years, subject to two years' notice.

5.29 The Second Lomé Convention, signed at Lomé on October 31, 1979, extends the stabilisation system (Stabex) to agricultural products and to a limited degree to some minerals (Sysmin) and increases the allocation to the European Development Fund, which distributed aid under the convention. Sysmin is a system of aid designed to help those ACP countries whose economies depend on mining products, its principal object-

[25] [1976] O.J. L25/1.

ive being to maintain production capacity at viable levels. The Third Lomé Convention (see below) increases its funding of Stabex, requiring for the first time a degree of ACP accountability to the Community for the use to which they put the Stabex transfers. It also increases funding to Sysmin and introduces some procedural alterations. The Fourth Lomé Convention (see below) has expanded the Stabex programme increasing funds and introducing new rules enabling countries in need of assistance to join the system automatically. The Sysmin system has been extended to cover gold and uranium.

The Third Lomé Convention, signed at Lomé on December 8, 1984, 5.30
entered into force for five years on March 1, 1985. It was implemented by Decision 86/125[26] amended by Regulation 1825/87.[27] Objects and principles of the convention aim at creating a model for relations between developed and developing countries. Most notable of the principles is Article 4 which stresses the concept of self-development, social and cultural values, ideas of human potential and capacity, recognition of the role of women and respect for the desires of the individual. The Community, however, was unsuccessful in its efforts to incorporate into the convention legally binding obligations regarding human rights in spite of the reference in the preamble.

The Fourth Lomé Convention, signed on December 15, 1989, entered into 5.31
force for 10 years on March 1, 1990. It was implemented by Council and Commission Decision 91/400.[28] This convention covers the same areas as the Third Lomé Convention, but introduces some notable changes. Article 5.1 and Article 5.2 link the development and co-operation of the convention to the enjoyment of fundamental human rights. It reafirms the contracting parties' commitment under international law to strive to eliminate discrimination of all types at all levels. Article 5.3 allows for financial resources to be allocated by the E.C. to the ACP countries, at their request, to promote and establish systems to promote human rights. In Part One Chapter 4 states the principles governing the instruments of co-operation, while Chapter 5 sets out the various institutions and their functions to ensure the operation of the convention. Part Two deals in detail with the areas of co-operation between the contracting parties. Articles 33 to 41 emphasise the importance the environment plays in the day to day survival of some of the ACP states. To ensure that enviromental damage is controlled and minimised the parties have agreed to prohibit all direct and indirect exports of hazardous and radioactive waste (Article 39), while the ACP countries deal equally with such imports.

[26] [1986] O.J. L86/1.
[27] [1987] O.J. L173/6.
[28] [1991] O.J. L229.

The parties have agreed to expedite legislation and administrative regulations to ensure that this occurs. The term "hazardous" waste will have the meaning given to it by the Basle Convention (Article 39.3). See further Chapter 16. Technical information is to be provided by the E.C. to the ACP States at their request to assist in this area (Article 40).

5.32 Like the Third Convention, the Fourth Convention gives prominence to agricultural and rural development (Articles 42 to 52) which includes drought and desertification control. Emphasis is placed on developing local agriculture to ensure food security and stability in the ACP States while safeguarding the environment and fighting drought, desertification and deforestation. With this object the E.C. undertakes to assist the ACP States in the areas of research and technical and financial co-operation (Articles 47 and 48). The successful development of agriculture at national and local level calls for the development of processing and storage facilities as well as successful marketing systems and procedures. Considerable importance is attached to the development of fisheries (Articles 58 to 68). and special attention is to be given to the landlocked and island ACP States, maximising their management of fishery resources and overcoming the difficulties encountered by landlocked States as a result of the sovereignty of coastal States. As in agriculture the Community undertakes to co-operate in the development of the infrastructure for rural communities, acquisition of equipment, boats, management and protection of fisheries' markets and the process and marketing of fishery products. Articles 69 to 76 provide for co-operation in the field of commodities, expressing the need to resolve the structural difficulties in any commodity sector by developing the processing, marketing, distribution and transport structure and by improving the competitiveness of the ACP States in this field. It includes co-operation in the enhancement of training and support for educational institutions. The contracting parties agree to exchange views on the requirements of existing international agreements in the process of developing this co-operation, which will be monitored by a commodities committee responsible for the examination of particular problems who will recommend measures to resolve them and will exchange views and information on the workings of the commodities co-operation.

5.33 Industrial, manufacturing and processing development is another major area of co-operation (Articles 77 to 98). The objective is the sustained industrial development of the ACP States. This is to be achieved by establishing an infrastructure to link the various sectors of the economy such as agriculture, manufacturing, mining and energy. The Community will assist in the establishment and expansion of all types of industry (Article 81). A Committee in Industrial Co-operation supervised by a Committee of Ambassadors will review progress made in this co-operation and the intervention in this field by the European Investment Bank, the Centre for the Development of Industry and the responsible ACP authorities (Articles 87 to 91). Special attention is again drawn to assisting the landlocked, least developed and island States to establish their industrialisation (Article 97). Other fields of co-operation include mining development which under the Sysmin system is expanded to include gold and uranium (Article 215.1(a) and (b)), energy (Articles 105 to 109) and enterprise (Articles 110 to 113), stressing that efforts should be made to channel an increased proportion of financial resources in this field (Article 110(2)). Further co-operation is covered in the field of services (Articles 114 to 134), such as support services for economic development, tourism, transport, communication and information. Articles 135 to 138 deal with trade co-operation promoting trade within the wider market of the Community and the ACP States. Cultural and social co-operation (Articles 139 to 155) involves understanding the cultural and social dimensions of the milieu, promoting cultural identies and intercultural dialogue (Article 145). It covers the safeguarding of cultural heritage (Article 146), education and training (Article 151), scientific and technical co-operation (Article 152), the development of women in all fields (Article 153), health and nutrition and ensuring that adequate health care is available to all. The field of regional co-operation is covered by Articles 155 to 166.

Part Three of the convention lays down the Instruments governing ACP/ E.C. co-operation. Articles 167 to 181 deal with trade co-operation mainly covering procedures to ensure accessibility of the Community markets to products from ACP States. Article 168 sets out procedures for the applicability of the tariff and preferential treatment accorded by the contracting parties to one another. Restrictions on imports and exports or goods in transit are prohibited (Article 169) but the prohibition on the movement of hazardous and radioactive waste provided for by Part Two, Article 39, still applies. Articles 182 to 184 set out special undertakings on rum and bananas while Article 185 recognises that the long-term aim is to liberalise trade, taking into account national policies and the level of development of ACP States. This article further states that the Council of Ministers will negotiate amendments to the convention incorporating the advantages resulting from the GATT agreement. Articles 186 to 212 provide for co-operation in the field of commodities, namely the stabilisation of earnings from export of agricultural commodities, excluding sugar cane, which is covered by Article 213 and Protocol 8 of the convention, thereby retaining the agreement reached under the Lomé Convention signed on February 28, 1975. Articles 214 to 219 provide a special financing facility for mining products (Sysmin) stating the various procedures by which ACP States may obtain financial assistance for existing and new projects in this area. The aim is to establish a solid 5.34

and wider basis for the mining industry in ACP States and to ensure diversification of mining products to promote economic growth. Emphasis is placed on the development of financial co-operation (Articles 221 to 257). Its main objectives are to support and promote the efforts of ACP States towards self-reliance and self-sustainable growth in social, cultural and economic areas by assisting them to raise their standard of living, mobilise initiatives for implementing new projects, provide support to develop human resources, develop and implement measures to ensure non-debt creating transfers and encourage co-operation in and between ACP States. Two important areas of the financial co-operation are (i) to enable ACP States faced with major economic and social difficulties to benefit from emergency assistance, provided that, if such difficulties are economic, they are not man-made (Articles 254 to 257). The various principles, guidelines, scope and eligibility for financial aid and co-operation are covered in Articles 221, 222(3), 224 to 228 and 230. Financial co-operation is covered by Articles 231 to 251 providing for resources, terms and conditions, co-financing of major projects between States or agencies and micro-projects for individual ACP States.

**5.35** The Fourth Convention enhances the shift away from public sector investment started by the Third Convention and recognises the importance of encouraging private investment in the promotion and development of ACP States (Articles 258 to 274). The objective is to encourage fair and equitable treatment of private investors who comply with the APC/E.C. objectives and priorities, to create and maintain a secure and predictable investment climate, to facilitate a greater flow of resources between the contracting parties and to promote the development of a dynamic private sector (Article 258). In order to achieve this, the contracting parties undertake to support and promote European private investment in APC States, encourage the flow and dissemination of information on investment opportunities, provide assistance to small and medium-sized enterprises and overcome or reduce the risk of individual investment which could hamper economic progress in the ACP States (Article 259). With that aim, the contracting parties have agreed to conclude investment promotion and guarantee schemes (Article 260). But discrimination between the contracting parties is prohibited and account must be taken of obligations under international agreements (Article 261). The Community will support investment financing by providing financial assistance in the form of risk capital or loans from its own Bank's resources. Such risk capital will be devoted to support private sector investment (Article 263). Other forms of support are participation in financial assistance (including equity participation), technical and advisory assistance and information co-ordination services (Articles 267 to 272). Article 273 covers the procedures for current payments and capital movements. Articles 275 to 280 provide the procedures for technical co-operation to assist ACP States in the development of their national and regional economies and to sustain further such development. Various implementing procedures are provided in Articles 281 to 310 such as the planned financial requirements for each ACP State and measures to attain the objectives and programme of planned projects. Financing and agreements for such projects are provided for in Articles 291 to 293. A major aspect of the Finance Co-operation Instrument is the promotion of competitiveness for projects financed by the fund. Contracts must be awarded on equal terms for all, whether individuals, organisations or states through a system of open tender (Articles 294 to 298). The use of direct labour of the State or States concerned is encouraged (Articles 299 to 303) while selection of contractor must be made on the basis of the tender most responsive to the invitation to tender documents and the best commercial, technical and social proposals submitted (Article 304). Tax and customs arrangements are provided for in Articles 308 to 310. The management of financial co-operation is provided for by Articles 311 to 327, establishing various authorising and controlling bodies including an ACP/E.C. Development Finance Co-operation Committee which is responsible to the Council of Ministers (Articles 324 to 327). The ACP/E.C. Committee is responsible, among others, for collecting all information, examining specific problem areas, ensuring that the general objectives of the Convention are attained and examining various socio-economic aspects of private investment.

The Convention is managed by a Council of Ministers (Part Four, Articles 338 to 345), consisting of members of the Council of the E.C., one member of the Commission and a minister of each ACP State. It meets once a year and its proceedings are only valid if half of the members of the E.C. Council, one member of the Commission and two-thirds of the ACP States are present. A Committee of Ambassadors and a Joint Assembly (Articles 346 to 355), both being consultative bodies, meet every six months. The Joint Assembly may adopt resolutions on matters concerning the convention. 5.36

Part Five, Final Provisions, provides for various undertakings by the contracting parties (Articles 356 to 369); accession by a third country to the Community (Articles 356 to 358), ratification and the coming into force of the convention (Articles 359 to 361), accession by a country or territory to the convention (Articles 362 to 365), and notice for amendments to the convention which must be given not later than 12 months before the expiry of the first five years of the convention (Article 366.2). 5.37

Protocols have been annexed to the convention which implement and define various areas of it. A financial protocol has been annexed which 5.38

states that, for the initial five years of the convention, the Community's financial assistance will be 12,000 million ECUs. It further states the amounts to be allocated to the various institutions, organisations and projects. A new financial protocol will be negotiated for the second five year term of the convention. Protocol 1 lays down rules of origin. Protocol 2 provides for financial accountability by the individual States and for expenditure incurred by them as a result of their participation within the convention. Protocol 3 provides for privileges and immunities which each party accords to the other in respect of representatives, staff, property, funds, assets, official communication and Commission delegations. Protocol 4 provides for measures to be adopted for the implementation of Article 177 of the convention which deals with the safeguards to be applied in the event of major disturbances in any sector of the economy of any of the contracting States. Protocol 5 deals with the export of bananas. In it, the contracting parties agree to maintain access to the markets and the advantages acquired by each ACP State which exports bananas to the Community. Protocol 6 allows for the duty-free import of rum to the Community, subject to an established yearly quota until 1st February 1995, after which it is intended that tariff quotas will be abolished. Protocol 7 deals with beef and veal imports to the Community stating yearly quotas of boneless meat (subject to 10 per cent. of import duties), from Botswana, Kenya, Madagascar, Swaziland and Zimbabwe. Protocol 8 reproduces Protocol 3 of the Lomé Convention of 1975, dealing with imports of sugar cane into the Community. Protocol 9 concerns products within the sphere of the European Coal and Steel Community.

5.39 The Community has drawn up an internal agreement on the financing and administration of Community aid under the Fourth ACP/E.C. Convention stipulating the financial commitment of each Community Member State (Decision 91/401).[29] Another internal agreement (Decision 91/402)[30] is concerned with the measures and procedures required for the implementation of the Fourth Convention. Eighteen months prior to the expiry of the Convention (February 28, 2000) the contracting parties must enter into negotiations to determine future relations between them.

5.40 Articles 329–337 list the least developed, landlocked and island ACP States which are eligible for more favourable arrangements. (They are listed in the Annex to this chapter.)

[29] [1991] O.J. L229/288.
[30] [1991] O.J. L229/301.

## Asian Nations

The Community has a co-operation agreement with the Association of South-East Asian Nations (Indonesia, Malaysia, The Philippines, Singapore, Thailand-ASEAN) signed in 1980. The Community and ASEAN grant each other most favoured nation status, and they have agreed to study means of fostering investment, technological co-operation and other similar measures. This agreement is based on Articles 113 and 235 of the Treaty (Regulation 1440/80)[31] and it was extended to Brunei in 1985.[32] Co-operation agreements have also been drawn up with other Far East nations. Regulation 2616/85[33] concludes an agreement pursuant to Articles 113 and 235 of the Treaty between the Community and China. The aim is to promote and intensify trade between the parties and encourage the steady expansion of economic co-operation. The two parties grant each other most favoured nation treatment. They have further agreed to diversify their economic links and encourage scientific and technological progress. Decision 92/605[34] represents a similar agreement with Macao, but covers a wider area of co-operation than with China. In this agreement the parties reaffirm their reciprocal commitment under the GATT agreement. Similar agreements were concluded with Mongolia (Decision 93/101)[35] and with Pakistan (Regulation 1196/86).[36] Commercial co-operation agreements have been drawn up under Article 113 of the Treaty with Bangladesh (Regulation 2785/76)[37] and with Pakistan (Regulation 1503/76).[38] Within these agreements the parties are determined to develop their commercial exchanges on the basis of mutual benefit so as to contribute to their economic and social progress. An agreement concluding a protocol for the production, marketing and trade in manioc renewing the co-operation agreement was concluded with Thailand (Decision 90/637).[39] Decision 89/149 (Euratom)[40] represents co-operation with Japan in the areas of fusion programmes. 5.41

## North America

The agreements with North American countries are comparatively limited in number and scope. There are agreements negotiated under Art- 5.42

[31] [1980] O.J. L144/2.
[32] [1985] O.J. L81/2.
[33] [1985] O.J. L250/1.
[34] [1992] O.J. L404/26.
[35] [1993] O.J. L41/45.
[36] [1986] O.J. L108/1.
[37] [1976] O.J. L319/1.
[38] [1976] O.J. L168/1.
[39] [1990] O.J. L347/23.
[40] [1989] O.J. L57/62.

icles XXVIII and XXIV of GATT with the United States on olive oil residues,[41] on certain types of manufactured tobacco and on petroleum products[42] going back to 1967. There are arrangements in the form of an exchange of letters with the United States concerning trade in certain steel products.[43] More important is an agreement concerning fisheries off the coast of the United States, amended and extended in 1989.[44] (Also see Chapter 7.) In 1993 the parties concluded under Article 113 an agreement in the form of a Memorandum of Understanding (Decision 93/323)[45] on government procurement.

**5.43** Canada equally has agreements negotiated under the GATT Articles[46] and further agreements for commercial and economic co-operation with the European Community and the European Coal and Steel Community.[47] There are specific agreements covering trade in certain products, and their nature is best illustrated by the subject of the agreements, such as those covering alcoholic beverages (Decision 89/189)[48] women's and girls' footwear (Decision 86/123),[49] and boneless manufacturing beef (Decision 86/101).[50] There is an agreement covering fisheries (Decision 81/1053)[51] with implementing subsidiary agreements, an example of which is represented by Decision 93/493[52] dealing with health conditions required for importing fishery products from Canada. A Joint E.C. Canada Committee deals with economic co-operation. In the field of atomic energy Canada and the European Community are involved in co-operation in several sectors.

## Central and Latin America

**5.44** Decision 91/627[53] drawn up under Articles 113 and 235 of the Treaty, concludes a framework agreement for co-operation between the Community and the United Mexican States. This agreement provides for co-operation in the economic field, investment, industrial measures, trade,

[41] [1967] O.J. L292/46.
[42] [1967] O.J. L131/15.
[43] [1985] O.J. L9/2, L355/20.
[44] [1984] O.J. L272/13, [1989] O.J. L63/23.
[45] [1993] O.J. L125/1.
[46] [1967] O.J. L292/46, [1968] O.J. L97/15, [1980] O.J. L111/18.
[47] [1976] O.J. L260/228.
[48] [1989] O.J. L71/41.
[49] [1986] O.J. L100/26.
[50] [1986] O.J. L87/33.
[51] [1981] O.J. L379/53.
[52] [1993] O.J. L268/15.
[53] [1991] O.J. L340/1.

science and technology, agriculture, mining, information and technology and other similar measures. In 1984 a co-operation agreement was concluded between the Community and the members of the Cartagena Agreement (Bolivia, Colombia, Ecuador, Peru and Venezuela) (Regulation 1591/84).[54] The parties grant each other most favoured nation treatment. The Community recognises that the Andean Group is a developing region and that the Cartagena Agreement embraces less-developed countries and is ready to take into account the Andean region development policies. Various framework agreements have been concluded with other South American countries: with Argentina (Decision 90/530)[55] with Brazil (Regulation 2613/82)[56] with Chile (Decision 91/158)[57] and with Paraguay (Decision 92/509).[58] Each party in each of these agreements grants each other most favoured nation treatment and provide for co-operation in economic, investment, industrial, trade, science and technology and other similar measures, with the exception of the agreements with Brazil and Argentina which are limited to trade and economic co-operation.

## General

Various agreements have been concluded with other nations under Article 113 of the Treaty and which relate to trade in mutton, lamb and goatmeat: with Argentina and Australia (Decision 89/673),[59] with New Zealand (Decision 89/572),[60] with Uruguay (Decision 90/114)[61] (goatmeat not included), with Argentina, Australia, New Zealand and Uruguay (Decision 93/61).[62] All these agreements are in the form of an exchange of letters concerning the trade of meat. The 1993 agreement is, again, in the form of an exhange of letters dealing with the voluntary restraints agreements. Two further agreements deal with the trade in cheese: with Australia (Decision 84/560)[63] and with New Zealand (Decision 84/561).[64] 5.45

[54] [1984] O.J. L153/1.
[55] [1990] O.J. L295/66.
[56] [1982] O.J. L281/1.
[57] [1991] O.J. L79/1.
[58] [1992] O.J. L313/71.
[59] [1989] O.J. L396/17.
[60] [1989] O.J. L318/13.
[61] [1990] O.J. L396/17.
[62] [1993] O.J. L17/16.
[63] [1984] O.J. L308/54.
[64] [1984] O.J. L308/59.

## Conclusion

5.46 Looking at the whole of Community legislation in force, one can say that there are some agreements with most of the sovereign countries in the world, some agreements being more limited than others, but all the same enabling the Community to develop closer trade links, should the opportunity arise. Another example of action following political developments is the co-operation agreement between the European Community and the Co-operation Council of the Arab States of the Gulf, implemented by Decision 89/147.[65]

# ANNEX

## List of the ACP States

*Africa*

Angola
Benin
Botswana
Burkina Faso
Burundi
Cameroon
Cape Verde
Central African Republic
Chad
Comoros
Congo
Djibouti
Equatorial Guinea
Ethiopia
Gabon
Gambia
Ghana
Guinea
Guinea-Bissau
Ivory Coast
Kenya
Lesotho
Liberia
Madagascar
Malawi
Mali
Mauritania
Mauritius
Mozambique
Niger
Nigeria
Rwanda
São Tome & Principe
Senegal
Seychelles
Sierra Leone
Somalia
Sudan
Swaziland
Tanzania
Togo
Uganda
Zaire
Zambia
Zimbabwe

*Caribbean*

Antigua and Barbuda
Bahamas
Barbados
Belize
Dominica
Dominican Republic
Grenada
Guyana
Haiti
Jamaica
St Christopher & Nevis
St Lucia
St Vincent & the Grenadines
Suriname
Trinidad and Tobago

[65] [1989] O.J. L54/1.

*Pacific*

Fiji
Kiribati
Papua New Guinea
Solomon Islands
Tonga
Tuvalu
Vanuatu
Western Samoa

## The least-developed, landlocked and island ACP States

Title IV of Part Three of the Convention specifies which ACP States are regarded as the least-developed, landlocked and island ACP States (see below). These countries are eligible for more favourable arrangements in the following areas of the Convention:

(a) agricultural and food co-operation
(b) fisheries
(c) industrial development
(d) transport and communication
(e) development of trade and services
(f) regional co-operation
(g) general trade arrangements
(h) Stabex and Sysmin
(i) financial and technical co-operation
(j) investment
(k) rules of origin
(l) structural adjustment
(m) micro and major projects
(n) specific regional co-operation

*The least developed ACP States (Article 330)*

Antigua and Barbuda
Belize
Benin
Botswana
Burkina Faso
Burundi
Cape Verde
Central African Republic
Chad
Comoros
Djibouti
Dominica
Equatorial Guinea
Ethiopia
Gambia
Grenada
Guinea
Guinea-Bissau
Kiribati
Lesotho
Malawi
Mali
Mauritania
Mozambique
Niger
Rwanda
St Christopher and Nevis
St Lucia
St Vincent and the Grenadines
São Tome and Principe
Seychelles
Sierra Leone
Solomon Islands
Somalia
Sudan
Swaziland
Tanzania

| | | |
|---|---|---|
| Togo | Tuvalu | Vanuatu |
| Tonga | Uganda | Western Samoa |

*Landlocked ACP States (Article 333)*

| | | |
|---|---|---|
| Botswana | Chad | Rwanda |
| Burkina Faso | Lesotho | Swaziland |
| Burundi | Malawi | Uganda |
| Central African Republic | Mali | Zambia |
| | Niger | Zimbabwe |

*Island ACP States (Article 336)*

| | | |
|---|---|---|
| Antigua and Barbuda | Haiti | São Tome and Principe |
| Bahamas | Jamaica | Seychelles |
| Barbados | Kiribati | Solomon Island |
| Cape Verde | Madagascar | Mauritius |
| Comoros | Mauritius | Suriname |
| Dominica | Papua New Guinea | Tonga |
| Dominican Republic | St Christopher and Nevis | Trinidad and Tobago |
| Fiji | St Vincent and the Grenadines | Tuvalu |
| Grenada | | Vanuatu |
| | | Western Samoa |

# CHAPTER 6

# AGRICULTURE

## I. GENERAL

### The scope of the common agricultural policy

The adoption of a "common policy in the sphere of agriculture and fisheries" is an activity which the Community was obliged to pursue by Article 3(e) of the Treaty, and by virtue of Article 38 the common market extends to "agriculture and trade in agricultural products". 6.01

The extension of the common market to agriculture means that conceptually there is, throughout the Community, only one market for agricultural products instead of 12 national markets. Thus when, in the context of sugar quotas, an Italian producer alleged that Italian producers should not be obliged to assist in financing surpluses for which other producers were responsible, the Court replied that "such a view is incompatible with the very principle of a common market, in which the undertakings of the Member States responsible for any surplus production cannot be identified": see Case 250/84, *Eridania v. Cassa Conquaglio Zucchero.*[1] 6.02

### Definition of "agricultural products"

The word "agriculture" is not defined in the Treaty, but the term "agricultural products" is defined in Article 38(1) as "the products of the soil, of stock-farming and of fisheries and products of first-stage processing directly related to these products". A list of such products was provided in Annex II of the Treaty, which has on occasion been supplemented under the authority of Article 38(3) of the Treaty. 6.03

[1] [1986] E.C.R. 117.

6.04 The expression "products of first-stage processing directly related to these products" was discussed in Case 185/73, *Hauptzollamt Bielefeld v. Konig*.[2] Here, in holding that the dilution of alcohol after its distillation did not prevent the resulting product from falling within the expression, the Court stated that the concept of direct relationship implies "a clear economic interdependence between basic products and the processed products, irrespective of the number of processing operations involved". The Court added, however, that where "processed products have undergone a productive process, the cost of which is such that the price of the basic agricultural raw materials becomes a completely marginal cost", they are excluded from the definition.

## Objectives of the common agricultural policy

6.05 Article 38(4) of the Treaty states that "the operation and development of the common market for agricultural products must be accompanied by the establishment of a common agricultural policy among the Member States". Thus there must be an agricultural policy common to all Member States rather than merely a co-ordination of national agricultural policies. The objectives of the common agricultural policy are set out in Article 39(1) of the Treaty as follows:

"(a) to increase agricultural productivity by promoting technical progress and by ensuring the rational development of agricultural production and the optimum utilisation of the factors of production, in particular labour;
(b) thus to ensure a fair standard of living for the agricultural community, in particular by increasing the individual earnings of persons engaged in agriculture;
(c) to stabilise markets;
(d) to assure the availability of supplies;
(e) to ensure that supplies reach consumers at reasonable prices."

6.06 In working out the common agricultural policy, account must also be taken of:

"(a) the particular nature of agricultural activity, which results from the social structure of agriculture and from structural and natural disparities between the various agricultural regions;
(b) the need to effect the appropriate adjustments by degrees;
(c) the fact that in the Member States agriculture constitutes a sector closely linked with the economy as a whole."

[2] [1974] E.C.R. 607.

Since these objectives are for the protection of competing interests, that of agricultural producers as well as that of consumers, they must sometimes conflict. When a choice has to be made between these objectives or factors, it is for the Community institutions to decide on which to give priority, taking account, where necessary, of the principle of Community preference in favour of the farmers: see Case 5/67, *W. Beus GmbH & Co. v. Hauptzollamt München.*[3] However, the European Court has also made it clear that

> "efforts to achieve objectives of the common agricultural policy, in particular under common organisations of the markets, cannot disregard requirements relating to the public interest such as the protection of consumers or the protection of the health and life of humans and animals, requirements which the Community institutions must take into account in exercising their powers": see Case 68/86, *Re Agricultural Hormones: U.K. v. Council.*[4]

## Background to the CAP

In 1960 the Council drew up guidelines for working out and implementing the common agricultural policy, based on proposals of the Commission submitted under Article 43 of the Treaty. These guidelines stressed the importance of the free movement of agricultural products, a joint agricultural and commercial policy, a common price level for agricultural products and the co-ordination of structural reform: see Council Resolution of December 20, 1960. The general guidelines having been drawn up by virtue of Article 43, Member States were then to "develop the common agricultural policy by degrees during the transitional period" (ending on December 31, 1969) and to "bring it into force by the end of that period at the latest". In the case of most products, this was in fact done. Basic regulations for Common market organisations in certain products were adopted from 1962 on, and in 1964 the first common price was agreed (for cereals), with the first common organisation based on a single price system following in 1967. The next year the Customs Union was introduced, replacing national duties for common duties in respect of all agricultural products by January 1, 1970. Since then the CAP, whose burden on the Community taxpayer grew to be excessive, has undergone radical changes which are reflected below. 6.07

[3] [1968] E.C.R. 83, [1968] C.M.L.R. 131.
[4] [1988] E.C.R. 855, [1988] 2 C.M.L.R 543.

### Legal powers

6.08 Legislation in the agricultural sector is generally made under, or implements, legislation made under Articles 42 and 43 of the Treaty. Article 42 makes provision for the Council to determine to what extent the Treaty rules on competition shall apply to the production of and trade in agricultural products, and Article 43(3) empowers the Council, subject to certain conditions, to replace national market organisations by common organisations. The legislation adopted by the Community in relation to agriculture is very extensive and only the broad outline of it can be described here.

## II. COMMON ORGANISATIONS

### The European market organisation

6.09 Article 40(2) of the Treaty provided that in order to attain the objectives set out in Article 39 a common organisation of agricultural markets was to be established. Such common organisation was to take one of the following forms, depending on the product concerned:

(a) common rules on competition;
(b) compulsory co-ordination of the various national market organisations;
(c) a European market organisation.

6.10 In fact, the European market organisation has been the form chosen for common organisations and nearly all products are now covered by such an organisation. A European market organisation is "based on the concept of the open market to which every producer has access and which is regulated solely by the instruments provided for by these organisations", see Case 83/78, *Pigs Marketing Board v. Redmond,*[5] and involves the abolition of barriers to intra-Community trade, the establishment of a common system of border regulations for imports and exports, and the application of common rules on competition.

### Procedure in relation to common organisations

6.11 The procedure the Council adopts in relation to common organisations is to lay down the main principles but to delegate the laying down of

[5] [1978] E.C.R. 2347, [1979] C.M.L.R. 177.

the details to the Commission, which has power under Article 155 of the Treaty to "exercise the powers conferred on it by the Council for the implementation of the rules laid down by the latter". It was held in Joined Cases 279–280 & 285–286/84, *Firma Walter Rau Lebensmittel Werke v. EEC*[6] that, since only the Commission is in a position to keep track of agricultural market trends and to act quickly when necessary, the Council may confer on it wide powers of discretion and action in that sphere, and when it does so the limits of those powers must be determined in the light of the essential aims of the market organisation. The overall financing of the CAP is governed by Regulations 729/70[7] and 3187/83.[8]

## General rules relating to common organisations

*1. Exclusion of discrimination*

Article 40(3) of the Treaty states that the common organisation shall exclude any discrimination between producers or consumers within the Community. As pointed out in Case 5/73, *Balkan-Import-Export GmbH v. Hauptzollamt Berlin-Packhof*,[9] this provision is part and parcel of the Community principle of equality of treatment. It was held in Joined Cases 279–280 & 285–286/84, *Firma Walter Rau Lebensmittel Werke v. EEC*[10] that agricultural products "which compete with each other and are partial substitutes for each other are covered by the rule in Article 40(3) regarding discrimination". But this does not prevent comparable situations being treated differently if such a difference in treatment is justified. The Court went on to decide that there is such objective justification where: 6.12

(a) the common organisation of the market in one product (here, milk, including butter) is conceived in a very special context compared to that of the other competing product (here, vegetable fats, including margarine),
(b) the place occupied by the two competing products is entirely different, and
(c) one product but not the other is subject to a structural imbalance which requires special measures.

In the event the Court held that the introduction of the Christmas butter 6.13

[6] [1988] 2 C.M.L.R. 704.
[7] [1970] O.J. L94/13, as last amended by Reg. 2048/88, [1988] O.J. L185/1.
[8] [1987] O.J. L304/1.
[9] [1973] E.C.R. 1091.
[10] [1988] 2 C.M.L.R. 704.

scheme by Commission Regulation 2956/84,[11] whereby intervention butter was sold over Christmas at reduced prices, thereby undercutting the price of margarine, was within the powers of the Commission as delegated to it by Council Regulation 804/68.[12]

*2. Exclusion of national rules*

6.14 Where there is a common organisation of an agricultural market the Member States are obliged to abstain from all measures which would derogate from it: see Case 177/78, *Pigs and Bacon Commission v. McCarren & Co. Ltd.*[13] This doctrine applies in respect of all unilateral measures, even those which would help to achieve the common policy: see Case 274/87, *Commission of the European Communities v. Federal Republic of Germany.*[14] However, Member States "remain competent to make such measures as they consider appropriate to improve structures in [a] sector, so long as they observe the mechanisms and principles governing the common organisation of the market": see Case 148/85, *Procureur de la République v. Forest (Sangoy).*[15]

## General arrangements

6.15 A common organisation may "include all measures required to attain the objectives set out in Article 39" of the Treaty, "in particular regulation of prices, aids for the production and marketing of the various products, storage and carry over arrangements and common machinery for stabilising imports and exports": Article 40(3) of the Treaty. The organisations vary considerably from one product to another.[16] In the case of

[11] (Now repealed).
[12] [1968] O.J. L148/13.
[13] [1979] E.C.R. 2161, [1979] 3 C.M.L.R. 389.
[14] [1989] E.C.R. 229, [1989] 2 C.M.L.R. 733.
[15] [1986] E.C.R. 3449, [1988] 2 C.M.L.R. 577.
[16] Common organisations exist for markets in a wide variety of sectors of which the following are among the main provisions:
—cereals: Reg. 1766/92, [1992] O.J. L181/21, as last amended by Reg. 2193/93, [1993] O.J. L196/22;
—pigmeat: Reg. 2759/75, [1975] O.J. L282/1, as last amended by Reg. 1249/89, [1989] O.J. L129/12;
—eggs: Reg. 2771/75, [1975] O.J. L282/49, as last amended by Reg. 1574/93, [1993] O.J. L152/1;
—poultrymeat: Reg. 2777/75, [1975] O.J. L282/77, as last amended by Reg. 1574/93, [1993] O.J. L152/1;
—fresh fruit and vegetables: Reg. 23/62, [1962] O.J. Spec. Ed. 97, as last amended by Reg. 1108/91, [1991] O.J. L110/67; Reg. 1035/72, [1972] O.J. L118/1, as last amended by Reg. 746/93, [1993] O.J. L77/14;
—wine: Reg. 822/87, [1987] O.J. L84/1, as last amended by Reg. 1566/93, [1993] O.J. L154/39;

some products, such as cereals and milk, there is a price and trading system, while other products, such as various meats and eggs, only receive external protection, and a scheme for quality standards is imposed in the fresh fruit and vegetable sector. In addition, a variety of rules applies to certain sectors, for instance on the maintenance of minimum stocks to prevent shortages (in the sugar sector) and the provision of aids for the formation of producer's organisations (*e.g.* in the fisheries sector). Measures often taken include the following.

*1. Price policies*

Article 40(3) of the Treaty states that "any common price policy shall be based on common criteria and uniform methods of calculation". Member States are precluded from adopting unilateral measures which conflict with such a policy: see Case 31/74, *Galli.*[17] A typical price structure makes use of the following concepts: 6.16

*(a) Target or guide prices.* These are the prices set by the Council which it is hoped producers will achieve during the marketing season for which they are fixed. They do not bind anyone and are intended merely to help producers to plan the year ahead with some indication of likely prices, although in the case of some products, such as oil seeds, there is a production subsidy equivalent to the difference between the target and 6.17

—milk: Reg. 804/68, [1968] O.J. L148/13, as last amended by Reg. 2071/92, [1992] O.J. L215/64;
—beef and veal: Reg. 805/68, [1968] O.J. L148/24, as last amended by Reg. 747/93, [1993] O.J. L77/15;
—rice: Reg. 1418/76, [1976] O.J. L166/1, as last amended by Reg. 1544/93, [1993] O.J. L154/5;
—oil and fats: Reg. 136/66, [1966] O.J. Spec. Ed. 221, as last amended by Reg. 3179/93, [1993] O.J. L285/9;
—live trees, etc.,: Reg. 234/68, [1968] O.J. L55/1, as last amended by Reg. 3336/92, [1992] L336/1;
—dried fodder: Reg. 1117/78, [1978] O.J. L142/1, as last amended by Reg. 3996/87, [1987] O.J. L377/35;
—processed fruit and vegetables: Reg. 426/86, [1986] O.J. L49/1, as last amended by Reg. 1569/92, [1992] O.J. L166/5;
—flax and hemp: Reg. 1308/70, [1970] O.J. L146/1, as last amended by Reg. 2057/92, [1992] O.J. L215/16;
—hops: Reg. 1696/71, [1971] O.J. L175/1, as last amended by Reg. 3124/92, [1992] O.J. L313/1;
—seeds: Reg. 2358/71, [1971] O.J. L246/1, as last amended by Reg. 3695/92, [1992] O.J. L374/40;
—sheepmeat and goatmeat: Reg. 3013/89, [1989] O.J. L289/1, as last amended by Reg. 363/93, [1993] O.J. L42/1;
—miscellaneous Annex II products: Reg. 827/68, [1968] O.J. L151/16, as last amended by Reg. 2430/93, [1993] O.J. L223/9.

[17] [1975] E.C.R. 47, [1975] 1 C.M.L.R. 211.

intervention prices: Regulation 136/66.[18] Member States may not make laws, see Case 31/74, *Galli*[19] or adopt practices, see Case 60/75, *Russo*[20] which could prevent producers from having the opportunity of obtaining a price approximating to the target price.

6.18 *(b) Intervention prices.* These, in principle, are the prices at which the intervention agencies (in the United Kingdom, the Intervention Board Executive Agency) purchase all Community-produced commodities offered to them. They are fixed below the target price of the relevant product. Nowadays, however, the full intervention price is not always paid.

*2. Trading systems*

6.19 The typical trading system may include threshold prices, levies and refunds, and import and export licences.

6.20 *(a) Threshold prices.* These are entry prices for certain imports into the Community from third countries and are used to calculate levies. They are fixed by the Council (acting on a proposal from the Commission) at a level which makes the selling price of the products concerned the same as the target price for those products. In this way Community farmers are protected from cheap, and perhaps subsidised, imports from third countries. In some sectors a "sluice-gate" price takes the place of the threshold price.

6.21 *(b) Levies.* Levies are amounts charged on imports or exports of agricultural products to compensate for the difference between world prices and Community prices. They are "primarily intended to protect and stabilise the Community market, in particular by preventing price fluctuations on the world market affecting prices within the Community": Case 113/75, *Frecassetti v. Italian Finance Administration.*[21] Import levies are fixed, often daily, by Commission regulations at a rate which ensures that the price in the Community of products imported into the Community is the same as, or higher than, the price of Community products.

6.22 Levies are collected *as* customs duties but are not customs duties and they have a very different purpose, with the result that different rules apply to them. Thus, for instance, changes in prices on the world market (and therefore in levies) after the date of acceptance by Customs of an

[18] [1966] O.J. Spec. Ed. 221.
[19] [1975] E.C.R. 47, [1975] 1 C.M.L.R. 211.
[20] [1976] E.C.R. 45.
[21] [1976] E.C.R. 983.

import declaration were not reflected in the rate of levies in *Frecassetti v. Italian Finance Administration.*[22] Export levies have been introduced in respect of some agricultural products whose prices are higher on the world market than on the Community market. They are collected in the United Kingdom by the Intervention Board pursuant to section 6(4) of the European Communities Act 1972. Regulation 120/89[23] lays down common rules for export levies on agricultural products.

*(c) Export refunds.* These are payments made to exporters of agricultural products to compensate in whole or in part for the difference between the Community prices of agricultural products exported and the generally higher world prices. They are fixed for each product periodically in accordance with the management Committee procedure and are the same throughout the Community, although they may vary according to the destination of the exports. Where goods are trans-shipped within the Community they are regarded, for the purpose of the payment of export refunds, as goods exported from the first European Community port in which the customs export formalities are carried out: Case 337/85, *Commission v. Ireland.*[24] Regulation 386/90[25] sets the framework for measures to monitor the payment of export refunds. 6.23

The common detailed rules for the system of export refunds are laid down in Regulation 3665/87,[26] and rules relating to the advance payment of export refunds are laid down in Regulation 565/80.[27] To ensure uniform presentation of the lists of agricultural products on which refunds are granted an agricultural product nomenclature for export refunds appears in Regulation 3846/87,[28] which correlates with the Combined Nomenclature in the Common Customs Tariff. 6.24

## Advance fixing of levies and refunds

In order to enable importers and exporters to know what rate of levy or refund will be applicable to goods at the time when trading contracts are made, levies and refunds may be fixed in advance. The rate of levy or refund is then applicable on the day of application for an advance fixing certificate, adjusted according to the threshold price which will be in force in the month of importation, with a premium added to take account 6.25

[22] *Ibid.*
[23] [1989] O.J. L16/19, as amended by Reg. 1431/93, [1993] O.J. L140/27.
[24] [1987] E.C.R. 4237.
[25] [1990] O.J. L42/6.
[26] [1987] O.J. L351/1, as last amended by Reg. 2805/93, [1993] O.J. L256/7.
[27] [1980] O.J. L62/5, as last amended by Reg. 2026/83, [1983] O.J. L199/12.
[28] [1987] O.J. L366/1, as last amended by Reg. 3198/93, [1993] O.J. L288/10.

of future trends in world prices. A levy fixed in advance should do no more than compensate for the difference between the prices ruling outside and those ruling within the Community: Case 6/77, *Schouten v. Hoofproduktschap voor Akkerbouwprodukten*.[29] The issue of an advance fixing certificate imposes an obligation on the trader to import or export the stated quantity during the period of the validity of the licence, plus or minus a small percentage, and the rules relating to deposits in relation to such certificates are the same as those in relation to import and export licences which are spelt out below. Common detailed rules relating to advance fixing certificates are laid down in Regulation 3719/88.[30]

## Import and export licences

**6.26** Generally speaking, agricultural products may not be imported into or exported from the Community without an import or export licence. In the United Kingdom licences are issued by the Intervention Board. Common detailed rules for the application of the system of import and export licences are also contained in Regulation 3719/88, and rules applying to particular products are laid down in the rules on the common organisation of the product concerned.

**6.27** Regulation 3719/88 describes certain general exceptions to the requirement for licences. Thus licences are not required for operations which do not in the strict sense constitute imports or exports, for example for products:

(a) which are not placed in free circulation within the Community;
(b) in respect of which export is effected under a customs procedure which allows import free of customs duties, charges having equivalent effect or levies, or under special arrangements which allow export free of export duties;
(c) which are placed in free circulation under provisions governing the treatment of returned goods;
(d) for re-export in respect of which the exporter provides proof of a favourable decision for the repayment or remission of import duties.

**6.28** Nor are licences generally required, in cases in which advance fixing of a levy or a refund is not requested, for the purpose of operations:

(a) for the victualling within the Community of seagoing vessels or aircraft, to international organisations established within the

[29] [1977] E.C.R. 1291.
[30] [1988] O.J. L331/1, as last amended by Reg. 2697/93, [1993] O.J. L245/75.

Community, or to armed forces stationed within the territory of, but not subject to the flag of, a Member State;
(b) of a non-commercial nature; and,
(c) relating to products in small quantities.

One of the main aims of the system of licences is to provide statistics to enable the Community to assess market developments and thus to manage the market more effectively. The system also goes some way towards ensuring that the rules concerning the common organisations are uniformly applied. A licence therefore constitutes an obligation as well as an authorisation to carry out the transaction to which it relates (Article 8 of Regulation 3719/88), and a transaction is regarded as having been carried out when customs formalities have been completed, subject to the product being actually put into free circulation (Article 29 of that Regulation). A 5 per cent. variation on the quantity stated in a licence is generally permitted (and the special rules applying to particular products sometimes allow a wider variation, for instance 7 per cent. in the case of cereals and rice: Regulation 891/89).[31] **6.29**

Generally, the issue of a licence is conditional upon the lodging of a deposit guaranteeing that the transaction will be carried out during the period of validity of the licence. Where it is not, the deposit will be forfeited, in whole or in part. Some or all of a deposit will also be forfeited where proof of the completion of customs formalities has not been furnished within a specified period of the expiry of a licence. Common detailed rules for the application of the system of securities for agricultural products are set out in Regulation 2220/85.[32] **6.30**

Forfeiture of the deposit is excluded in cases of *force majeure. Force majeure* is not limited to absolute impossibility but must be understood in the sense of "unusual circumstances, outside the control of the importer or exporter, the consequences of which, in spite of the exercise of all due care, could not have been avoided except at the cost of excessive sacrific" (Case 158/73, *Kampffmeyer v. Einfuhr- und Vorratsstelle für Getreide und Futtermittel,*[33] where it was held that the loss of a licence or certificate may constitute a case of *force majeure*). The false assurance of a national customs official that the period of validity of a licence could be extended does not in itself constitute *force majeure,* see Case 125/83, *Corman;*[34] nor does a change in the law of a foreign state: see Case C–124/92, *An Bord Bainne Co-operative Limited v. Intervention Board for Agricultural Produce.*[35] **6.31**

[31] [1989] O.J. L94/13, as last amended by Reg. 3224/93, [1993] O.J. L292/15.
[32] [1985] O.J. L205/3, as last amended by Reg. 3745/89, [1989] O.J. L364/54.
[33] [1974] E.C.R. 101.
[34] [1985] E.C.R. 3039.
[35] [1993] 3 C.M.L.R. 856.

## Quality standards

6.32 An example of the scheme of quality standards is that laid down in the fresh fruit and vegetable sector. Here, the preamble to the main regulation concerned, Regulation 1035/72,[36] states that the scheme is intended to keep products of unsatisfactory quality off the market and to guide production to consumers' requirements. The scheme is exhaustive; there are Community procedures for adopting the standards in question and when such norms have been adopted the products to which they apply may not be displayed or offered for sale, sold, delivered or marketed in any other manner unless they conform to the standards, subject to the exceptions spelt out in Regulation 1035/72.

## The safeguard clause

6.33 When the market for a product undergoes, or is threatened by, serious disturbances as a result of imports or exports of the product, certain actions may be taken by the Commission, and in certain urgent cases, by a Member State in trade with third countries pending the Commission's decision. The measures taken by the Commission may be referred to the Council by a Member State. Depending on the products concerned, the measures that may be taken are total or partial suspension or the predetermination of levies or refunds; total or partial suspension of the issue of import or export certificates; total or partial refusal of pending applications for predetermination and licences; the suspension of imports or exports; or the levy of duties on exports.

## Intervention buying

6.34 Intervention buying is, in principle, the buying of agricultural products on behalf of the Community at guaranteed minimum ("intervention") prices. The system of intervention buying is a major feature of several of the common organisations of markets and constitutes one of the main supports for the farmer. Although originally designed as a safety net, it rapidly became seen as a guarantee of an unlimited market for production, and this gave rise to problems of overproduction. The intervention price is the price which will be paid to a farmer for his product if he cannot sell it on the market at a higher price. Once an offer has been made and has come to the knowledge of an intervention agency that agency has, in principle, a binding obligation to buy the quantity offered:

[36] [1972] O.J. L118/1, as last amended by Reg. 746/93, [1993] O.J. L77/14.

see Case 49/71, *Hagen v. Einfuhr- und Vorratsstelle für Getreide*.[37] Various other means of intervening in the market for agricultural products are adopted by the Council as it considers appropriate.[38]

## III. FINANCIAL MECHANISMS

### European Agricultural Guidance and Guarantee Fund

All these interventions are financed by the European Agricultural Guidance and Guarantee Fund (EAGGF) whose principal financing provisions are contained in Regulation 1883/78.[39] Regulations 4045/89,[40] 1863/90,[41] 307/91[42] and 967/91[43] provide extensively for the scrutiny of EAGGF expenditure, and Regulation 3002/92[44] details the rules for verifying the use or destination of products from intervention. Regulation 1068/93[45] now governs the determination and application of the agricultural conversion rates. **6.35**

[37] [1972] E.C.R. 23, [1973] C.M.L.R. 35.

[38] The main sector intervention provisions are:
—cereals: Reg. 689/92, [1992] O.J. L74/18, as last amended by Reg. 3134/93, [1993] O.J. L280/15.
—pigmeat: Reg. 391/68, [1968] O.J. L80/5, as last amended by Reg. 3498/88, [1988] O.J. L306/32.
—fresh fruit and vegetables: Reg. 3587/86, [1986] O.J. L334/1, as last amended by Reg. 2868/93, [1993] O.J. L262/27.
—wine: Reg. 1059/83, [1983] O.J. L116/77, as last amended by Reg. 2192/93, [1993] O.J. L196/19.
—butter and cream: Reg. 985/68, [1968] O.J. L169/1, as last amended by Reg. 2045/91, [1991] O.J. L187/1.
—beef and veal: Reg. 2226/78, [1978] O.J. L261/5, as last amended by Reg. 3492/88, [1988] O.J. L306/20.
—rice: Reg. 470/60, [1960] O.J. 204/8, as last amended by Reg. 3528/92, [1992] O.J. L358/6; Reg. 1424/76, [1976] O.J. L166/24, as last amended by Reg. 749/91, [1991] O.J. L82/5.
—oil seeds: Reg. 282/67, [1967] O.J. 151/1, as last amended by Reg. 1904/91, [1991] O.J. L169/41.
—olive oil: Reg. 3472/85, [1985] O.J. L333/5, as last amended by Reg. 1767/93, [1993] O.J. L162/6.
—raw tobacco: Reg. 1469/70, [1970] O.J. L164/35, as last amended by Reg. 1332/90, [1990] O.J. L132/52.
—sheepmeat and goatmeat: Reg. 2644/80, [1980] O.J. L275/8.

[39] [1978] O.J. L216/1, as last amended by Reg. 1571/93, [1993] O.J. L154/46.

[40] [1989] O.J. L388/18.

[41] [1990] O.J. L170/23.

[42] [1991] O.J. L37/5.

[43] [1991] O.J. L100/18.

[44] [1992] O.J. L301/17, as last amended by Reg. 1938/93, [1993] O.J. L176/12.

[45] [1993] O.J. L108/106, as amended by Reg. 1713/93, [1993] O.J. L159/94.

6.36 Under Regulation 17/64,[46] the EAGGF was split into two sections: the Guarantee Section, which finances the common marketing and price policy, and the Guidance Section, which finances Community structural reforms. The general administration of the EAGGF is the responsibility of the Commission but at national level the Commission relies on the national authorities, who collect monies due under the common agricultural policy on behalf of the Community and make payments due under Community rules. Cash advances are made to Member States in accordance with periodical estimates of expenditure by virtue of Regulation 729/70. The question inevitably arises, what happens if Community money runs out? It was held in Case 99/74, *Grands Moulins des Antilles v. Commission*[47] that if the EAGGF refuses, or is unable, to reimburse payments, the Member States are nevertheless still liable to make payments under Community rules, and in 1987, when it appeared that the Community budget might become exhausted, Regulation 3183/87 required the Member States to continue to make payments when the guarantee allocation for 1987 had been used up on the basis that the Member States must bear the costs of the policies to which they have agreed.

## Control of EAGGF money

6.37 Article 4(2) of Council Regulation 729/70 as amended by Regulation 2048/88[48] obliges Member States to ensure that the credits made available to them are used without delay and solely for authorised purposes. It also requires Member States to take the measures, in the form of administrative and judicial procedures, necessary to enable them:

(a) to satisfy themselves that transactions financed by the fund are actually carried out and executed correctly,
(b) to prevent and deal with irregularities, and
(c) to recover sums lost as a result of irregularities or negligence.[49]

6.38 Member States can only recover from the EAGGF money which has been spent in accordance with correctly interpreted Community legislation (correct interpretation being settled, if necessary, by the European Court). Thus, for instance, financing by the EAGGF of expenditure by the Netherlands on export refunds for mackerel caught in excess of the national quota allowed by Community conservation measures was

[46] [1964] O.J. L586/94.
[47] [1975] E.C.R. 1531.
[48] [1988] O.J. L185/1.
[49] See also Reg. 595/91, [1991] O.J. L67/11.

refused in Case 262/87, *Kingdom of the Netherlands v. Commission.*[50] Moreover, where Member States adopt national practices which are incompatible with Community law it is not only the resulting net increase in expenditure which is disallowed but the whole of monies wrongfully paid, disregarding any resulting decreases in expenditure which would, but for the illegality, have been recoverable from the EAGGF: see Case 347/85, *Re United Kingdom Dual Milk Pricing.*[51] The only exceptions to this rule are that expenditure falling within a reasonable exercise of a discretion may be recoverable, and that where an incorrect application of Community law is attributable to a Community institution, the Community ought to bear the financial consequences of it: see Case 11/76,[52] Case 18/76,[53] and Joined Cases 15–16/76.[54]

## Common prices

A basic tenet of the common agricultural policy is that prices of agricultural products should be the same throughout the Community, and Article 40(3) of the Treaty provides that "any common price policy shall be based on common criteria and uniform methods of calculation." Thus the common price policy is based on the fixing of a single price, which is measured now in ECUs. 6.39

## The ECU

Regulation 3813/92[55] now settles, following the advent of the Single Market without internal frontiers and without the former elaborate structure of Monetary Compensatory Amounts, the rules for the conversion rates to be used for the purpose of the CAP. The actual rates are laid down by frequently changing regulations, often proper to each sector of the market: see generally Regulation 3822/92[56] fixing the agricultural conversion rates and Regulation 1068/93[57] on determining and applying the rates. 6.40

[50] [1989] E.C.R. 225.
[51] [1988] E.C.R. 1749, [1988] 2 C.M.L.R. 487.
[52] [1979] E.C.R. 245.
[53] [1979] E.C.R. 343.
[54] [1979] E.C.R. 321.
[55] [1992] O.J. L387/1.
[56] [1992] O.J. L387/26.
[57] [1993] O.J. L108/106, as last amended by Reg. 1713/93, [1993] O.J. L159/94.

## IV. STRUCTURAL AND GUIDANCE MEASURES

**6.41** One of the objectives of the common agricultural policy is:

> "to increase agricultural productivity by promoting technical progress and by ensuring the rational development of agricultural production and the optimum utilisation of the factors of production, in particular labour"[58]

Article 39(2) goes on to provide that in working out the common agricultural policy account shall be taken of:

> "(a) the particular nature of agricultural activity, which results from the social structure of agriculture and from structural and natural disparities between the various agricultural regions."

**6.42** When the Community was established, its farming was characterised by large numbers of small, inefficient farms and it was recognised from the start that structural reforms were necessary if the objectives of the common agricultural policy were to be achieved. When the EAGGF was split into two sections by Regulation 17/64[59] structural measures were added to the guidance section.

### Measures taken

**6.43** Measures taken to increase or reduce production, and to deal with allied matters, include:

(a) Member States are obliged to introduce an aid scheme to encourage the set-aside of arable land. Under the "set-aside" scheme applicable from 1993/94 onwards, a producer who sets aside at least 15 per cent. of his arable land is granted aid, the rate varying according to the use of the set-aside land and whether or not the land iso situated in a less-favoured area. Regulations 2328/91[60] and 1765/92[61] establish much of the current system, though the regulations governing the common organisation of markets also contain sectorally-related provisions. Land set aside can be used for non-agricultural production, and Regulation 2296/92[62] lays down the products which are allowed together with their permitted end uses, and the control methods applicable.

[58] Article 39(1)(a) of the Treaty.
[59] [1964] O.J. Spec. Ed. 103.
[60] [1991] O.J. L218/1, as last amended by Reg. 1992/93, [1993] O.J. L182/12.
[61] [1992] O.J. L181/12, as last amended by Reg. 1551/93, [1993] O.J. L154/19.
[62] [1992] O.J. L221/31, as last amended by Reg. 334/93, [1993] O.J. L38/12.

(b) Member States are to introduce an aid scheme to promote extensification for surplus products. This is for the purpose of adjusting the various production sectors to market requirements, in particular reducing production where there is a surplus. "Extensification" means reducing the output of the product concerned by at least 20 per cent. for a period of at least five years without other production capacity being increased, and surplus products are those for which there are consistently, at Community level, no normal unsubsidised outlets; the products are listed in Regulation 4115/88,[63] which lays down detailed rules for applying this aid scheme.

(c) Regulation 2078/92[64] now provides for aids to be granted to farmers to promote the use of farming practices which reduce the polluting effects of agriculture, environmentally favourable extensification methods, ways of using agricultural land compatible with the protection of the environment, the upkeep of abandoned farmland and land management for public access and leisure activities. The aids available are partly financed by the EAGGF, at the rates of either 75 per cent. or 50 per cent.

(d) Regulation 3669/93[65] brings together and updates various initiatives on the adjustment of production, processing and marketing structures and further amends Regulation 2328/91.[66]

(e) Early retirement from farming has long been a method by which the Community has sought to ease rationalisation of farming structures. A new system detailed in Regulation 2079/92[67] is now in operation. It seeks to provide an income for elderly farmers who decide to stop farming, to encourage their replacement by farmers able to improve the economic viability of their holdings and to reassign agricultural land to non-agricultural uses where it cannot be farmed economically.

(f) Forestry has long been part of the CAP and its development is seen as an alternative to surplus crop or livestock farming, with the added advantage of reducing the shortage of forestry products within the Community. Accordingly, a Community aid scheme for forestry measures has been adopted by Regulation 2080/92.[68] This also amends Regulation 2328/91 and introduces premiums to compensate farmers for the loss of income during the non-productive period of afforested agricultural land, and to

[63] [1988] O.J. L361/13, as last amended by Reg. 838/93, [1993] O.J. L88/16.

[64] [1992] O.J. L215/85, and see also Reg. 2062/93, [1993] O.J. L187/22.

[65] [1993] O.J. L338/26.

[66] [1991] O.J. L218/1, as last amended by Reg. 870/93, [1993] O.J. L91/10.

[67] [1992] O.J. L215/91.

[68] [1992] O.J. L215/96.

offer incentives to non-farmers (including local authorities) to undertake afforestation.

## V. RULES RELATING TO COMPETITION

6.44 The competition rules of the Treaty do not automatically apply to the production of and trade in agricultural products. By virtue of Article 42 of the Treaty they apply

> "only to the extent determined by the Council ... account being taken of the objectives set out in Article 39 [the CAP].
> The Council may, in particular, authorise the granting of aid:
> (a) for the protection of enterprises handicapped by structural or natural conditions;
> (b) within the framework of economic development programmes."

6.45 The Council has determined the extent to which the competition rules apply in Regulation 26/62[69] and in various regulations establishing common organisations of the market. The broad effect of these determinations is as follows.

### Rules applying to undertakings (Articles 85–90 of the Treaty)

6.46 Articles 85 to 90 of the Treaty apply to the production of or trade in agricultural goods by virtue of Article 1 of Regulation 26/62, subject to the derogations relating to Article 85(1) set out in Article 2(1) of that regulation. According to Article 2(1) of Regulation 26/62, Article 85(1) of the Treaty shall not apply to such of the agreements, decisions, and practices as:

(a) form an integral part of a national market organisation,[70] or
(b) are necessary for the attainment of the objectives set out in Article 39 of the Treaty.

Article 2 of the regulation also states that Article 85(1) of the Treaty:

> "shall not apply to agreements, decisions, and practices of farmers, farmers' associations, or associations of such associations belonging

[69] [1962] O.J. Spec. Ed. 129, as amended by Reg. 49/62, [1962] O.J. Spec. Ed. 201 (and derogated from by Reg. 2077/92, [1992] O.J. L215/80).

[70] For a definition of national market organisation see Case 48/74, *Charmasson*: [1974] E.C.R. 1383, [1975] 2 C.M.L.R. 48.

> to a single Member State which concern the production or sale of agricultural products or the use of joint facilities for the storage, treatment or processing of agricultural products, and under which there is no obligation to charge identical prices, unless the Commission finds that competition is thereby excluded or that the objectives or Article 39 of the Treaty are jeopardised."

The Commission has sole power, subject to review by the European Court, to determine which agreements, decisions and practices fulfil these conditions. Where its determination is in the negative, the agreement, etc., will be void under Article 85(2) of the Treaty.

These derogations are not as useful as they may appear, for the following reasons: 6.47

(a) That spelt out in paragraph 6.46(a) above is now of little significance, since most national market organisations have been replaced by common organisations.
(b) In the case of that spelt out in paragraph 6.46(b) above, it has proved to be somewhat difficult to establish that an agreement, etc., is "necessary for the attainment of the objectives" of the common agricultural policy unless the common organisation for the product concerned has expressly contemplated or impliedly permitted such an agreement: see *Preserved Mushrooms*.[71] Moreover, it appears that to come within this exception an agreement must be necessary for the attainment of all, and not merely some, of the objectives of Article 39 of the Treaty: see Case 71/74, *Frubo v. Commission*.[72]
(c) The second sentence of Article 2(1) gives examples of the type of agreement which could fall within the first sentence and is not a separate exception in its own right: see *Meldoc*.[73]

## State aids (Articles 92–94 of the Treaty)

In the case of products in respect of which there is no common organisation, the substantive rules on state aids do not apply. However, where there is a common organisation, first, state aids may not interfere with the operation of that common organisation: see Case 177/78, *Pigs and Bacon Commission v. McCarren*,[74] and secondly, the regulations setting up common organisations very often specifically provide for Articles 92 to 6.48

[71] [1975] O.J. L29/26, [1975] C.M.L.R. D83.
[72] [1975] E.C.R. 563, [1975] 2 C.M.L.R. 123.
[73] Dec. 86/595, [1986] O.J. L348/50.
[74] [1979] E.C.R. 2161, [1979] 3 C.M.L.R. 389.

94 of the Treaty to be applied "save as otherwise provided in this regulation." The Treaty provisions on state aids do not have direct effect, and this is so even when those provisions have been incorporated into regulations which themselves have direct effect: see Case 78/76, *Steinike und Weinlig v. Germany*.[75]

**6.49** Apart from the substantive rules on state aids, Article 4 of Regulation 26/62 provides that the provisions of Article 93(1) and the first sentence of Article 93(3) of the Treaty shall apply to aids granted for the production of or trade in the products listed in Annex II to the Treaty. Article 93(1) places an obligation on the Commission to "keep under constant review all systems of aid existing in the Member States and to propose to them any appropriate measures required by the progressive development or by the functioning of the common market", and the first sentence of Article 93(3) states that the "Commission shall be informed, in sufficient time to enable it to submit its comments, of any plans to grant or alter aid". However, the real substance of this article, which provides that the Member States shall not put their proposed measures into effect until the Commission has reached a final decision on the aid, has not been applied in relation to agricultural products.

## Countervailing charges

**6.50** Where there is no common organisation the rules on state aids do not apply, but the free movement of goods rules do. An example of the unfairness to which this situation can give rise was the inability of France legally to prevent or restrict the import of lamb which had benefited from the United Kingdom system of deficiency payments. Article 46 of the Treaty therefore provides that:

> "Where in a Member State a product is subject to a national market organisation or to internal rules having equivalent effect which affect the competitive position of similar production in another Member State, a countervailing charge shall be applied by Member States to imports of this product coming from the Member State where such organisation or rules exist, unless the State applies a countervailing charge on export."

**6.51** The effect of this provision is to enable the Commission to adopt immediate safeguards where competition is distorted by Member States' national support measures encouraging low-priced exports. In each case "it is for the Commission to ensure that the duration and the amount of

[75] [1977] E.C.R. 595, [1977] 2 C.M.L.R. 688.

the charge remain within the limits circumscribed by the need to re-establish equilibrium": see Case 337/82, *St Nikolaus Brennerei v. Hauptzollamt Krefeld*.[76] In deciding upon the appropriate safeguards, the Commission does not have to "set up a highly complex system of data gathering and calculation" which would delay the adoption of those safeguards: see Case 181/85, *Re Countervailing Charge on French Ethyl Alcohol: France v. Commission*.[77] In this case it was held that the Commission had not exceeded its discretion or made an error in law in adopting a method for calculating the charge based on a single export price, even though there were in fact different export prices for different grades of alcohol.

## VI. HARMONISATION OF LEGISLATION

### Harmonisation of veterinary laws

The objectives of harmonisation measures taken so far in the veterinary field have been to protect human and animal health and animal well-being, to control epizootic diseases, and to eliminate obstacles to intra-Community trade in livestock and livestock products. Most of the directives in this field concern the public health requirements of the Member States in relation to trade between one other. By and large these directives allow certain animals and meats to be exported from one Member State to another for the purposes of breeding, production or slaughter only if accompanied by a veterinary certificate issued by the exporting Member State certifying that the animals or meats comply with the health requirement of the relevant directive. The health requirements generally relate to standards of vaccination, inspections and freedom from certain specified diseases. As to verification, the ultimate objective of the Community is that the same health checks on animals and products should be applied whether they are intended for the home market or for intra-Community trade, with checks being made at the place of production and destination rather than at the internal frontiers of the Community.[78] In the meantime, checks and controls at frontiers are simplified as much as possible, and the Court takes a fairly restrictive view of those frontier controls which are permitted: see Case 186/88, *Commission v. Germany*.[79] 6.52

In particular, measures have been taken: 6.53

[76] [1984] E.C.R. 1051, [1985] 3 C.M.L.R. 83.
[77] [1987] E.C.R. 689, [1988] 2 C.M.L.R. 225.
[78] See Dir. 90/675, [1990] O.J. L373/1 on veterinary checks on products entering the Community from third countries, as last amended by Dir. 92/1601, [1992] O.J. L173/13.
[79] [1989] E.C.R. 3997.

(a) in respect of intra-Community trade, concerning animal health problems of cattle and pigs: Directive 64/432;[80]
(b) laying down animal health requirements applicable to intra-Community trade in, and importers from third countries of, deep-frozen bovine semen: Directive 88/407,[81] and porcine semen: Directive 90/429;[82]
(c) in respect of the pure-bred breeding of cattle: Directive 77/504;[83] and of sheep and goats: Directive 89/361;[84] and to oblige Member States to accept pure-bred cattle for breeding purposes: Directive 87/328;[85]
(d) in respect of zootechnical standards applicable to breeding pigs: Directive 88/661;[86]
(e) relating to health problems affecting intra-Community trade in fresh meat from domestic animals: Directives 64/433[87] and 72/461;[88]
(f) relating to health problems affecting trade in fresh poultrymeat: Directive 71/118;[89]
(g) relating to health problems affecting intra-Community trade in meat products: Directive 77/99;[90] and to animal health problems affecting that trade: Directive 80/215;[91]
(h) relating to health and animal problems affecting intra-Community trade in heat-treated milk; Directive 85/397;[92]
(i) to control certain animal diseases, in particular for the eradication of brucellosis, tuberculosis and leucosis in cattle: Directive 77/391;[93] the control of foot-and-mouth disease: Directive 85/511;[94] the control and eradication of swine fever in pigs: Directives 80/217[95] and 80/1095;[96] and the acceptance of pure-bred breeding pigs for breeding: Directive 90/118;[97]
(j) to deal with problems concerning the health and veterinary

80 [1964] O.J. Spec. Ed. 164, as last amended by Dir. 92/102, [1992] O.J. L355/32.
81 [1988] O.J. L194/10, as last amended by Dir. 93/60, [1993] O.J. L186/28.
82 [1990] O.J. L224/62.
83 [1977] O.J. L206/8, as last amended by Dir. 91/174, [1991] O.J. L85/37.
84 [1989] O.J. L153/30.
85 [1987] O.J. L167/54.
86 [1988] O.J. L382/36.
87 [1964] O.J. Spec. Ed. 185, as last amended by Dir. 91/497, [1991] O.J. L268/69.
88 [1972] O.J. L302/24, as last amended by Dir. 92/118, [1992] O.J. L62/49.
89 [1971] O.J. L55/23, as last amended by Dir. 92/116, [1992] O.J. L62/1.
90 [1977] O.J. L26/85, as last amended by Dir. 92/118, [1992] O.J. L62/49.
91 [1980] O.J. L47/4, as last amended by Dir. 91/687, [1991] O.J. L377/16.
92 [1985] O.J. L226/13, as last amended by Dir. 92/46, [1992] O.J. L268/1.
93 [1977] O.J. L145/44, as last amended by Dir. 85/3768, [1985] O.J. L362/8.
94 [1985] O.J. L315/11, as last amended by Dir. 92/380, [1992] O.J. L198/54.
95 [1980] O.J. L47/11, as last amended by Dir. 93/384, [1993] O.J. L166/34.
96 [1980] O.J. L325/1, as last amended by Dir. 91/686, [1991] O.J. L377/15.
97 [1990] O.J. L71/34.

inspection of cattle and pigs and of fresh meat imported from third countries. The Council is authorised, on a proposal from the Commission, to designate third countries or parts of them from which Member States may authorise imports: Directive 72/462;[98]

(k) to provide for the identification and registration of animals: Directive 92/102,[99] and introducing general Community measures for the control of certain animal diseases and swine vesicular disease in particular: Directive 92/119;[1]

(l) to prohibit the use in livestock farming of certain substances having a hormonal action: Directive 88/146;[2]

(m) laying down hygiene and health requirements concerning the production and placing on the market of egg products: Directive 89/437;[3]

(n) to lay down minimum standards for the production of laying hens kept in battery cages: Directive 88/166;[4] and to approximate laws regarding the protection of animals used for experimental and scientific purposes: Directive 86/609;[5]

(o) to protect animals during international transport;[6] and relating to the stunning of animals before slaughter: Directive 74/577;[7]

(p) laying down conditions governing animal health controls on intra-Community trade in, and import from third countries of embryos of domestic cattle: Directive 89/556.[8]

## Harmonisation of legislation on animal feeds

Measures have been taken to harmonise control of the composition and marketing of animal feeds. These have necessitated the introduction of Community methods of sampling and analysis and the Commission has been authorised, in consultation with a Standing Committee for Feedingstuffs set up under Article 3 of Directive 70/373[9] to issue directives laying down Community rules establishing uniform methods for sampling and analysing animal feedstuffs. 6.54

[98] [1972] O.J. L302/28, as last amended by Dir. 92/1601, [1992] O.J. L173/13.
[99] [1992] O.J. L355/32.
[1] [1992] O.J. L62/69.
[2] [1988] O.J. L70/16.
[3] [1989] O.J. L212/87, as last amended by Dir. 91/684, [1991] O.J. L376/38.
[4] [1988] O.J. L74/83.
[5] [1986] O.J. L358/1.
[6] Dir. 90/425, [1990] O.J. L224/29 on intra-Community trade in live animals, as last amended by Dir. 92/118, [1992] O.J. L62/49;
[7] [1974] O.J. L316/10.
[8] [1989] O.J. L302/1, as last amended by Dir. 93/52, [1993] O.J. L175/21.
[9] [1970] O.J. L170/2, as last amended by Dir. 85/3768, [1985] O.J. L362/8.

6.55 To control the composition of animal feeds measures have been taken:

(a) to control the addition of additives (substances added to feedingstuffs to enhance their nutritional value: Directive 70/524).[10] The directive lists the authorised substances and specifies the quantities which are permitted as additives and lays down that feedingstuffs which contain additives may only be marketed if the additives are specified on the packaging or by means of a label giving prescribed particulars;

(b) to fix maximum permitted levels for certain identified undesirable substances and products in feedingstuffs: Directive 74/63.[11] "Undesirable substances" are substances either found naturally in feedingstuffs or their constituents, or present as residues from processing which, if present in excessive quantities, can endanger animal or human health;

(c) to control the use as, or as constituents of, animal feedingstuffs of certain products used in animal nutrition: Directive 82/471.[12] This directive requires Member States to prescribe that feedingstuffs belonging to certain product groups or containing certain products may only be marketed if they comply with the requirements of the directive.

6.56 These rules do not apply to products intended for export to third countries, and amendments to the lists of additives, substances and products may be made by the Commission in the light of scientific or technical developments. Guidelines for the assessment of certain products[13] and additives[14] used in animal nutrition have been fixed.

6.57 To control the marketing of animal feeds harmonised rules have been laid down on the marketing of straight feedingstuffs: Directive 77/101;[15] and compound feedingstuffs: Directive 79/373.[16] The directives regulate the presentation, packaging and labelling of feedingstuffs. Generally, feedingstuffs may only be marketed if they are wholesome, unadulterated, of merchantable quality and do not represent a danger to animal or human health, and are not presented or marketed in a manner which is likely to mislead.[17]

[10] [1970] O.J. L270/1, as last amended by Dir. 93/55, [1993] O.J. L206/11.
[11] [1974] O.J. L38/31, as last amended by Dir. 93/74, [1993] O.J. L237/23.
[12] [1982] O.J. L213/8, as last amended by Dir. 93/74, [1993] O.J. L237/23.
[13] Dir. 83/228, [1983] O.J. L126/23.
[14] Dir. 87/153, [1987] O.J. L64/19.
[15] [1977] O.J. L32/1, as last amended by Dir. 90/654, [1990] O.J. L353/48.
[16] [1979] O.J. L86/30, as last amended by Dir. 93/74, [1993] O.J. L237/23.
[17] See also Dir. 93/74 on feedingstuffs intended for particular nutritional purposes, [1993] O.J. L237/23.

## Harmonisation of plant health and marketing laws

Rules for the protection of plants from diseases and for the progressive eradication of diseases have been harmonised. At the same time measures have been taken to protect human and animal health by fixing maximum levels for pesticide residues. The aim of the Community regarding verification in this area is that checks will be restricted to places of production, supervised by a Community inspectorate, with compliance ensured by an official stamp. 6.58

Directive 77/93[18] lays down protective measures against the introduction into Member States of harmful organisms of plants or plant products. Plants, plant products, their packaging and vehicles in which they are transported must all be officially examined before entering the territory of a Member State to ensure that they are not contaminated by a prohibited organism and that other requirements of the regulation have been met in respect of them. Once plants or plant products have been issued with a phytosanitary certificate on the basis of the official examination they may not be prohibited or restricted from entry into another Member State on plant health grounds unless a Member State considers that it is in imminent danger of the introduction or spread of harmful organisms. In such a case that Member State may take temporary protective measures, which may then be amended or rescinded by the Commission in consultation with the Standing Committee on Plant Health set up by Decision 76/894.[19] 6.59

Directives have been issued which lay down minimum measures to be taken by the Member States to control certain diseases, maximum levels for pesticide residues in and on fruit and vegetables and foodstuffs of animal origin. The placing on the market and use of plant protection products containing certain active substances have also been prohibited.[20] 6.60

[18] [1977] O.J. L26/20, as last amended by Dir. 93/19, [1993] O.J. L96/33.

[19] [1976] O.J. L340/25.

[20] See also:

—Dir. 91/414 on the placing of plant protection products on the market, [1991] O.J. L230/1;

—Dir. 91/682 on the marketing of ornamental plant propagating material, [1991] O.J. L376/21, as amended by Dir. 93/399, [1993] O.J. L177/26;

—Dir. 92/34 on the marketing of fruit plant propagating material, [1992] O.J. L157/10, as amended by Dir. 93/401, [1993] O.J. L177/28;

—Dir. 93/85 on the control of potato ring rot, [1993] O.J. L259/1;

—Dir. 92/33 on the marketing of vegetable propagating and planting material, [1992] O.J. L157/1, as amended by Dir. 93/400, [1993] O.J. L177/27.

6.61 Directives[21] restrict the marketing of seeds and young plants to those of which the identity, varietal purity and value for cultivation and use has been officially verified in accordance with minimum conditions specified in the directives. Member States may impose additional or more stringent requirements for the certification of seed in their own territory. Subject to certain exemptions, seed which satisfies the prescribed criteria must not be subject to any other marketing restrictions. Directives incorporating similar provisions have been issued in respect of the marketing of forest reproductive material.

6.62 Council Directive 70/457[22] provides for a common catalogue of varieties of agricultural plant species. This catalogue is based on the national catalogues of the Member States. The directive establishes criteria for inclusion in the common catalogue of those varieties of beet, fodder plant, cereal, potato and oil and fibre plants the marketing of the seeds of which is subject to the directives specified above.

## Human health

6.63 A series of measures is designed to benefit human health in regard to animal products. Thus Directive 92/46[23] lays down health rules for the production and placing on the market of raw milk, heat-treated milk and milk-based products. Directive 92/48[24] deals with hygiene rules for fishery products caught on board certain vessels. Newcastle disease among poultry is the subject of Directive 92/66[25] and wild game is dealt with in Directive 92/45.[26] Other measures have been adopted laying down the health rules applying to meat intended for the domestic market: Directive 88/409,[27] and to the production of, and trade in, minced and small-chopped meat and meat preparations: Directive 88/657.[28]

21 *e.g.* Dir. 66/402, [1966] O.J. Spec. Ed. 143 (as last amended by Dir. 93/2, [1993] O.J. L54/20) on marketing of cereal seed, and Dir. 66/404, [1966] O.J. Spec. Ed. 161 (as last amended by Dir. 91/44, [1991] O.J. L23/32) on marketing of forest reproductive material.
22 [1970] O.J. L225/1, as last amended by Dir. 90/654, [1990] O.J. L353/48.
23 [1992] O.J. L268/1.
24 [1992] O.J. L187/41.
25 [1992] O.J. L260/1.
26 [1992] O.J. L268/35, as amended by Dir. 92/116, [1992] O.J. L62/1.
27 [1988] O.J. L194/28, as amended by Dir. 91/498. [1991] O.J. L268/105.
28 [1988] O.J. L382/3, as last amended by Dir. 92/110, [1992] O.J. L394/26.

## VII. E.C. AGRICULTURAL LAW IN THE UNITED KINGDOM

### The Intervention Board

Section 6(1) of the European Communities Act 1972 established the Intervention Board for Agricultural Produce (now known as the Intervention Board Executive Agency or IBEA) as follows: 6.64

> "There shall be a Board in charge of a government department, which shall be appointed by and responsible to the Ministers [*i.e.* MAFF and the Secretaries of State respectively concerned with agriculture in Scotland and Northern Ireland, acting jointly] and shall be by the name of the Intervention Board for Agricultural Produce a body corporate . . .; and the Board (in addition to any other functions that may be entrusted to it) shall be charged, subject to the direction and control of the Ministers, with such functions as they may from time to time determine in connection with the carrying out of the obligations of the United Kingdom under the common agricultural policy of the Economic Community."

The board has responsibility for administering the EAGGF legislation and of recovering agricultural levies charged on goods exported from the United Kingdom or shipped as stores (section 6(4) of the 1972 Act) (import levies being the responsibility of the Commissioners of Customs and Excise under section 6(5)). The 1972 Intervention Board for Agricultural Produce Order[29] enabled the board, with the approval of the ministers, to arrange for the performance of any of its functions by another statutory body concerned with agriculture or agricultural produce. By virtue of this power functions are from time to time delegated to various bodies. 6.65

### Section 6(5) of the European Communities Act 1972

This provision stipulates that import levies are to be levied, collected and paid as if they were Community customs duties and they are therefore collected by the Commissioners of Customs and Excise. Since it is the national agencies who collect levies, it is for the Member States themselves to take the necessary criminal or civil proceedings to enforce or recover them: see Joined Cases 178–180/73, *Belgium and Luxembourg v.* 6.66

[29] S.I. 1972 No. 1578.

*Mertens.*[30] Vice versa, a trader who thinks he has been wrongfully charged levies must proceed against the national authorities and not against the Community, see Case 96/71, *Haegeman v. Commission,*[31] and a trader who thinks money is due to him under Community legislation must act against the national authorities, see Case 99/74, *Grands Moulins des Antilles v. Commission.*[32]

[30] [1974] E.C.R. 33.
[31] [1972] E.C.R. 1005, [1973] C.M.L.R. 365.
[32] [1975] E.C.R. 1531.

# CHAPTER 7

# FISHERIES

## Basis

Article 38 of the Treaty defines agricultural products to include the products of fisheries and the products of first stage processing therefrom. Accordingly, the common fisheries policy (CFP) emerged from the common agricultural policy, of which in principle it remains part: see Case 141/78, *France v. United Kingdom*;[1] although in practice it now stands on its own as the organisation of a common market in fishery products. Since 1983, the CFP has provided for the limiting of fish catches, price support and quality control, conservation measures and third country agreements. **7.01**

From the very earliest stages of Community development, however, it was established that the basic principle of non-discrimination found throughout Community law must be applied to fishing within the waters over which Member States enjoyed sovereignty or exercised jurisdiction. Thus, Regulation 101/76,[2] replacing even earlier legislation, established that there was to be no discrimination in regard to access to the fishing waters of each Member State by vessels flying the flag of any other Member State. A Council resolution of November 6, 1976 urged Member States to extend their overall fishing zones along North Atlantic and North Sea coasts to 200 nautical miles from January, 1977, and Resolution 507/81[3] offered detailed guidance on its application. The principles of Community law apply in zones thus extended, or in any less extensive zone actually claimed by a Member State. **7.02**

Article 227(5)(c) of the Treaty provides that the Treaty applies to the **7.03**

[1] [1979] E.C.R. 2923, [1980] 1 C.M.L.R. 6.
[2] [1976] O.J. L20/19.
[3] [1981] O.J. C105/1.

Channel Islands and the Isle of Man to the extent necessary for the implementation of the arrangements concerning them included in the 1972 Act of Accession of the United Kingdom, Ireland and Denmark.[4] Protocol 3 of that Act makes provision accordingly. The general effect is to require the islands to apply Community rules to the extent necessary for their enforcement, but to exclude them from the scope of the common fisheries policy as such: see Case 32/79, *Commission v. United Kingdom*.[5] Equal access to Spanish and Portuguese waters will not be established before 2002.[6]

7.04 Regulation 3760/92[7] consolidates the law on fisheries on access to waters and resources and the regulation of fishing, and is now the basic legislative instrument for the CFP. It provides for the entire range of Community control measures: the establishment of zones, permitted rates and quantities of catch, periods at sea, the size and composition of fleets, net sizes and the types of fish which may be taken. The regulation declares the fundamental principle that all Community waters are open to all fishermen from E.C. states, but it permits the previous exclusive fishing zone for each State up to a maximum of 12 nautical miles to be maintained until the end of the year 2002; previously existing arrangements between Member States allowing rights to each others' fishermen in reserved waters may be continued and there are special restrictions relating to fishing by larger vessels in the Orkney/Shetlands "box".

## Total allowable catches and quotas

7.05 The regulation of fishing activity to ensure conservation of resources is well established as a matter within the Community's competence rather than that of the Member States: see Case 804/79, *Commission v. United Kingdom*.[8] As has been seen, Regulation 3760/92 provides the framework within which overall limits for the quantity of fish which may be taken are laid down by subsequent detailed regulations. These are normally made by reference to particular fish types, and are now in principle dealt with according to a multiannual programme. The total allowable catch, or TAC as it is known, is calculated globally in the first instance, by reference to species and areas; alternatively, regulation may proceed by reference to a concept known as "total allowable fishing effort"—a for-

[4] [1972] O.J. L73.
[5] [1980] E.C.R. 2403, [1981] 1 C.M.L.R. 219.
[6] [1985] O.J. L302.
[7] [1992] O.J. L389/1. See also Dec. 94/15, [1994] O.J. L10, setting the objectives and rules for restructuring the Community fisheries sector from January 1, 1994 to December 31, 1996.
[8] [1981] E.C.R. 1045, [1982] 1 C.M.L.R. 543.

mula based on the capacity and periods of activity of fishing vessels. These measures are then (generally) allocated among Member States, who must report the manner in which they implement them to the Commission with a view to overall Community control. The States may, within limits, trade allowances between themselves.

Regulation 3676/93[9] lays down TACs for 1994. The detailed management regulations are made in the light of advice from the Scientific and Technical Committee for Fisheries, based on research on the capacity of the fishing grounds. Because the greater part of the Community waters is subject to common access, overfishing by fishermen from State B can lead to State A's fishermen being prejudiced by being unable themselves to use up their own quotas; or underuse of a quota by State A can lead to part of the TAC being unused even if States B, C and D exhaust their own quotas entirely. This problem is dealt with by means of quota exchanges between States under Regulation 3760/92. 7.06

Regulation 3760/92 also provides for the Commission and the Member States to determine the detailed rules for the utilisation of the quotas allocated to them, for example by discouraging the tendency for all the quotas to be used up as soon as possible, with the attendant flooding of the market early in the season and shortages later on. Under previous legislation, the Court held in Case 207/84, *De Boer v. Produktschap voor Vis en Visprodukten*,[10] that Member States might in this context limit the taking of part of their quotas to vessels of a certain size. 7.07

Where the figures indicate that a national quota has been used up, the Member State must issue a provisional prohibition order to stop further fishing; the Commission subsequently makes a definitive order after checking that there are no unused quotas from the same TAC in other Member States. If a Member State is prevented, by the adoption of conservation measures, from utilising its full TAC, measures may be adopted to compensate its fishing interests for the prejudice suffered. Regulation 3094/86[11] lays down detailed technical measures which, in addition to the system of TACs, are designed to promote conservation of fish stocks. These measures include minimum mesh sizes, restrictions on the type of fishing gear and vessels which may be used, specification of the minimum size of fish of certain types which may be taken and the designation of closed areas and closed seasons. 7.08

A claim by a Member State to be entitled to prevent the practice known as "quota-hopping", where vessels of State A register to fly the flag of 7.09

[9] [1993] O.J. L341/1.
[10] [1985] E.C.R. 3210, [1987] 2 C.M.L.R. 515.
[11] [1986] O.J. L288, as last amended by Reg. 3919/92, [1992] O.J. L397.

State B in order to gain access to the latter's national quota, was referred to the Court by the House of Lords in Case C–221/89, *R. v. Secretary of State for Transport, ex parte Factortame and others*[12] and the Court held that national residence requirements for the crews of Community vessels could not be used for that purpose. But in Case 223/86, *Pesca Valentia v. Ministry of Fisheries and Forests*[13] the Court upheld the right of a Member State to require that a specified minimum proportion of the crews of vessels flying the flag of that State and fishing in Community waters should be Community nationals.

**7.10** In Case C–3/87, *R. v. Ministry of Agriculture, ex parte Agegate Ltd.* and Case C–216/87, *R. v. Ministry of Agriculture, ex parte Jaderow Ltd.*[14] the Court held that Member States could insist on a real economic link with the State whose flag a vessel is flying and therefore stipulate that the vessel should operate out of national ports, but not that it should land its catch, nor that a proportion of its crew should reside, in the State in question; and one State could also require the crew to contribute to its social security system.

## Enforcement measures

**7.11** Although enforcement measures are, as usual, primarily a matter for the Member States, specific Community provisions exist and Regulation 2241/87[15] consolidates the Community legislation on controls. This legislation covers the recording of information about catches by means of logbooks kept by skippers, landing records and the inspection and control of fishery vessels. It also lays down the conditions in which nets which may not be used lawfully must be stored meanwhile. Member States are required to report the statistics thus established to the Commission.

**7.12** The Commission has power to monitor enforcement by means of inspectors who accompany national officials, but who do not deal direct with the fishermen. Detailed rules about recording catches are contained in Regulation 2807/83,[16] and a classification of fishing vessels is laid down by Regulation 2930/86.[17] The inspection of vessels is provided for by Regulation 1382/87,[18] with a view to harmonising the methods used

[12] [1991] I E.C.R. 3905, [1991] 3 C.M.L.R. 589.
[13] [1988] E.C.R. 83, [1988] 1 C.M.L.R. 888.
[14] [1989] E.C.R. 4459, [1991] 1 C.M.L.R. 366.
[15] [1987] O.J. L207, as last amended by Reg. 3483/88, [1988] O.J. L306.
[16] [1983] O.J. L276, as last amended by Reg. 473/89, [1989] O.J. L53.
[17] [1986] O.J. L274.
[18] [1987] O.J. L132.

by Member States; the marking and recording of vessels, enabling them to be identified at sea and their catches assessed, is provided for by Regulation 1381/87.[19]

Regulation 1956/88[20] makes provision in the context of the North Atlantic Fisheries Organisation (see paragraph 7.17 below) for the designation of Community inspectors (assigned by Member States) and their functioning in conjunction with the inspectors of other contracting parties to the Convention, and the conditions under which inspections take place are also prescribed. The registration of vessels remains a function of the Member States, but Regulation 163/89[21] provides for details of all vessels registered or removed from the registers to be reported to the Commission monthly. This gives the Commission an overall view of the Community fishing fleet, and the individual items of information thus centrally held may only be divulged to the Member State from whose register they are drawn. 7.13

## Structural policy

This refers to the measures taken to update and improve the economic and material features of the fishing industry. The central instruments by reference to which this is done are the Multiannual Guidance Programmes (MGP) which are approved by the Commission. Yearly reports on these programmes are made to the Commission, together with proposals as necessary for adjustments during a programme's validity. The various types of grant outlined below must all be approved in the context of the MGP. The principal legislation is contained in Regulation 4028/86,[22] though there is much implementing and subsidiary legislation based on this regulation. 7.14

The regulation provides for a series of grants, funded jointly by the Member States and the Commission, to be available within the parameters referred to above, for the following purposes: 7.15

(a) the purchase or construction of individual fishing vessels, with a bias towards owner-operated vessels replacing one more than 15 years old;
(b) the modernisation of fishing fleets as a whole;

[19] *Ibid.*
[20] [1988] O.J. L175.
[21] [1989] O.J. L20.
[22] [1986] O.J. L376, as last amended by Reg. 3946/92, [1992] O.J. L401. See also Reg. 4022/89, [1989] O.J. L388.

(c) the development of fish-farming installations and structural works in coastal waters;
(d) exploratory operations to establish the viability of long-term exploitation of fishery resources by Community vessels in Community waters or elsewhere;
(e) joint venture projects relating to the catching, marketing and processing of fish and the use of the technology relevant to it;
(f) temporary or permanent withdrawal of certain vessels from fishing activity;
(g) the improvement of port facilities, and obtaining new outlets and markets for surplus or underfished species.

## External relations

7.16 The counterpart of the CFP is necessarily a common external policy with regard to trade with non-Community countries. The Common Customs Tariff applies to third country imports, and Regulation 3796/81[23] prohibits Member States from applying any charge equivalent to a customs duty or any quantitative restriction to such trade. The Court has held that the corollary of internal Community competence in the area of fisheries is that the Community is now solely empowered to deal with third countries or international organisations: See Joined Cases 3, 4 & 6/76, *Kramer*.[24] The Community has accordingly made agreements with a very wide range of individual countries allowing for fishing rights to be exercised in their waters by Community fishermen, *i.e.* by vessels flying the flag of a Member State, or in Community waters by vessels flying the flag of the third country.

7.17 Likewise, the Community has entered as a contracting party into several conventions, such as the Northwest Atlantic Fisheries Convention in 1978[25] (the NAFO Convention) and the Northeast Atlantic Fisheries Convention in 1981[26] (the NEAFO Convention). Article 234 of the Treaty expressly preserves the operation of international agreements entered into before the Treaty itself, and a similar provision is contained in Article 5 of the 1972 Act of Accession of the United Kingdom, Ireland and Denmark.[27] This means that, to the extent that Member States' bilateral agreements have not been superseded by Community-wide treaties, they remain binding. The same appears from the Court's judgment in Case

[23] [1981] O.J. L379, as last amended by Reg. 3571/90, [1990] O.J. L353.
[24] [1976] E.C.R. 1279, [1976] 2 C.M.L.R. 440.
[25] [1978] O.J. L378.
[26] [1981] O.J. L227.
[27] [1972] O.J. L73.

181/80, *Arbelaiz-Emazabel*[28] to be the case in relation to agreements entered into after the date of the Treaty (or the Accession), but before the Community actually assumed internal competence in the area.

When setting the TAC of fish which migrate to or from Community waters, the Community will attempt to do so in agreement with the third countries affected by the migrations. A large number of bilateral agreements between the Community and third countries now exists regulating the conduct of fishing and mutual rights. An example is the bilateral European Community-United States agreement. Regulation 3928/92[29] lays down detailed rules for the NAFO pilot observer scheme; Regulation 3927/92[30] establishes a system for the conservation and management of fishery resources in the NAFO area. **7.18**

## Regulation of the internal market

As in the case of the common agricultural policy, the CFP aims to create an organised and controlled market in fish and fish products. The object of doing this, in contrast with the rules designed to ensure free markets in industrial products and in services, is to stimulate productivity by stabilising the market, ensuring a fair standard of living for those engaged in it, and to provide for continuity of supplies and reasonable prices for consumers. This is done primarily by regulating price levels for a defined range of products: fresh, dried, salted, frozen, chilled and smoked fish, crustaceans or molluscs, and certain other fish-related products. The principal legislation is now contained in Regulation 3759/92.[31] **7.19**

By reference to fish species, the Council sets a guide price at the start of each year, and this is done taking account of market conditions, supply availability and the objectives of the CFP generally. There is then established a Community withdrawal price or, depending on the type of fish product concerned, a Community selling price. These prices are always below the guide price, but may be adjusted for specified ports in order to compensate for any distortion likely to result from a port's remoteness from the main centres of consumption. When actual market prices fall to the withdrawal price or Community selling price, the goods are taken off the market by intervention buying. Special provision is made in respect of certain species where required by market conditions. **7.20**

[28] [1981] E.C.R. 2961.
[29] [1992] O.J. L397.
[30] *Ibid.*
[31] [1992] O.J. L388, as last amended by Reg. 694/93, [1993] O.J. L76.

7.21 Regulation 3759/92[32] deals with the recognition by Member States of producers' organisations, who open their membership to all Community producers within their area, according to detailed criteria laid down in subsequent regulations. In general, they must provide for their members to market their produce through them, and adopt measures designed to improve product quality. They may receive aid within prescribed limits from the Member States, but may not occupy a dominant position in the Common Market unless necessary in pursuance of Treaty objectives. Their marketing and production rules may now be imposed upon non-members if the Member State in question so authorises.

7.22 The producer organisations are empowered to operate the withdrawal system and to buy in produce when prices fall below the withdrawal price, and they receive the financial support necessary for that purpose and, in certain cases, for the purpose of storing produce bought in. The intervention arrangements are structured to encourage producers to gear supply to actual demand by reducing progressively the level of payments for withdrawals, so that the more production exceeds demand, the less the producer is compensated for his output.

7.23 In order to be eligible for financial compensation in this way, or to be marketed within the Community, produce must conform to Community standards relating to quality, size, weight, packing, and labelling which are prescribed in supplementary regulations. Thus, for example common marketing standards were laid down by Regulation 103/76[33] for fresh or chilled fish. These provisions are in general applicable equally to Community-caught fish and that caught by vessels flying the flag of a third country. Detailed rules governing the financial compensation applied by producers' organisations are contained in Regulation 3902/92.[34]

7.24 In dealing with imports to the Community of fish or fish products, the same principles are applied as in the case of other goods where there is a Common Market organisation. A reference price is established for each type of fish product on the Community market, and duties are imposed if it is considered necessary to bring their value up to the relevant Community level in order to prevent disturbance to the internal market. Conversely, export refunds are available to enable the export of products to the world market (or to a particular third country market) where the price is lower than the Community price, and the export of the product in question is considered to be

[32] [1992] O.J. L388, as last amended by Reg. 697/93, [1993] O.J. L76.
[33] [1976] O.J. L20, as last amended by Reg. 33/89, [1989] O.J. L5.
[34] [1992] O.J. L392.

important to the Community economy. General rules for the grant of export refunds, and the criteria by reference to which the amounts are fixed, are the subject of Regulation 110/76.[35]

[35] [1976] O.J. L20.

# CHAPTER 8

# FREE MOVEMENT OF WORKERS AND SOCIAL SECURITY

**8.01** Title III of the Treaty under the heading of "Free movement of persons, services and capital" covers in Chapter 1 free movement of workers, in Chapter 2 the right of establishment, and the right of business enterprises to move across national frontiers, and in Chapter 3 the right to provide services across national frontiers. Chapter 4 deals with the right to move capital between the Member States.

## The principle of free movement of workers

**8.02** Article 48 of the Treaty is concerned with the free movement of workers. It specifies the right which are involved in such free movement and provides that the freedom of movement shall entail the abolition of any discrimination based on nationality between workers of Member States as regards employment, renumeration and other conditions of work and employment; it entails the right, subject to limitations justified on grounds of public policy, public security or public health:

(a) to accept offers of employment actually made;
(b) to move freely within the territory of Member States for this purpose;
(c) to stay in a Member State for the purpose of employment in accordance with the provisions governing the employment of nationals of that State;
(d) to remain in the territory of a Member State after having been employed in that State.

Employment in the public service is excluded from the scope of the article.

Article 49 of the Treaty provides for the Council to issue directives or make regulations setting out the measures required to bring about freedom of movement for workers as defined in Article 48. It should be noted that the Court of Justice has established the scope of the Article by deciding that the Article has direct effect: see Case 167/73, *Commission v. French Republic*,[1] and Case 41/74, *Van Duyn v. Home Office*.[2] 8.03

The term "worker" covers all persons working under a contract of employment and it covers salaried employees and executives as well as manual workers. The Court of Justice, however, has gone further and in Case 53/81, *Levin v. Staatssecretarie van Justitie*[3] ruled that a person was a worker as long as he performed paid work of some substantial duration; full-time work was not required, but the work had to be of more than a casual nature. The term "worker" is also defined in Regulation 1408/71[4] in terms of being insured by a social security scheme. The question of who is to be considered as a national of a Member State must normally be determined by national law. As far as the United Kingdom is concerned the term "nationals" refers to individuals who have the right of abode in the United Kingdom and therefore are exempt from United Kingdom immigration control. Restrictions cannot be imposed on the right of a national of any Member State to enter the territory of another Member State, to stay there and to move within it unless his presence or conduct constitutes a genuine and sufficiently serious threat to public policy: see Case 36/75, *Rutili v. Ministre de l'Interieur*,[5] in which case it was held that reasons must be given to enable the worker to assess whether or not the restriction imposed on him is supported by reference to considerations of public policy, and to exercise effectively his right to challenge the restriction if appropriate. However in Case 175/78, *R. v. Saunders*,[6] the Court held that a Member State may limit the freedom of movement of one of its own nationals in its own territory (a British court had required a United Kingdom national to reside for three years outside England and Wales as a condition of suspending a sentence for theft). The principle of free movement of workers is further qualified to the extent that it is not contrary to the provisions of Community law to provide that a national of another Member State, who entered the territory of the host State in order to seek employment, may be required to leave the territory of that State (subject to appeal) if he has not found employment there after six months unless there is evidence that he is continuing to seek employment with genuine chances of being engaged: 8.04

[1] [1974] E.C.R. 359, [1974] 2 C.M.L.R. 216.
[2] [1974] E.C.R. 1337, [1975] 1 C.M.L.R. 1.
[3] [1982] E.C.R. 1035, [1982] 2 C.M.L.R. 454.
[4] [1971] O.J. L149/2.
[5] [1975] E.C.R. 1219, [1976] 1 C.M.L.R. 140.
[6] [1979] E.C.R. 1129, [1979] 2 C.M.L.R. 216.

see Case C–292/89, *The Queen v. Immigration Appeal Tribunal, ex parte Antonissen.*[7]

## Public service exception

8.05 The provision of Article 48(4) dealing with employment in the public service is subject to varying interpretation. The Court of Justice in Case 152/73, *Sotgiu v. Deutsche Bundespost,*[8] held that the exception provided by the article applies only to the access to public service occupations and not to the functions performed. In Case 149/79, *Kingdom of Belgium v. Commission,*[9] the Court seemed to indicate that it is the functions which are performed which may involve the protection of the public interest. In Case 225/85, *Commission v. Italian Republic,*[10] the Court stated that for the exception to apply it must be shown that the persons employed are charged with the exercise of powers conferred by public law or are responsible for safeguarding the general interests of the State. In Case C–4/91, *A. Bleis v. Ministère de l'Education National,*[11] the Court ruled that employment as a secondary school teacher does not constitute employment in the public service within the meaning of Article 48(4). Article 48(2), dealing with the abolition of discrimination based on nationality, is more specific than the general rule on non-discrimination embodied in Article 7 of the Treaty.

## Prohibition of discrimination

8.06 The anti-discrimination rules contained in the provisions mentioned are not validly given effect by a Member State if as a matter of administrative practice such a State simply does not apply existing legislation of a discriminatory nature to nationals of other Member States. The discriminatory rules must be amended to make them formally inapplicable to Community nationals: see Case 167/73, *Commission v. French Republic.*[12] The Treaty also prohibits discrimination during the course of employment and the Court of Justice has made it clear that this implies equal treatment over dismissals. A national rule which prohibits dismissal of certain employees (*e.g.* handicapped persons) without prior authorisation, but which applies to nationals and residents only, must be extended to all

[7] [1991] I E.C.R. 745, [1991] 2 C.M.L.R. 373.
[8] [1974] E.C.R. 153.
[9] [1980] E.C.R. 3881, [1981] 2 C.M.L.R. 413.
[10] [1987] E.C.R. 2625, [1988] 3 C.M.L.R. 635.
[11] Not yet reported.
[12] [1974] E.C.R. 359, [1974] 2 C.M.L.R. 216.

Community nationals: see Case 44/72, *Marsman v. Rosskamp*.[13] The Court of Justice has reaffirmed the Community national's right to enter another Member State and to reside there in connection with the free movement of workers. The Court ruled that the right to take up residence is conferred by the Treaty and does not depend upon the discretion of national authorities: see Case 48/75, *Royer*,[14] and Case 8/77, *Sagulo*.[15] In *Royer* the Court stressed that the right of entry and residence conferred by Community law is equally conferred on members of workers' families.

Article 48 is administered by legislation made under Article 49. This legislation is represented by a number of Community instruments. Regulation 1612/68[16] lays down the principles governing the freedom of movement of workers within the Community. It provides that any national of any Member State, irrespective of his residence, has a right to take up an activity as an employed person and to pursue this activity within the territory of another Member State in accordance with the provisions laid down by law, regulation or administrative action governing the employment of nationals of that State. He must have the right to take up available employment in the territory of another Member State with the same priority as nationals of that State. The questions of residence permits, access to education and funding of studies were considered in Case C–357/89, *Raulin v. Netherlands Ministry of Education and Science*[17] and, in Case C–3/90, *Bernini v. Netherlands Ministry of Education and Science*,[18] both in the scope of Regulation 1612/68. The right to take employment is extended to the family of the worker. The worker is entitled to all the rights and benefits accorded to national workers in housing matters and his children are entitled to education and vocational training as nationals of the State concerned. This includes grants for higher education. In Case C–308/89, *Carmina de Leo v. Land Berlin*,[19] the Court ruled that Article 12 of the regulation must be interpreted as meaning that the children falling within its scope are to be treated as nationals for the purpose of awarding educational or training grants, not only when the education or training takes place in the host State but also when is is provided in a State of which those children are nationals. In addition, Directive 77/486[20] provides for special free tuition to facilitate the initial reception of the children in the new Member State, including training in the official language. The regulation provides for equal rights to become **8.07**

[13] [1972] E.C.R. 1243, [1973] C.M.L.R. 501.
[14] [1976] E.C.R. 497, [1976] 2 C.M.L.R. 619.
[15] [1977] E.C.R. 1495, [1977] 2 C.M.L.R. 585.
[16] [1968] O.J. L257/2.
[17] [1994] 1 C.M.L.R. 227.
[18] [1992] I E.C.R. 1071.
[19] [1990] I E.C.R. 4185.
[20] [1977] O.J. L199/32.

members of trade unions but here the workers are excluded from certain workers' tribunals. Directive 68/360[21] complements the regulation by requiring the abolition of restrictions on the movement and residence of nationals of the Member States and members of their families to whom the regulation applies. Passports and identity cards must be issued or renewed by Member States, which must allow entry to their territory simply on production of a valid identity card or passport. A valid identity card is sufficient even if it does not allow the holder to leave the territory of the Member State in which it was issued: see Case C–376/89, *Giagounidis v. City of Reutlingen*.[22] No entry visa or equivalent may be demanded except for those members of the worker's family who are not nationals of a Member State: see Case 157/79, *R. v. Stanislaus Pieck*.[23] Nationals of a Member State are not required to answer questions by border officials regarding the purpose and duration of their journey and the financial means at their disposal: see Case C–68/89, *Commission of the European Communities v. Kingdom of the Netherlands*.[24] The directive lists documents on the production of which a residence permit must be issued by the Member State. Such a permit is valid for a least five years and is automatically renewable. Commission Regulation 1251/70[25] regulates the position of workers who have worked in the territory of another Member State. It deals with their right to remain in the territory of the Member State in which the worker has ceased working. Directive 90/365[26] extends the right of residence in a Member State to all employees and self-employed persons who have ceased their occupational activity and their families, provided they are in receipt of benefits which preclude their being a burden on the social security system and provided they are covered by sickness insurance. The right of residence is further conferred by Directive 90/364[27] on all nationals of Member States and their families if they do not enjoy this right under other provisions of Community law, provided they are covered by sickness insurance and would not become a burden on the social assistance system of the host Member State. Again, the right of residence is conferred on students, their spouse and children for the duration of their course of studies by Directive 90/366,[28] provided they will not become a burden on the social assistance system. The Court of Justice, however, in Case C–295/90, *European Parliament v. Council of European Communities*[29] annulled this dir-

[21] [1968] O.J. L257/13.
[22] [1991] I E.C.R. 1069, [1993] 1 C.M.L.R. 537.
[23] [1980] E.C.R. 2171, [1980] 3 C.M.L.R. 220.
[24] [1993] 2 C.M.L.R. 389.
[25] [1970] O.J. L142/24.
[26] [1990] O.J. L180/28.
[27] [1990] O.J. L180/26.
[28] [1990] O.J. L180/30.
[29] [1992] 3 C.M.L.R. 281.

ective on the ground that its legal basis (Article 235) was inappropriate and it should have been based on Article 7, while maintaining the effects of the annulled directive until the entry of a directive adopted on the appriopriate legal basis. The new Directive 93/96[30] reiterates the right of residence of students attending a vocational training course, their spouse and children. The effects of the old directive are maintained until December 31, 1993. Regulation 2434/92[31] amended Regulation 1612/68[32] with a view to giving all nationals of the Member States equal priority on the labour market, particularly under the mechanism for clearing vacancies and applications for employment.

Article 48(3) subjects the freedom of movement of workers to exceptions on the grounds of public policy, public security or public health. Directive 64/221[33] effected the co-ordination of national provisions regulating these exceptions. This directive was extended by Directive 72/194[34] to nationals of Member States and members of their families who remain in the territory of a Member State after having been employed in that State. Directive 64/221 provides that grounds of public policy, public security or public health must not be invoked to serve economic ends. Measures taken on the ground of public policy or public security must be based exclusively on the personal conduct of the individual concerned. Previous criminal convictions do not in themselves constitute grounds for taking such measures. The expiry of the identity card or passport used by the person concerned to enter the country does not justify expulsion from the territory and the State which issued the identity card or passport shall allow the holder of such document to re-enter the territory without any formality although the document is no longer valid or the nationality of the holder is in dispute. Article 3 of the directive was held to be directly applicable in Case 41/74, *Van Duyn v. Home Office*.[35] In Case 30/77, *R. v. Bouchereau*,[36] the court laid down as a test of the application of the public policy exception the existence of a genuine and sufficiently serious threat affecting one of the fundamental interests of society. In that case the Court held that previous convictions do not on their own constitute grounds for imposition of restrictions authorised by Article 48 on the grounds of public policy and public security. The only diseases or disabilities justifying refusal of entry into a territory or refusal to issue a first residence permit under Directive 68/360[37] are those listed 8.08

30 [1993] O.J. L317/59.
31 [1992] O.J. L245/1.
32 [1968] O.J. L257/2.
33 [1964] O.J. L56/850.
34 [1972] O.J. L121/32.
35 [1974] E.C.R. 1337, [1975] 1 C.M.L.R. 1.
36 [1977] E.C.R. 1999, [1977] 2 C.M.L.R. 800.
37 [1968] O.J. L257/13.

in the Annex to Directive 64/221,[38] *e.g.* drug addiction or active tuberculosis.

8.09 Article 50 states that Member States shall, within the framework of a joint programme, encourage the exchange of young workers. The current programme is the third joint programme embodied in Decision 84/636.[39] The Community is in fact going further in the operation of joint programmes in the labour sector by the establishment of a European system for the international clearing of vacancies and applications for employment (the SEDOC system) and since 1982 there has been in operation a mutual information system on employment policies in Europe set up to collect, exploit and disseminate information.

## Social Security

8.10 Social security systems form an intrinsic part of the freedom of movement of workers in the Community. An uneven distribution of rights and benefits throughout the Member States will affect the Common Market by charges imposed on commerce or industry and thus the ability to compete. Unequal social security systems, however, are significant obstacles to the free movement of labour, since workers will be reluctant to seek employment in another Member State when that employment involves loss of rights and benefits. Article 51 of the Treaty provides that the Council shall adopt such measures in the field of social security as are necessary to provide freedom of movement for workers; to this end, it must make arrangements to secure for migrant workers and their dependants:

(a) aggregation, for the purpose of acquiring and retaining the right to benefit and of calculating the amount of benefit, of all periods taken into account under the laws of the several countries; and
(b) payment of benefits to persons resident in the territories of Member States.

The Court of Justice has construed Article 51 and its implementing legislation in a large number of cases and the Court's decisions have had great influence on the drafting and implementing of the Community rules relating to social security and led to frequent revision of the appropriate regulations; the interpretations of the Court were incorporated in the new regulations. In interpreting Article 51 the Court has frequently paid attention to Articles 48 and 49.

38 [1964] O.J. L56/850.
39 [1984] O.J. L331/36.

8.11 The scope of Article 51 and its implementing regulations is wide. Regulation 1408/71[40] states in Article 4(1) that it shall apply to sickness, maternity benefits, invalidity benefits, old age and survivors' benefits, benefits arising out of workmen's compensation and occupational diseases, death grants, unemployment benefits and family benefits. The regulation applies only to social security schemes and not to public assistance benefits nor to some types of special legislation. This regulation is the central provision on social security for families moving within the Community. It has been extended by Regulation 1390/81[41] to apply to self-employed persons and their families. Thus the regulation now applies to employed or self-employed persons who are or have been subject to legislation of one or more Member States, and who are Community nationals or stateless persons or refugees residing within the territory of one of the Member States, and to members of their families. The principle underlying all this legislation is that a person residing in the territory of one of the Member States and to whom the legislation applies enjoys the same rights and obligations under the legislation of a Member State as its own nationals. As Article 51 requires, periods of employment and insurance completed in several Member States are to be aggregated for the calculation of benefits. The beneficiary may request the transfer of benefits from one Member State to another. Regulation 1408/71 underwent amendment by Chapter IX of Annex I of the Act of Accession of the United Kingdom, Denmark and Ireland and by Regulation 2001/83[42] to take account of the social security systems of new Member States. The regulation is governed in its application by rules contained in Regulation 574/72,[43] which has been amended to allow for changes in the social security systems of Member States and which has been extended to apply to self-employed persons by Regulation 3795/81.[44] Regulation 1209/76[45] introduced changes to enable workers insured in the United Kingdom who later became disabled in another country to obtain benefits in the United Kingdom. A spouse is entitled to the social advantage of a husband or wife, although she or he is not resident in the Member State where the employed person works: see Case C–78/91, *Hughes v. Chief Adjudication Officer, Belfast*.[46] However, a handicapped person's allowance which national legislation grants as a personal right and not by reason of the status of a member of a worker's family cannot be claimed by a national of a non-Member State, the spouse of a worker who is a national of a Member State moving within the Community: see Case C–243/91,

[40] [1971] O.J. L149/2.
[41] [1981] O.J. L143/1.
[42] [1983] O.J. L230/6.
[43] [1972] O.J. L74/1.
[44] [1981] O.J. L378/1.
[45] [1976] O.J. L138/1.
[46] [1992] 3 C.M.L.R. 490.

*Belgian State v. Taghavi.*[47] As a result of the accession of Greece some technical changes were made in the legislation and the same followed the admission of Spain and Portugal. Regulation 1305/89[48] further deals with social security schemes. Regulation 2332/89[49] amended Regulation 1408/71 and Regulation 574/72 to take account of changes made by Member States in their social security legislation and introduced some amendments of a technical nature to the implementation procedure. It covers employed persons, self-employed persons and members of their families. Further amendments to Regulation 1408/71 along these lines and to take account of the various judgments of the Court of Justice were effected by Regulation 2195/91,[50] Regulation 1247/92,[51] Regulation 1248/92[52] and Regulation 1249/92.[53] The various detailed provisions of Regulation 1408/71 and Regulation 574/72 were interpreted further by Case C–102/91, *Knoch v. Bundesanstalt für Arbeit.*[54] These two regulations and Regulation 1247/92 were amended by Regulation 1945/93.[55]

**8.12** The Court of Justice gives the article and regulations made in its pursuance a broad interpretation. Thus the implementing regulations can only increase a worker's rights under national laws and cannot diminish them: see Case 1/67, *Ciechelski v. Caisse Régionale de Sécurité Sociale.*[56] On the other hand, a worker from another Member State is not entitled to more than national treatment. If social security benefits of nationals are suspended during periods of imprisonment, the same rule may be applied to a worker from another Member State even if the imprisonment occurs in the home State and not in the State liable for benefits: see Case 1/78, *Kenny v. Insurance Officer.*[57] The rules on social security must always be interpreted in such a way that workers moving between Member States are not penalised by doing so. Thus periods of employment treated as periods of insurance in a Member State where the claimant has previously been employed must also be so considered in the other Member State where benefit is claimed: see Case 126/77, *Frangiamore v. Office National de l'Emploi.*[58] These principles were reiterated in Cases C–228/88, *Bronzino v. Kindergeldkasse*[59] and C–12/89, *Gatto v. Bun-*

[47] Not yet reported.
[48] [1989] O.J. L131/1.
[49] [1989] O.J. L224/1.
[50] [1991] O.J. L206/2.
[51] [1992] O.J. L136/1.
[52] [1992] O.J. L136/7.
[53] [1992] O.J. L136/28.
[54] Not yet reported.
[55] [1993] O.J. L181/1.
[56] [1967] E.C.R. 75, [1967] C.M.L.R. 77.
[57] [1978] E.C.R. 1489, [1978] 3 C.M.L.R. 651.
[58] [1978] E.C.R. 725, [1978] 3 C.M.L.R. 166.
[59] [1990] I E.C.R. 531.

*desanstalt für Arbeit*[60] where the Court held that where the conditions for grant of certain family benefits require that the unemployed member of the worker's family be at the disposal of the unemployment office for the territorial area in which the legislation applies, that condition must be regarded as fulfilled where the unemployed member of the family is at the disposal of the employment office of the Member State in which he resides. Again, benefits paid in one Member State must not be suspended where benefits or allowances are no longer payable in the Member State in which members of the family, solely because they have not been applied or re-applied for. See Case C–117/89, *K.J. Kracht v. Bundesanstalt für Arbeit.*[61] The periods which may be treated as a period of insurance must be determined solely by reference to criteria laid down by national legislation under which those periods were completed: See Case C–324/88, *Vella widow of Scadutta v. ANMC.*[62] Where the institution responsible for paying an invalidity benefit exercises the powers provided by Regulation 574/72[63] of having the recipient of the benefit residing in another Member State examined by a doctor of its choice, the person concerned may be required to go to the Member State where the competent institution is situated, provided that the travel and accomodation expenses thereby incurred are borne by the institution and the person concerned is fit enough to make the journey without impairment of his health: see Case C–344/89, *Vidal v. Gemenschappelike Medischeg Dienst.*[64] Article 46 of Regulation 1408/71 dealing with overlapping of benefits must be interpreted so that the worker is entitled to the highest amount of benefits: see Joined Case C 90–91/91, *ONP v. Crescenzo.*[65]

Each Member State declares the nature of its benefits, *e.g.* unemployment insurance or other measures of social security. This is important as it classifies the benefits for the purposes of Regulation 1408/71. To distinguish social security benefits from welfare benefits the Court of Justice appears to rely on the criterion of whether the entitlement to benefit is one of right or whether it depends on some degree of administrative discretion: see Case 7/75, *Mr & Mrs F. v. Belgium,*[66] concerning special benefits for the handicapped. Persons in employment but not insured as required in the place of their employment as a result of their employer's neglect fall within the ambit of the regulation: see Case 39/76, *Bestuur der Bedrijfvereniging v. Mouthaan.*[67] Benefits accruing under Community 8.13

[60] [1990] I E.C.R. 557.
[61] [1990] I E.C.R. 2781.
[62] [1990] I E.C.R. 257.
[63] [1972] O.J. L74/1.
[64] Not yet reported.
[65] Not yet reported.
[66] [1975] E.C.R. 679, [1975] 2 C.M.L.R. 424.
[67] [1976] E.C.R. 1901.

law may not be less than those available under national laws alone: see Case 112/76, *Manzoini v. Fonds National de Retraite*,[68] and this principle was used by the Court to declare Article 46(3) of Regulation 1408/71 invalid when it required a reduction of benefits due to overlap. In interpreting Article 76 of the regulation the Court held in Case 24/88, *Michel Georges v. ONAFTS*,[69] that if the amount of the family allowances actually paid in the Member State of residence was less than that provided for under legislation of another Member State, the worker was entitled to a supplementary allowance equal to the difference between the two amounts, the cost of which is to be borne by the institutions of the other Member State. However, the Court held in Case 313/86, *Lenoir v. Caisse d'Allocations Familiales des Alpes-Maritimes*,[70] that the terms of Article 77 of the regulation call for payment by the country of origin of "family allowances" only to the exclusion of other family benefits such as the schooling expenses allowance and single wage allowance provided for by the legislation of the country of origin. Voluntary or contributory insurance has been treated similarly to compulsory insurance in relation to the recognition of insurance periods completed in another Member State. In Joined Cases 82 & 103/86, *Laborero and Sabato v. OSSOM*,[71] the Court found a voluntary insurance scheme brought the insured person's survivor within the terms of Regulation 1408/71, even if the benefits provided by national rules were based on periods of employment in non-Member States. Residence requirements for the granting of childbirth and maternity allowances were held to be contrary to Article 7(2) of Regulation 1612/68, Article 18(1) of Regulation 1408/71 and Article 52 of the Treaty: see Case C–111/91, *Commission v. Grand Duchy of Luxembourg*.[72]

**8.14** An Administrative Commission on Security for Migrant Workers, consisting of one representative of each Member State, deals with coordination and administration in connection with the implementation of the Community rules on social security and gives (without prejudice to normal recourse to the courts) interpretation of the Community regulations, which are, however, not legally binding. It also establishes model forms and documents, provides a clearing system for balances of sums due among the various systems and calculates the sums due. Regulation 1408/71 has supplemented this Commission with an Advisory Committee on Social Security for Migrant Workers composed, in addition to two government representatives from each Member State, of two representat-

[68] [1977] E.C.R. 1647, [1978] 2 C.M.L.R. 416.
[69] [1989] E.C.R. 1905, [1991] 2 C.M.L.R. 251.
[70] [1988] E.C.R. 5391, [1990] 1 C.M.L.R. 543.
[71] [1987] E.C.R. 3401.
[72] Not yet reported.

ives of trade unions and similarly two representatives of employers' organisations. The Committee examines general questions and questions of principle arising under Article 51, formulates opinions for the Administrative Commission and makes proposals for revisions of the applicable regulations. It is this machinery which resulted in the provision of a degree of free medical care for Community nationals on short visits to other Member States, in addition to provision for migrant workers. The scheme covers dependants whatever their nationality and whether or not they travel alone. The scheme is invoked in the United Kingdom by the issue and production of Form E 111, obtained from the local social security office.

# CHAPTER 9

# SOCIAL POLICY

**9.01** Title III of the Treaty, under the heading Social Policy, deals with social provisions in Chapter 1 and the European Social Fund in Chapter 2. The social provisions deal with differing aspects of working conditions in the Community and contain only two specific legislative provisions in Articles 119 and 120, dealing with equal pay for men and women and holidays with pay respectively. The chapter begins in Article 117 with the belief in the harmonisation of improved working conditions and an improved standard of living for workers. Article 118 sets the task for the Commission of promoting closer co-operation between Member States in the social field, particularly in employment, labour law and working conditions, vocational training, social security, prevention of occupational accidents and diseases, occupational hygiene and the right of association and collective bargaining. The Single European Act added an Article 118a which calls for directives to obtain minimum requirements for harmonisation of improved conditions in the area of the health and safety of workers. The aims of Articles 117, 118a and 118b were expressed in terms by the European Council in 1989 when it adopted the Community Charter of the Fundamental Social Rights of Workers (the Social Charter). The United Kingdom dissented from its adoption. The provisions of the Charter are wide, providing for the right to freedom of association and collective bargaining, of employment and renumeration, the right to social protection, improvement of living and working conditions, the right of men and women to equal treatment, and the right to health and safety at work.

## Sex discrimination and equal pay

**9.02** Articles 119 and 120 represent what may be termed labour law provisions which deal in precise terms with two narrowly drawn requirements. Article 119 provides that each Member State shall, during the first stage, ensure and subsequently maintain the application of the principle that men and women should receive equal pay for equal work. For the purpose of this Article "pay" means the ordinary basic or minimum wage or salary and any other consideration, whether in cash or in kind, which the worker receives, directly or indirectly, in respect of his employment from the employer. Equal pay without discrimination based on sex means: (a) that pay for the same work at piece rate shall be calculated on the basis of the same unit of measurement; (b) that pay for work at time rates shall be the same for the same job. The article thus required each Member State to achieve equal pay during the first stage (*i.e.* by January 1, 1962) and to maintain it thereafter.

It was not till 1975 that the Council enacted Directive 75/117[1] on the approximation of laws of the Member States relating to the application of the principle of equal pay for men and women. Accordingly, equal pay must be given not only for identical work but for comparable work, work to which equal value is attributed. This concept was considered by the Court of Justice in Case 129/79, *Macarthys Ltd. v. Wendy Smith,*[2] where the Court ruled that equal pay must be considered in relation to workers performing the same work in succession, the comparison not necessarily involving the same work at the same time. Whether the discrimination is based on sex or other factors is a question of fact for national courts to decide. In Case 61/81, *Commission v. United Kingdom,*[3] the Court further stressed that the directive required equal pay for work of equivalent value, the United Kingdom being at fault in not requiring job classification schemes at all times. 9.03

The interpretation of the provisions of the directive has been overtaken by the decisions of the Court that Article 119 is of direct effect and is self-executing. In Case 43/75, *Defrenne v. Sabena,*[4] the Court ruled that Article 119 had become of direct effect at the end of the first stage and that employees could rely on it in proceedings in national courts against private employers. The Court further considered this article on the basis of its being directly applicable in Case 69/80, *Worringham v. Lloyds Bank Ltd.,*[5] and Case 96/80, *Jenkins v. Kingsgate (Clothing Productions) Ltd.*[6] The latter case suggests that Article 119 might be directly applicable even if the pay differentials were not identical. The former case indicated that fringe benefits are taken into account in defining wages. Considering 9.04

[1] [1975] O.J. L45/19.
[2] [1980] E.C.R. 1275, [1980] 2 C.M.L.R. 205
[3] [1982] E.C.R. 2601, [1982] 3 C.M.L.R. 284
[4] [1976] E.C.R. 455, [1976] 2 C.M.L.R. 98.
[5] [1981] E.C.R. 767, [1981] 2 C.M.L.R. 1.
[6] [1981] E.C.R. 911, [1981] E.C.R. 24.

private pension schemes, the Court decided in Case 19/81, *Burton v. British Railways Board*[7] that early retirement for women did not contravene equal pay provisions since Article 119 is only concerned with remuneration and not access to benefits. The same principle that Article 119 is not concerned with the access to pensions was repeated in Case 275/81, *Koks v. Raad van Arbeid*.[8]

9.05 The Court reiterated in Case 170/84, *Bilka Kaufhaus GmbH v. K. Weber von Hartz*,[9] that occupational pension schemes are covered by Article 119, and where the scheme did not cover part-time workers who were mainly women this amounted to indirect discrimination. This was reiterated in Case C–33/89, *Kowalska v. Freie und Hansestadt Hamburg*,[10] where Article 119 was held as precluding the application of a clause in a collective pay agreement which excluded part-time employees from payment of a severance grant, when in fact a considerably lower percentage of men than women work part-time, unless the exclusion is based on objectively justified factors unrelated to any discrimination on grounds of sex. Persons placed at a disadvantage must become subject to the same scheme, proportionately to the number of hours worked, as other workers. A provision in a collective wage agreement where reclassification in a higher grade depended upon seniority of workers, and only half of such seniority was taken into accout in the case of workers working between one half and three quarters of normal working hours, was held to amount to indirect discrimination and contravention of Article 119: see Case C–184/89, *Helga Nimz v. Freie und Hansestadt Hamburg*.[11] The problem of part-time workers and discrimination in relation to training courses was the subject of Case C–360/90, *A. W. S. B. v. Bötel*.[12] It is open to the employer to justify the provision by special factors relating to the nature of duties and experience afforded by a certain number of working hours worked. Again in Case 171/88, *Ingrid Rinner-Kuhn v. FWW Spezial-Gebaudereinigung GmbH & Co.*,[13] the Court ruled that the exclusion of part-time employees from the continued payment of wages during illness, where this affects a far greater number of women than men, would be interpreted as being contrary to Article 119, unless it could be shown that it was justified by objective factors unrelated to any discrimination on grounds of sex. These principles were re-affirmed by the House of Lords in *R. v. Secretary of State for Employment, ex parte Equal Opportunities*

[7] [1982] E.C.R. 555, [1982] 2 C.M.L.R. 136.
[8] [1982] E.C.R. 3031, [1983] 1 C.M.L.R. 626.
[9] [1985] E.C.R. 1607, [1986] 2 C.M.L.R. 701.
[10] [1990] E.C.R. 985.
[11] [1991] I E.C.R. 297, [1992] 3 C.M.L.R. 699.
[12] [1992] I E.C.R. 3591, [1992] 3 C.M.L.R. 446.
[13] [1989] E.C.R. 2743, [1993] 2 C.M.L.R. 932.

*Commission*[14] and will call for amendments to the legislation referred to in paragraph 9.10 below. However, all benefits which have economic value must be considered as pay: see Case 12/81, *Garland v. British Rail Engineering*.[15] Thus special travel facilities after retirement for male employees amount to discrimination under Article 119 when these facilities are denied to female employees.

Where a pay system is characterised by a total lack of transparency, the employer bears the burden of proof of demonstrating that the pay system was not in fact discriminatory. In Case 109/88, *Handels- og Kontorfunktionærernes Forbund i Danmark v. Dansk Arbejdsgiverforening*,[16] the system of individual increments applied to basic pay was operated in such a way that it was impossible for a female worker to identify the reasons for a difference between her pay and that of a male worker. The employer was bound to show how he had applied the incremental criteria and would therefore make his pay scheme transparent. In Case C–127/92, *Enderby v. Frenchay Health Authority*,[17] the Court ruled that where significant statistics disclosed an appreciable difference in pay between two jobs of equal value, one of which was carried out almost exclusively by women and the other predominantly by men, Article 119 required the employer to show that the difference was based on objectively justified factors unrelated to any discrimination on the groud of sex, and the fact that the respective rates of pay of two jobs of equal value were arrived at by a collective bargaining process was not sufficient objective justification for the difference in pay. It was for the national court to determine whether the need to attract canditates by higher pay constituted an objectively justified ground for the difference in pay between the jobs in question. 9.06

The principles enshrined in the Treaty and Article 119 were further given effect in Directive 76/207[18] on the implementation of the principle of equal treatment for men and women as regards access to employment, vocational training and promotion, and working conditions, and in Directive 79/7[19] on the progressive implementation of the principle of equal treatment for men and women in matters of social security (these two directives being based on Article 235 of the Treaty). The Court considered these two directives in Joined Cases 48 & 106–107/88, *Acterberg-ye-Riele v. Sociale Verzekeringsbank*,[20] holding that their purpose (and that of 9.07

14 Judgment of March 3, 1994; *The Times*, March 4, 1994.
15 [1982] E.C.R. 359, [1982] 1 C.M.L.R. 696.
16 [1989] E.C.R. 3199, [1991] 1 C.M.L.R. 8.
17 [1994] 1 C.M.L.R. 8.
18 [1976] O.J. L39/40.
19 [1979] O.J. L6/24.
20 [1989] E.C.R. 1963, [1990] 3 C.M.L.R. 323.

Article 119) was to bring about equal treatment of men and women, not in a general way but solely in their capacity as workers. Housing benefits under Directive 79/7 were the subject of Case C–243/90, *The Queen v. Secretary of State, ex parte Smithson.*[21] Directive 86/613[22] governs the application of the principle of equal treatment between self-employed men and women and deals with the protection of self-employed women during pregnancy and motherhood. Directive 86/378[23] governs the implementation of the principle of equal treatment in occupational social security schemes which are defined as schemes not covered by Directive 79/7. However, in Case C–9/91, *The Queen v. Secretary of State for Social Security, ex parte EOC,*[24] the Court ruled that Article 7(1) of Directive 79/7 must be interpreted as authorising the determination of a statutory pensionable age which differs according to sex. The derogation in Article 7(1) was limited to the form of discrimination existing under the other benefit schemes which were necessarily and objectively linked to the difference in retirement age: see Case C–328/91, *Secretary of State v. Thomas.*[25]

9.08 These directives gave rise to some questions which were to be decided by the Court of Justice. The Court ruled in the case of *Burton,*[26] dealing with a voluntary scheme with differing retirement dates for men and women, that the scheme fell to be considered under Directive 76/207.[27] The fact of differing pensionable age for men and women did not amount to discrimination under the directive. In Case 151/84, *Roberts v. Tate and Lyle Industries,*[28] the Court found that a provision laying down a single age for dismissal with an early retirement pension (where normal retirement for men and women differed) did not constitute discrimination on the ground of sex. In Case 152/84, *Marshall v. Southampton and South West Hampshire Area Health Authority,*[29] the Court decided that a Member State could set differing pensionable ages, but this did not entitle an employer to dismiss a woman who reached the normal retiring age for women but not for men. In Case C–173/91, *Commission v. Belgium,*[30] the Court held legislation which renders female workers who have attained the age of 60 ineligible for a supplementary allowance payable upon redundancy to be contrary to Article 119 of the Treaty or

[21] [1992] 1 C.M.L.R. 1061.
[22] [1986] O.J. L359/56.
[23] [1986] O.J. L225/40.
[24] [1992] 3 C.M.L.R. 233.
[25] [1993] 3 C.M.L.R. 880.
[26] [1982] E.C.R. 555, [1982] 2 C.M.L.R. 136.
[27] [1976] O.J. L39/40.
[28] [1986] E.C.R. 703, [1986] 1 C.M.L.R. 714.
[29] [1986] E.C.R. 723, [1986] 1 C.M.L.R. 688.
[30] [1993] 2 C.M.L.R. 165.

Directive 76/207. It is significant that the Court ruled that the provisions of the directive (requiring Member States to prohibit discrimination on the grounds of sex with regard to working conditions and dismissal) were available to an individual in proceedings against the State. In Case C–188/89, *Foster v. British Gas plc*,[31] the Court confirmed the basis of its judgment in *Marshall* and held that the directive may be relied upon in a claim for damages against a body, whatever its legal form, which has been made responsible for providing a public service under the control of the State and has for that purpose special powers beyond those which result from the normal rules applicable in relations between individuals. The Court further ruled in Case C–271/91, *Marshall v. Southampton and South West Hampshire Area Health Authority (No. 2)*,[32] that where financial compensation was the measure adopted in order to achieve the objective of real equality of opportunity, it had to be adequate in that it had to enable the loss and damage actually sustained as a result of a discriminatory dismissal to be made good in full, including the award of interest. A person might rely on the provisions of Article 6 of Directive 76/207 as against an authority of the State acting in its capacity as an employer in order to set aside a national provision which imposed limits on the amount of compensation recoverable by way of reparation. The operation of Article 119 and Directives 75/117[33] and 76/207[34] was again considered in detail in Case 262/88, *Barber v. Guardian Royal Exchange Assurance Group*,[35] where the Court held that the benefits paid by the employer to a worker in connection with the latter's compulsory redundancy fell within the second paragraph of Article 119. A pension paid under a contracted-out private occupational scheme falls within the scope of Article 119. It is contrary to Article 119 for a man made compulsorily redundant to be entitled to claim only deferred pension payable at a normal retirement age, when a woman in the same position is entitled to an immediate retirement pension as a result of the application of an age condition that varies according to sex in the same way as is provided for by the national statutory pension scheme. The application of the principle of equal pay must be ensured in respect of each element of remuneration and not only on the basis of a comprehensive assessment of the consideration paid to workers. However, a difference between the amount of a bridging pension paid to women and men between the ages of 60 and 65, which was based on an objective difference between their respective financial situations, could not be considered discriminatory: see Case C–132/92, *Birds Eye Walls Ltd. v. Roberts*.[36] In Case C–152/91, *Neath v. Steeper*

[31] [1990] I E.C.R. 3313, [1990] 2 C.M.L.R. 833.
[32] [1993] 3 C.M.L.R. 293.
[33] [1975] O.J. L45/19.
[34] [1976] O.J. L39/40.
[35] [1990] I E.C.R. 1989, [1990] 2 C.M.L.R. 513.
[36] [1993] 3 C.M.L.R. 822.

*Ltd.*,[37] the Court of Justice ruled that the judgment in *Barber* did not extend to the way employers choose to fund their schemes, and by extension non-pension benefits, and can calculate pension benefits, particularly transfer values and tax-free lump sums, differently for male and female members of final occupational pension schemes.

9.09 Article 119 of the Treaty may be relied upon before the national courts. It is for those courts to safeguard the rights which that provision confers on individuals, in particular where a contracted-out pension scheme does not pay to a man on redundancy an immediate pension such as would be granted in a similar case to a woman. The direct effect of Article 119 is not retroactive except in relation to claims initiated before the date of the judgment in *Barber*, May 17, 1990. The Court of Justice decided accordingly in Case C–109/91, *Ten Oever v. Stichtingchting Bedrijfspensioenfonds voor het Glazenwassers en Schoonmaakbedrijf*, [38] and the protocol concerning Article 119 to the Treaty on European Union made the same provision. The extent to which a Member State is allowed to derogate from the directive was considered in Case 222/84, *Johnston v. Chief Constable of the Royal Ulster Constabulary*.[39] The right of women members of the RUC to handle and use firearms could be limited by Article 2(2) of Directive 76/207[40] in the policing arrangements relating to public safety. The requirement for maternity leave does not extend to fathers: see Case 184/83, *Ulrich Hoffman v. Barmer Ersatzkasse*.[41] Refusal to employ a pregnant woman constitutes a direct contravention of Directive 76/207 if the candidate for employment is otherwise suitable: see Case 177/88, *Dekker v. VJV Centrum*.[42] The directive does not preclude dismissals resulting from absences due to an illness which originated in pregnancy or confinement: see Case 179/88, *Handels-og Kontorfunktionærernes Forbund v. Dansk Arbejdsgiverforening*.[43] Directive 76/207 was held to be precise enough to preclude national legislation prohibiting night-work only for women: see Case C–345/89, *Ministère Public v. A. Stoeckel*.[44]

9.10 In the United Kingdom the principle of equal pay is governed by the Equal Pay Act 1970, as amended, and the Sex Discrimination Act 1975, as amended. However, the Equal Pay Act 1970 has been found by the Court of Justice not to satisfy fully the requirements of the equal pay

[37] Not yet reported.
[38] Not yet reported.
[39] [1988] E.C.R. 1651, [1986] 3 C.M.L.R. 240.
[40] [1976] O.J. L39/40.
[41] [1984] E.C.R. 3047, [1986] 1 C.M.L.R. 242.
[42] [1990] I E.C.R. 3941.
[43] [1990] I E.C.R. 3979.
[44] [1993] 3 C.M.L.R. 673.

directive[45] and it ruled that each Member State must endow an authority with the powers to decide whether the work has the same value as other work: see Case 61/81, *Commission v. United Kingdom.*[46] This led to amendment of the Act by the Equal Pay (Amendment) Regulations 1983. Reference should also be made to the Industrial Tribunals (Rules of Procedure) (Equal Value Amendment) Regulations 1983. Complaints of breach of equal treatment are placed before an industrial tribunal. The Equal Opportunities Commission established under the 1975 Act supervises equal pay and may assist persons to establish their rights.

Sex discrimination is governed by the Sex Discrimination Act 1975. The legislation providing for an exception for firms employing five persons or fewer and for domestic service was found to be in breach of Community law by the Court of Justice in Case 165/83, *Commission v. United Kingdom,*[47] which also found the exception for midwives to be lawful. The Sex Discrimination Act 1986 gave effect to the ruling of the Court in *Marshall.*[48] Protection of the employment of women during pregnancy and after giving birth is further afforded in the United Kingdom by the Employment Protection (Consolidation) Act 1978. In the case of *Brown v. Stockton-on-Tees Borough Council,*[49] the House of Lords held that pregnancy should not affect reasons for redundancy. 9.11

## Protection of employment

This Act also implements Directive 75/129[50] which deals with arrangements for collective redundancies. Directive 77/187[51] further safeguards employees' rights in cases of transfer of businesses and is implemented in the United Kingdom by the Transfer of Undertakings (Protection of Employment) Regulations 1981. The directive was considered in Case 101/87, *P. Bork International A/S v. Foreningen af Arbejdsledere i Danmark,*[52] the Court of Justice holding that the directive applied where the workforce dismissed before the transfer could claim the benefit of the directive against the transferee. Both the directive and the United Kingdom regulations were reviewed by the House of Lords in the case of *Litster v. Forth Dry Dock and Engineering Co.,*[53] where it was held that the regulations 9.12

45 [1975] O.J. L45/19.
46 [1982] E.C.R. 2601, [1982] 3 C.M.L.R. 284.
47 [1983] E.C.R. 3431, [1984] 1 C.M.L.R. 44.
48 [1986] E.C.R. 723, [1980] 1 C.M.L.R. 688.
49 [1988] 2 W.L.R. 935.
50 [1975] O.J. L48/29.
51 [1977] O.J. L61/26.
52 [1990] 3 C.M.L.R. 701.
53 [1990] 1 A.C. 546.

must be read to give effect to the directive and an employee dismissed shortly before the transfer of a business, for a reason connected with the transfer, was deemed to have been a person employed immediately before the transfer and to have been unfairly dismissed (and if the transferor was insolvent the liabilities to the employee were transferred to the transferee). The directive was again considered and applied by the High Court in the case of *Kenny v. South Manchester College*.[54] The maintenance of workers'rights in the event of the transfer of undertakings were the subject of two cases, C–29/91, *Dr Stichting v. Bartol*,[55] and C–209/91, *Watson v. Kantinenservice*.[56] The rights of the employees under Articles 3(1) and 7 of Directive 77/187 were considered again in joined Cases C–132 & 138-139/91, *Katsikas v. Konstantinidis*.[57] The directive was held to apply when the transfer concerned only one employee and did not involve the transfer of any tangible assets. See Case C–392/92, *Schmidt v. Spar-und Leihkasse der fruheren Amter Bordesholm et al.*[57a] Directive 80/987,[58] amended by Directive 87/164,[59] deals with the protection of employees on the insolvency of the employer. Direct application of the main directive was subject of the Joined Cases C 40–141 & 278–279/91, *Suffritti v. INPS*.[60] In Case C–334/92, *T. Wagner Miret v. Fondo de Garantia Salarial*,[61] the Court dealt with the position of higher management under the directive. The implementation in the United Kingdom of Directive 77/187 was considered by the Court in Cases C 382–383/92 *Commission v. United Kingdom*[61a] where it was held that the United Kingdom had failed to implement properly the provisions relating to consultations with employees and had not included non-profit undertakings. Failure to implement Directive 80/987 within the prescribed period prevents the assertion of employees' rights before national courts and the Court held in Joined Cases C–6 & 9/90, *Francovich and Bonifaci v. Italian Republic*,[62] that a Member State is obliged to make good the damage suffered by individuals as a result of the failure to implement the directive. Directive 91/533[63] deals with an employer's obligation to inform employees of the conditions applicable to the contract or employment relationship.

9.13 Article 120 of the Treaty simply states that Member States shall endeav-

[54] *The Times*, April 6, 1993.
[55] Not yet reported.
[56] Not yet reported.
[57] [1993] 1 C.M.L.R. 845.
[57a] *The Times*, May 25, 1994.
[58] [1980] O.J. L283/23.
[59] [1987] O.J. L666/11.
[60] Not yet reported.
[61] Not yet reported.
[61a] Judgment of June 8, 1994.
[62] [1991] I E.C.R. 5357, [1993] 2 C.M.L.R. 66.
[63] [1991] O.J. L288/32.

our to maintain the existing equivalence between paid holiday schemes. The actual impact of the article appears to be limited since the tendency in all Member States is to increase paid holidays. Articles 121 and 122 of the Treaty indicate the part to be played by the Commission in the harmonisation of social conditions. Under Article 121 the Council may assign to the Commission tasks in connection with the implementation of common measures, particularly as regards social security for migrant workers referred to in Articles 48 to 51. The only implementing act refers to arrangements for the Secretariat for the Administrative Commission for the Social Security of Migrant Workers. Article 122 requires the Commission to include a section on social affairs in its annual report to the European Parliament and does not call for any implementing measures.

## The European Social Fund

Article 3 of the Treaty states that the activities of the Community shall include, as provided in the Treaty: "(i) the creation of a European Social Fund in order to improve employment opportunities for workers and to contribute to the raising of their standard of living." Article 123 established the fund, giving it the task of rendering the employment of workers easier, and of increasing their geographical and occupational mobility within the Community. The fund is to be administered by the Commission assisted by a Committee (Article 124). Article 125 sets out cases where reimbursement may be granted for expenditures by the Member States. They are limited to occupational retraining, resettlement allowances and conversion of enterprises. After the end of the transitional period the Council may, under Article 126, cease assistance under Article 125 or entrust to the fund new tasks within the framework of Article 123. 9.14

A reform of the fund first took place by Decision 71/66[64] and secondary legislation following from it. This proved inadequate and so the structure of the fund was recreated in a simpler form by Decision 83/516.[65] This decision sets out the tasks of the fund. Regulation 2950/83[66] deals with its implementation and Decision 83/673[67] with the management of the fund. Regulation 3824/85[68] amends Regulation 2950/83, extending it to self-employed persons. The assistance under Article 125 is no longer granted and Decision 71/66 is repealed. The fund is now concerned to 9.15

[64] [1971] O.J. L28/15.
[65] [1983] O.J. L289/38.
[66] [1983] O.J. L289/1.
[67] [1983] O.J. L377/1.
[68] [1985] O.J. L370/25.

assist in equipping the workforce with the skills for stable employment and generating employment opportunities, bearing in mind young people and disadvantaged workers, technological changes and regional imbalances. The Commission, following Decision 83/516, also adopted guidelines for the management of the fund (the latest for 1987 to 1989). Assistance under the fund is granted to operations carried out by public and private bodies. All applications for assistance are to be submitted through the appropriate national authority, which for the United Kingdom is the Department of Employment. Once the assistance is granted, the Commission may carry out checks on the operation under the terms of the Regulation 2950/83. The Treaty on European Union replaces the existing Article 125 by a new version which states that the Council shall adopt implementing decisions relating to the European Social Fund. Existing Articles 126, 127 and 128 are replaced by new versions, specifying development of quality education, vocational training policy and contribution to culture respectively. Directive 93/404[69] deals with professional retraining and access to continuing vocational training.

## The Treaty on European Union and the Social Charter

9.16 The Treaty on European Union contains a Protocol on Social Policy which contains an agreement between 11 Member States, the United Kingdom having opted out, to implement the 1989 Social Charter on the basis of the *acquis communautaire*. This agreement is without prejudice to the provisions of this Treaty, particularly those relating to social policy which constitute an integral part of the *acquis communautaire*. Acts adopted by the Council and financial consequences other than administrative costs on the basis of the protocol shall not be applicable to the United Kingdom.

9.17 The agreement in the protocol specifies as the objectives of the Community and Member States the promotion of employment, improved living and working conditions, proper social protection, dialogue between management and labour, the development of human resources with a view to lasting high employment, and the combating of exclusion (Article 1). With a view to achieving these objectives the Community shall support activities in the following fields: improvement of the working environment to protect workers' health and safety, working conditions, the information and consultation of workers, equality between men and women with regard to labour market opportunities and treatment at work, the integration of persons excluded from the labour market, without prejudice to Article 127 of the Treaty. The Coun-

[69] [1993] O.J. L181/37.

cil may adopt, by means of directives, minimum requirements for gradual implementation, but such directives shall avoid imposing constraints in a way which would hold back the creation and development of small and medium-sized undertakings. The Council shall act unanimously in the following areas: social security and social protection of workers, protection of workers when their employment is terminated, representation and collective defence of interests of workers and employers, including co-determination, subject to paragraph 6 (of Article 2), conditions of employment for third country nationals, financial contributions for promotion of employment and job-creation.

A Member State may entrust management and labour at their joint request, with the implementation of directives adopted pursuant to the foregoing. In this case the Member State concerned is required to take any necessary measure enabling it to be in a position to guarantee the results imposed by that directive. The provisions of Article 2 shall not apply to pay, the rights of association, the right to strike or the right to impose lock-outs (paragraph 6). Article 3 states that the Commission shall have the task of promoting the consultation of management and labour at Community level. The Commission shall consult management and labour on the possible direction of Community action in the social policy field and if the Commission considers Community action advisable it shall consult management and labour on the content of the envisaged proposal and they are to forward to the Commission an opinion or recommendation. On the occasion of such consultation, management and labour may inform the Commission of their wish to initiate the process provided for in Article 4. (The duration of the procedure shall not exceed nine months.) Article 4 provides that should management and labour so desire, the dialogue between them at Community level may lead to contractual relations, including agreements. Agreements concluded at Community level shall be implemented either in accordance with the procedures and practices specific to management and labour or, in matters covered by Article 2, by a Council decision. The Council shall act by qualified majority, except when a unanimous decision is required under Article 2 above. Article 5 requires the Commission to encourage co-operation between Member States and facilitate the co-ordination of their action in all social policy fields under this agreement. 9.18

Article 6 states that each Member State shall ensure that the principle of equal pay for male and female workers for equal work is applied. For the purpose of this article, "pay" means the ordinary basic or minimum wage or salary and any other consideration, whether in cash or in kind, which the worker receives directly or indirectly, in respect of his employment, from his employer. Equal pay without discrimination based on sex means: (a) that pay for the same work at piece rates shall be calculated 9.19

on the basis of the same unit of measurement; (b) that pay for work at time rates shall be the same for the same job. This article shall not prevent any Member State from maintaining or adopting measures providing for specific advantages in order to make it easier for women to pursue a vocational activity or to prevent or compensate for disadvantages in their professional careers. The Commission shall draw up a report each year on progress in achieving the objectives of Article 1. The European Parliament may invite the Commission to draw up reports on particular problems concerning the social situation.

## CHAPTER 10

# FREEDOM OF ESTABLISHMENT FOR PROFESSIONS AND BUSINESSES

### Freedom of establishment

*General rules*

The right of establishment, that is the right of business enterprises to move and set up shop across frontiers and the right to conduct non-salaried economic activities, is provided for in Articles 52 to 58 of the Treaty. These activities are specified in Article 52 of the Treaty, which provides for the abolition by progressive stages of restrictions on the freedom of establishment of nationals of a Member State in the territory of another Member State. The right of establishment covers not only the activities themselves but also activities incidental to the main ones, and covers the setting up of agencies, branches and subsidiaries. The right of establishment includes the right of nationals of other Member States to participate in existing firms or companies on the same conditions as nationals of the host State. This right also comprises the right of entry and residence of nationals of other Member States in the territory of the regulating State in so far as entry and residence are necessary for the performance of economic activity. **10.01**

Article 52, which provides for the abolition of restrictions based on nationality, has been held by the Court of Justice to have direct effect; it ruled in Case 2/74, *Reyner v. Kingdom of Belgium*,[1] that the requirement of national treatment had become self-executing at the end of the transitional period (January 1, 1970), so that it had to be given effect by all **10.02**

[1] [1974] E.C.R. 631, [1974] 2 C.M.L.R. 305.

national administrative authorities and courts. The same principle applies to new Member States since their respective dates of accession: see Case 11/77, *Patrick v. Ministre des Affaires Culturelles*.[2] The Court again emphasised in Case 221/85, *Commission v. Belgium*,[3] that Article 52 is intended to ensure that self-employed persons are treated in another Member State in the same way as nationals of that Member State and prohibits any discrimination based on nationality. Article 52 does not limit in any way the obligation of Member States to abolish any national rules which are discriminatory: see Case 159/78, *Commission v. Italy*.[4] The right of establishment entitles a national of a Member State to pursue his activity in another Member State under the conditions laid down by law for the nationals of that country. The right of establishment applies, in relation to his home State, to a national of a Member State who has been resident in another Member State and subsequently returns to the State of his nationality: See Case 115/78, *Knoors v. Secretary of State for Economic Affairs*.[5] The rules on the right of establishment cover not only Community nationals, but also members of their families who want to join them: see Case 48/75, *Royer*.[6]

**10.03** Article 53 of the Treaty prohibits the introduction of any new restrictions on the right of establishment. In Case 6/64, *Costa v. ENEL*,[7] the Court ruled that this provision had direct effect. It also held that the Article was satisfied if no new and more onerous requirements were imposed than those applicable to nationals.

**10.04** Article 54 provides for the implementation of the Treaty establishment provisions by means of a General Programme[8] and the enactment of directives. The article sets out a number of guidelines which the Council and the Commission should follow in enacting the implementing directives. There are guidelines as to time schedules, the right of establishment of migrant workers, acquisition and use of real property, the right to set up agencies, branches and subsidiaries, the abolition of subsidies and the standardisation of company law in relation to shareholders' and creditors' protection. The judgments of the Court of Justice in relation to the direct applicability of the Treaty provisions concerned with restrictions on nationality have rendered the number of required directives smaller than it would have been, but the number of enacted directives is still very large, covering a wide range of activities of economic life.

[2] [1977] E.C.R. 1199, [1977] 2 C.M.L.R. 523.
[3] [1987] E.C.R. 719, [1988] 1 C.M.L.R. 620.
[4] [1979] E.C.R. 3247, [1980] 3 C.M.L.R. 446.
[5] [1979] E.C.R. 399, [1979] 2 C.M.L.R. 357.
[6] [1976] E.C.R. 497, [1976] 2 C.M.L.R. 619.
[7] [1964] E.C.R. 585, [1964] C.M.L.R. 426.
[8] [1962] O.J. 2/36.

*Implementing directives*

10.05 The directives deal with the right of establishment and the right to supply services (see paragraph 10.12 below.) Under Directive 64/220,[9] concerned with the removal of restrictions on entry and residence of nationals of the Member States, such persons had to be admitted to any Member State for the purpose of establishment or the provision of services upon presentation of a passport or national identity card. No visa might be required and the same applied to relatives of the persons concerned. This directive is replaced by Directive 73/148[10] but the changes are minor. The Court went further in Case C–68/89, *Commission of the European Communities v. Kingdom of Netherlands*,[11] in prohibiting border questioning of such entrants. A national of a Member State who possesses at the same time the nationality of a non-Member State cannot be denied the freedom of establishment under the provisions of Community law on the ground that the host State regards him as a national of a non-Member State: see Case C–169/90, *Micheletti v. Delegación del Gobierno en Cantabria.*[12] Directive 73/148 was the subject of the ruling by the Court of Justice in Case 81/87, *The Queen v. HM Treasury and Commissioners of Inland Revenue, ex parte Daily Mail and General Trust plc*,[13] that, properly construed, it confers no right on a company to transfer its central management and control to another Member State. Again, Article 52 and this directive were considered in Case C–370/90, *The Queen v. Immigration Appeal Tribunal and Surinder Singh*,[14] where the Court ruled that a Member State must grant leave to enter and reside in its territory to the spouse of whatever nationality of a national of that Member State who has gone with that spouse to another Member State and returns to establish himself in the State of which he is a national. A spouse must enjoy at least the same rights as would be granted to him under Community law if his spouse entered and resided in another Member State.

*Freedom to pursue specific occupations*

10.06 Business activities are the subject of directives in this context: Directive 64/222[15] and Directive 64/223[16] deal with activities in the wholesale trade, and Directive 68/363[17] and Directive 68/364[18] with activities of

9 [1964] O.J. Spec. Ed. 115.
10 [1973] O.J. L172/14.
11 [1993] 2 C.M.L.R. 389.
12 Not yet reported.
13 [1988] E.C.R. 5483, [1988] 3 C.M.L.R. 713.
14 [1992] 3 C.M.L.R. 358.
15 [1964] O.J. Spec. Ed. 120.
16 [1964] O.J. Spec. Ed. 123.
17 [1968] O.J. L260/1.
18 [1968] O.J. L160/6.

self-employed persons in the retail trade. The coal trade (Directives 70/522[19] and 70/523[20]) and trade in toxic products (Directives 74/556[21] and 74/557[22]) are singled out. Self-employed commercial agents are the subject of Directive 86/653.[23] A wide range of directives dealing with particular types of businesses and profession has now been established. Included among them are:

(a) Architects, covered by Directive 85/384.[24] The four-year period of study referred to in this directive was considered by the Court of Justice in Case C–310/90, *Conseil National de l'Ordre des Architectes v. Egle*,[25] and Case C–166/91, *Bauer v. Conseil National de l'Ordre*.[26]
(b) Dentists, covered by Directives 78/686[27] and 78/687.[28]
(c) Doctors, covered by Directives 75/362,[29] 75/363[30] and 86/457.[31] Directive 93/16[32] facilitates the free movement of doctors and the mutual recognition of their diplomas, certificates and other evidence of formal qualifications.
(d) Nurses, subject to Directives 77/452[33] and 77/453[34]; and
(e) Veterinary surgeons, subject to Directives 78/1026[35] and 78/1027.[36]

Directive 81/1057[37] completes the above directives relating to doctors, nurses, dentists and veterinary surgeons. There are also directives dealing with midwives (80/154[38] and 80/155[39]) and pharmacists (85/432[40] and 85/43[41] Provisions in Italy restricting to Italian citizens the pos-

[19] [1970] O.J. L267/14.
[20] [1970] O.J. L267/18.
[21] [1974] O.J. L307/1.
[22] [1974] O.J. L307/5.
[23] [1986] O.J. L382/17.
[24] [1985] O.J. L223/15.
[25] [1992] 2 C.M.L.R. 113.
[26] [1993] 1 C.M.L.R. 141.
[27] [1978] O.J. L233/1.
[28] [1978] O.J. L233/10.
[29] [1975] O.J. L167/1.
[30] [1975] O.J. L167/14.
[31] [1986] O.J. L267/26.
[32] [1993] O.J. L165/1.
[33] [1977] O.J. L176/1.
[34] [1977] O.J. L176/8.
[35] [1978] O.J. L362/1.
[36] [1978] O.J. L362/7.
[37] [1981] O.J. L385/25.
[38] [1980] O.J. L33/1.
[39] [1970] O.J. L33/8.
[40] [1985] O.J. L253/34.
[41] [1985] O.J. L253/37.

sibility of obtaining recognition of foreign qualifications to work in the field of health care were held to be in breach of Articles 48, 50 and 59 of the Treaty: see Case C–58/90 *Commission of the European Communities v. Italian Republic*.[42] All these principles were reiterated by the Court of Justice in Case C–351/90, *Commission of European Communities v. Grand Duchy of Luxembourg*,[43] where it held that by preventing medical practitioners, dentists and veterinary surgeons established in another Member State from establishing themselves in Luxembourg while retaining their practice in the other Member State, the Grand Duchy was in breach of Articles 48 and 52 of the Treaty. Directive 67/43[44] refers to matters of "real estate" and the provision of certain "business services not elsewhere classfied". The position of estate agents was considered by the Court in the light of this directive and Articles 52 and 57 of the Treaty. In Case C–104/91, *Colegio Oficial de Agentes v. Aguirre Newman SA*,[45] the Court held that qualifications obtained in the State of origin can be assessed by the host State before permission to exercise the profession,including the necessity for an examination. The directive does not preclude national legislation reserving certain activities to persons exercising the regulated profession of estate agent: see Case C–147/91, *Proceedings against M. Ferrer Lederer*.[46]

10.07 All these directives deal with mutual recognition of formal qualifications to facilitate the effective exercise of the right of establishment and freedom to provide services as well as dealing with these two freedoms. Other directives deal with freedom of establishment in farming, hairdressing, industry and commerce, transport, the film industry and many other occupations. Personal services in restaurants, cafés, taverns, hotels and rooming houses are subject to Directives 68/367[47] and 68/368;[48] and Directive 70/451[49] deals with freedom to provide services by self-employed persons in film production. Goods haulage operation is governed by Directive 74/561[50] and passenger transport operation by Directive 74/562.[51] Mutual recognition of their qualifications is governed by Directive 77/796.[52] Directive 87/540[53] deals with the occupation of a car-

42 Not yet reported.
43 [1992] 3 C.M.L.R. 124.
44 [1967] O.J. L10/140.
45 Not yet reported.
46 [1992] 3 C.M.L.R. 273.
47 [1968] O.J. L260/16.
48 [1968] O.J. L260/19.
49 [1970] O.J. L218/37.
50 [1974] O.J. L308/18.
51 [1974] O.J. L308/23.
52 [1977] O.J. L334/37.
53 [1987] O.J. L332/20.

rier of goods by waterway. Insurance brokers and agents are dealt with in Directive 77/92[54] and hairdressers in Directive 82/489.[55]

*Lawyers*

**10.08** Lawyers are governed by Directive 77/249.[56] The directive was the subject of Case 427/85, *Commission v. Federal Republic of Germany*,[57] where the Federal Republic was found to be in breach of the terms of the directive by requiring in the circumstances of that case the involvement of a German lawyer in addition to the lawyer from another Member State. The Court also held in Case 292/86, *Claude Gullung v. Conseil de l'Ordre du Barreau de Colmar*,[58] that the directive could not be relied upon by a lawyer who was established in one Member State in order to be permitted to provide legal services in another Member State where he had been barred from access to the profession for reasons relating to dignity, good reputation and integrity. The Court further reiterated the principle (already stated in Case 115/78, *Knoors*)[59] that the directive must apply without discrimination to nationals of all member States who satisfy the conditions for its application. A State cannot deny its application to its own nationals who are established in another Member State of which they are also a national. The directive and Articles 59 and 60 of the Treaty were further considered in Case C–294/89, *Commission of the European Communities v. French Republic*,[60] where the French Republic was found to be in breach of its obligations by depriving French nationals, who practise law in a Member State other than the French Republic, of the benefit of the right under the directive by requiring the lawyer providing services to act in conjunction with a lawyer established in a French territory, even in the case where it is not mandatory to have a lawyer, and by subjecting the lawyer providing services to the principle of territorial exclusivity in representing a client.

**10.09** However, Article 52 must be interpreted as meaning that the national authorities of a Member State to which a request for authorisation to practise as a lawyer is made, by a Community national practising in his country of origin, are required to examine to what extent the knowledge and qualifications attested by the qualifications acquired in his country of origin correspond to those required by the rules of the host State; where there is only partial equivalence of qualifications, the person con-

[54] [1977] O.J. L26/14.
[55] [1982] O.J. L218/24.
[56] [1977] O.J. L78/17.
[57] [1988] E.C.R. 1123, [1989] 2 C.M.L.R. 677.
[58] [1988] E.C.R. 111, [1988] 2 C.M.L.R. 57.
[59] [1979] E.C.R. 399, [1979] 2 C.M.L.R. 357.
[60] [1991] I E.C.R. 3591, [1993] 3 C.M.L.R. 569.

cerned has to establish that he or she has acquired the knowledge and qualifications lacking: see Case C–340/89, *Vlassopoulou v. Ministerium für Justiz Baden Württemberg*.[61] The Court went further in Case C–19/92, *Kraus v. Land Baden Württemberg*,[62] stating that Article 52 was to be interpreted as not preventing a Member State from prohibiting one of its own nationals, who held a post-graduate university diploma issued in another Member State, from using that diploma in its territory without having obtained an administrative authorisation for that purpose, provided that the authorisation procedure was, *inter alia*, for the sole purpose of establishing that the post-graduate university diploma had been correctly issued. Article 59 precludes the restricting of patent monitoring services to holders of special professional qualifications such as a qualification as a patent attorney: see Case C–76/90, *M. Sager v. Société Dennemeyer & Co. Ltd.*[63]

All these provisions must be read together with Article 57 of the Treaty. (The Treaty on European Union introduces a new text of Article 57 by referring to Article 189b, retaining the basic principles of Article 57 unamended.) Article 57(1) provides that the Council shall issue directives for mutual recognition of diplomas, certificates and other evidence of qualifications. The Court of Justice held in Case 71/76, *Thieffry v. Conseil de l'Ordre des Avocats*,[64] that in the absence of Community directives on mutual recognition of qualifications, if a person wishes to practise his profession in a Member State other than his own, and passes the professional examination in the host State, he must be admitted to do so even if his basic degree is regarded by the State in question as equivalent for academic purposes only. Such a limitation on equivalence cannot justify refusal to admit the applicant to practise and the Member States must apply their law, taking into account the requirement of Community law. In this case it was held that completion of Belgian law studies entitled a Belgian student to take the French bar examination. The same principle was applied to a veterinary surgeon with an Italian diploma who wanted to establish himself in France before the enactment of a directive: see Case 136/78, *Ministère Public v. Auer*.[65] The principles enunciated by Articles 52, 54 and 57 were upheld in Case 107/83, *Ordre des Avocats v. Klopp*,[66] where the Court ruled that even in the absence of any directive, Articles 52 *et seq.* prevent the authorities of a Member State from denying, in accordance with national provisions in force, to national of another Member State the right to enter and to exercise the legal profes- 10.10

[61] [1991] I E.C.R. 2357, [1993] 2 C.M.L.R. 221.
[62] Not yet reported.
[63] [1991] I E.C.R. 4221, [1993] 3 C.M.L.R. 639.
[64] [1977] E.C.R. 765, [1977] 2 C.M.L.R. 373.
[65] [1979] E.C.R. 437, [1979] 2 C.M.L.R. 373.
[66] [1984] E.C.R. 2971, [1985] 1 C.M.L.R. 99.

sion solely on the ground that he simultaneously maintains chambers in another Member State.

*Other professions*

10.11 However, the position is clarified with the enactment of Directive 89/48[67] on a general system for the recognition of higher education diplomas awarded on completion of professional education and training of at least three years' duration. This directive does not apply to professions which are the subject of separate directives establishing arrangements for the mutual recognition of diplomas by Member States (Article 2). It introduces the concept of regulation of professional activity which leads to a diploma or its equivalent; activity also qualifies as such if it is pursued by a member of an association or organisation which awards a diploma and ensures that its members respect the rules of professional conduct which it prescribes. The Annex to the directive contains a non-exhaustive list of such associations, which in the case of the United Kingdom contains 38 entries, commencing with the Institutes of Chartered Accountants, proceeding through Institutes of Actuaries, Bankers and Energy and the Engineering Council and ending with the British Computer Society. The directive deals in detail with any adaptation period, aptitude tests and procedures involved in exercising the profession in the host Member State. The Member States have to comply with the directive by January 4, 1991. The Council further recommended by Recommendation 89/49[68] that Member States should apply the provisions of the directive for persons who hold diplomas or other formal qualifications awarded in a third State and are in a position comparable to one of those described in the directive. In Case C–106/91 *C. Ramrath v. Ministère de la Justice*,[69] the Court held that a person cannot be prohibited from establishing himself on the territory of a Member State practising there as an auditor on the ground that he is established and authorized so to practise in another Member State, subject to objectively necessary conditions concerning compliance with professional rules.

## Exceptions

*Exercise of official authority*

10.12 Parallel to provisions of Article 48(4) in relation to free movement of workers, Article 55 excludes from the right of establishment activities

[67] [1989] O.J. L19/16.
[68] [1989] O.J. L19/24.
[69] [1992] 3 C.M.L.R. 173.

which are connected with the exercise of official authority. Article 55 should be construed narrowly: see Case 7/68, *Commission v. Italy*;[70] it refers to specific activities and not to types of occupation. Case 2/74, *Reyner v. Belgium*,[71] dealt with Article 55, stressing that the purpose of the article is to exclude non-nationals from access to activities which involve the exercise of official authority and which are linked to an activity covered by Article 52. This purpose is served when the exclusion is limited to those activities which, taken in themselves, constitute a direct and specific participation in official authority. The extension of the exception to a whole profession is only permissible if the activities concerned constitute an element which is not separate from the entire professional activity concerned. The directive dealing with the provision of services by lawyers (77/249)[72] allows for Article 55 in excluding certain groups with activities exercising public authority who have a monopoly and whose numbers are limited (*e.g.* notaries in some Member States). In the United Kingdom the directive excludes from its provisions by virtue of Article 55, and on the same basis, solicitors concerned with conveyancing.

*Public policy, public security and public health*

The general exception of this article is complemented by the more specific exceptions of Article 56, which on grounds of public policy, public security and public health also permits Member States to derogate from the principle of freedom of establishment. Article 56 reflects similar provisions concerning the free movement of workers (Article 48 (3)) and the directives enacted in pursuance of Article 56 reflect these principles. The first directive implementing the article, Directive 64/221,[73] as extended by Directive 75/35,[74] deals with nationals who are employed, self-employed or rendering a service, and their dependants. In pursuance of Article 56(2) it provides for the co-ordination of national provisions on the derogations of freedom of establishment and freedom to provide services. This directive and the issues involved are dealt with in greater detail in Chapter 8 on freedom of movement of workers and Article 48 (3). The social security legislation extends to self-employed persons and the legislation now covers employed persons and self-employed persons in one instrument (see paragraph 8.11 above). Directive 75/34[75] is concerned with the rights of nationals of a Member State to remain in the **10.13**

[70] [1968] E.C.R. 423, [1969] C.M.L.R. 1.
[71] [1974] E.C.R. 631, [1974] 2 C.M.L.R. 305.
[72] [1977] O.J. L78/17.
[73] [1964] O.J. Spec. Ed. 117.
[74] [1975] O.J. L14/14.
[75] [1975] O.J. L14/10.

territory of another Member State after having pursued therein an activity in a self-employed capacity.

## Provision of services

**10.14** Article 59 provides that restrictions on freedom to provide services within the Community should be abolished in respect of nationals of Member States who are established in a State of the Community other than that of the person for whom the services are intended. The article also enables the Community to extend the provisions on services to nationals of a third country who provide services and who are established within the Community. Article 59 was invoked by the Commission in the actions against France, Italy and Greece respectively: see Cases Joined C 154, 180 & 198/89, *Commission v. France, Italy and Greece*,[76] where the Court ruled that the requirement of a licence (which involved the passing of an examination) to provide services as a tourist guide accompanying tourists from another Member State was incompatible with Article 59 of the Treaty. A requirement of the law of a Member State that a national of another Member State who, in his capacity as executor of a will had brought proceedings before one of its courts, had to lodge security for costs while a national of the first Member State was not subject to such a requirement, was discrimination on the ground of nationality prohibited by Articles 59 and 60 of the Treaty: see Case C–20/92, *Hubbard v. Hamburger*[77] which further stated that the fact that the main proceedings were based upon the law of succession could not set aside the application of the right of freedom to provide services laid down by Community law in respect of a member of a profession responsible for that transaction. The Court also ruled that the right to equality of treatment upheld by Community law cannot be dependent on the existence of international agreements concluded by Member States. The provisions of the Treaty on freedom of establishment do not apply to situations arising entirely within one Member State, such as the position of nationals of a Member State engaging in its territory in a professional capacity on a self-employed basis in regard to which they cannot claim to have any previous training or experience in another Member State; see Cases C–54/88, C–91/88 and C–14/89, *Nino, Pradini & Goti and Pierini* respectively,[78] dealing with the exercise of paramedical profession.

**10.15** The non-discriminatory restrictions are not affected. The General Programme for the Abolition of the Restrictions on the Freedom to Provide

[76] [1991] I E.C.R. 659.
[77] Not yet reported.
[78] [1990] I E.C.R. 3537, [1992] 1 C.M.L.R. 83.

Services[79] indicates that this involves abolition of regulations which, though applicable regardless of nationality, in fact restrict predominantly the furnishing of services by foreign nationals. Restrictions on the transfer of funds to pay for services are also to be eliminated. Case 36/74, *Walrave & Koch v. Union Cycliste*,[80] would imply that in certain circumstances discrimination by a private individual may be covered. This case and Case 33/74, *Van Binsbergen v. Bestuur van de Bedrijfsvereniging*,[81] indicate that Article 59, after the end of the transitional period in 1970, now has direct effect.

Article 60 defines services as "services" within the meaning of the Treaty where they are normally provided for renumeration, in so far as they are not governed by the provisions relating to freedom of movement for goods, capital and persons. "Services" include activities of an industrial or commercial character, and activities of craftsmen and of the professions. The article states that a person providing a service may, in order to do so, temporarily pursue his activity in the State where the service is provided under the same conditions as are imposed by that State on its own nationals. Medical termination of pregnancy, performed in accordance with the law of the State in which it is carried out, constitutes a service within the meaning Article 60; it is not contrary to Community law for a Member State in which medical termination of pregnancy is forbidden to prohibit students associations from distributing information about the identity and location of clinics in another Member State, and the means of communicating with those clinics: see Case C–159/90, *The Society for the Protection of Unborn Children v. S. Grogan*.[82] Article 62 prevents Member States from introducing any new restrictions on the freedom to provide services and it has direct effect. Article 63, calling for a general programme, has been implemented by the General Programme. It has also been implemented by the actions of the Community in the field of the right of establishment and services, and in addition by Directive 63/340[83] on currency transfers where the services are limited only by restrictions on payments relating to them. Films form the subject of a directive under this article (Directive 65/264).[84] 10.16

Article 66 applies the provisions of Articles 55 to 58 to the chapter on services. Services and establishment are closely related and at times it is 10.17

[79] [1962] O.J. 2/32.
[80] [1974] E.C.R. 1405, [1975] 1 C.M.L.R. 320.
[81] [1974] E.C.R. 1299, [1975] 1 C.M.L.R. 298.
[82] [1991] I E.C.R. 4685, [1991] 3 C.M.L.R. 849.
[83] [1963] O.J. Spec. Ed. 31.
[84] [1965] O.J. Spec. Ed. 62.

difficult to distinguish between the two, particularly so in the case of the professions which are already governed by legislation under the right of establishment.

## CHAPTER 11

# TAXATION

### Introduction

11.01 Customs duties and agricultural levies are charged on imports into the Community (or in some cases on exports from it), and constitute a fiscal fence within which the Community economy operates. They represent fully-fledged Community taxes, imposed and varied by the Community legislature, and are the subject of directly applicable regulations. Member States, of course, remain free to impose taxation and that is known generically in Community law as *internal taxation*. All types of internal taxation—an expression often interpreted widely to include any charge or levy which is compulsory—are subject to the Treaty rules and to the general principles of Community law. Indirect taxes charged by each Member State on the supply, production or sale of goods are the types of internal tax most likely to be affected by the specific rules in Articles 95 to 99.

### Fiscal neutrality

11.02 The principle of fiscal neutrality requires that tax legislation should as far as possible operate so as not to distort economic activity. It flows from the concept of a single market economy, and in Community law it manifests itself in a number of different contexts. It is seen first as one of the implications of the general prohibition against discrimination on grounds of nationality in Article 7 of the Treaty. Secondly, it is an underlying feature of the harmonised system of value added tax, which in general aims to be neutral as between different types of business activity. Thirdly, it is seen in the provisions of Articles 95 to 99 specifically on indirect taxation, which interlock with the prohibition in Articles 12 and 30 against customs duties and quantitative restrictions in trade between

Member States. And finally, it is reflected in the Court's approach to tax avoidance.

*1. Nationality discrimination*

**11.03** Taking the broad concept of "tax" as any charge payable compulsorily, the Court held in Case 293/83, *Gravier v. City of Liège*,[1] that the imposition upon students from another Member State of a special tax for attending a vocational training course, which was not payable by Belgian nationals, was contrary to Article 7, and therefore recoverable by the students who had paid it. By contrast, a Member State which chooses to tax national production more heavily than imports does not infringe Community law: see Case 86/78, *Grandes Distilleries Peureux*.[2]

**11.04** The nationality provisions of Community law apply to all fiscal situations, whether or not they are directly governed by Community legislation. Thus in Case C–330/91, *R. v. Inland Revenue Commissioners, ex parte Commerzbank AG*,[3] a rule of United Kingdom corporation tax legislation that repayment supplement on overpaid tax could only be paid to companies resident for tax purposes in Britain was held to be contrary to Community law and void; it was held to be irrelevant that the particular refund was only available to non-resident companies—the general rule depriving them of entitlement to repayment supplement was discriminatory. By contrast, in Case C–112/91, *Werner v. Finanzamt Aachen*[4] the Court decided that Member States were not prohibited from imposing heavier tax burdens on non-residents *if they were nationals of the taxing state*; less favourable treatment by a state of its own nationals seems therefore to escape the prohibition on nationality discrimination.

*2. Value added tax*

**11.05** The concept of value added tax is that of a turnover tax which discriminates as little as possible between one form of economic activity and another, and between businesses in one Member State and another;[5] it is thus in principle applicable to all supplies of goods or services, except those which are exempted, rather than being applicable only to defined categories of supply. It is, in its harmonised form, entirely compatible with the principles of Article 95 because it is levied on imported goods

[1] [1985] E.C.R. 606, [1985] 3 C.M.L.R. 1.
[2] [1979] E.C.R. 897, [1980] 3 C.M.L.R. 337.
[3] [1993] 3 C.M.L.R. 457.
[4] Not yet reported.
[5] Recitals to the First Dir. 67/227, [1967] O.J. Spec. Ed. 14, and to the Sixth Dir. 77/388, [1977] O.J. L145/1.

on the same basis, and at the same rate, as upon internally supplied goods. The following illustrations show how this concept has influenced the Court's approach to questions of construction of the Community legislation. It should be noted that since January 1, 1993, the final suppression of customs barriers between Member States has rendered the concept of imports in *intra*-Community trade obsolete.

In Case 269/86, *Mol v. Inspecteur der Invoerrechten en Accijnzen*,[6] and Case 294/82, *Einberger v. Hauptzollamt Freiburg*,[7] the question arose whether value-added tax should be charged in one case on the supply, and in the other case on the import, of illegal drugs. Noting that the principle of tax neutrality opposed a general differentiation between lawful and unlawful transactions, the Court held that in the exceptional case of transactions which in no circumstances can be carried out lawfully no tax could be payable since the transactions were outside the contemplation of the directive. Thus in Case C–111/92, *Lange v. Finanzamt Furstfeldenbruck*,[8] exports in breach of legitimately imposed national sanctions were nonetheless entitled to export zero-rating. In normal circumstances, therefore, neutrality requires that a breach of the law in the course of carrying out a transaction should not lead to it being treated differently for tax. 11.06

In Case 50/88, *Kuehne v. Finanzamt München*,[9] the question arose whether depreciation on a car used by a lawyer, partly for professional use and partly for private use, could be charged to tax in circumstances in which the car had been acquired secondhand from a private individual, who had accordingly not charged tax on the price, and in respect of which therefore no input deduction could be claimed. Article 6(2) of the Sixth VAT Directive[10] provides that the use of goods forming part of the assets of a business by the taxable person for his private use is taxable if input tax on them is deductible. Member States, however, have the right to derogate from this provision on condition that the derogation does not lead to distortion of competition. But the Court held that the right to derogate from the rule in Article 6(2) could not be used to tax goods where the input on them was not deductible, since to do so would entail double taxation contrary to the principle of fiscal neutrality inherent in the Community system of value added tax. 11.07

[6] [1988] E.C.R. 3627, [1989] 3 C.M.L.R. 729.
[7] [1984] E.C.R. 1177, [1985] 1 C.M.L.R. 765.
[8] [1994] 1 C.M.L.R. 573.
[9] [1989] E.C.R. 1925, [1990] 3 C.M.L.R. 287.
[10] [1977] O.J. L145/1.

### 3. *Internal excise taxation of goods*

**11.08** It is in the context of the Treaty rules on internal taxation that the concept of fiscal neutrality has its clearest expression. The general principles are laid down in Articles 95 to 99, and in the extensive case law of the Court interpreting them. They are designed to prevent the effect of establishing the Customs Union and then the common commercial policy being lost as a consequence of Member States maintaining fiscal barriers to commerce within the Community. As noted above, the harmonised value added tax (established under the same Treaty chapter on taxation) complies with the basic requirements of a neutral tax; it is the first tax to do so to such a high degree, but Article 99 envisages similar harmonisation of excise duties and similar indirect taxes. Meanwhile, the Court has held that penalties affecting value added tax on imports from other Member States must not be more severe than the equivalent penalties for tax offences committed within the State.[11]

**11.09** Full harmonisation will involve approximating rates and the elimination of special derogations, matters which have still not been achieved fully even in relation to value added tax. Limited steps have been taken in relation to excise duty on tobacco products by Directive 72/464[12] and Directive 79/32.[13] The first of these directives seeks to establish a uniform basis for the duty, with a view to the eventual harmonisation of rates, and the second provides definitions of the products concerned. Directives 92/79 and 92/80[14] laid down agreed bands for duty rates. Similar developments have occurred with respect to mineral oil duties in Directives 92/81 and 92/82,[15] and alcohol duties in Directives 92/83 and 92/84.[16]

**11.10** The abolition of fiscal frontiers which formed part of the Single Market programme was implemented in the excise field by Directive 92/12,[17] which applied to all excise duties on mineral oils, alcohol and tobacco, and which laid down detailed provisions with regard to duty points and transit and warehousing of excise goods. Regulation 2719/92[18] laid down

[11] Case C–276/91, *Commission v. France*: not yet reported; "imports" between Member States can no longer take place, and it is uncertain whether this doctrine will apply to imports from outside the Community.
[12] [1974] O.J. L303, as last amended by Dir. 92/78, [1992] O.J. L316.
[13] [1979] O.J. L10, as last amended by Dir. 92/78, [1992] O.J. L316.
[14] [1992] O.J. L316.
[15] [1992] O.J. L316; see also Dir. 92/108, [1992] O.J. L390 and Decision 92/510, [1992] O.J. L316.
[16] [1992] O.J. L316.
[17] [1992] O.J. L76, as amended by Dir. 92/108, [1992] O.J. L390.
[18] [1992] O.J. L276.

procedures for the movement of excise goods under duty suspension regimes approved by Directive 92/12.

*4. Equal taxation for similar products*

In the meantime, Articles 95 to 99 provide for internal taxation in which there is equality of treatment between goods from other Member States and similar or competing domestic products. Article 95(1) prohibits Member States, directly or indirectly, imposing internal taxation on the products of other Member States in excess of that imposed on similar domestic products. Typically, but not always, taxation of goods from other Member States takes the form of import taxes which are designed to compensate for internal taxes on home-produced goods. Although in this case the mechanism of charging at import may involve differences from that used for home produce, see Case 127/75, *Bobie v. Hauptzollamt Aachen*,[19] the effect of the prohibition is only that the burden of the charge may not be greater. In Case 57/65, *Lutticke v. Hauptzollamt Saarlouis*,[20] Article 95(1) was held to have direct effect. 11.11

In an early decision which has been affirmed on many occasions, the Court in Joined Cases 2 & 3/62, *Commission v. Belgium and Luxembourg*,[21] laid down principles that: 11.12

(a) an import charge with no internal counterpart would fall under Articles 9 and 12 on customs duties and charges having equivalent effect (see Chapter 3); and

(b) an import charge would come under the provisions of Article 95 if a similar tax charge fell on national production. An internal charge for non-tax purposes would not justify an import charge by way of compensation. The concept of tax was given a wide interpretation (though consistent with the underlying objective of neutrality) in Case C–29/87, *Dansk Denkavit ApS v. Landbrugs ministeriet*,[22] where it was held that a charge levied both on import and internally, for the purpose of financing the checking by the State of additives in feedingstuffs, satisfied the criteria of Article 95.

Case 112/84, *Delville v. Administration des Impots*,[23] illustrates the point that a discriminatory tax may not be chargeable at the moment of import. 11.13

[19] [1976] E.C.R. 1079; see also Case C–327/90, *Commission v. Hellenic Republic*: not yet reported.

[20] [1966] E.C.R. 205, [1971] C.M.L.R. 199.

[21] [1962] E.C.R. 425, [1963] C.M.L.R. 199.

[22] [1990] 1 C.M.L.R. 203.

[23] [1986] 2 C.M.L.R. 338.

In that case, France levied a vehicle excise duty, by means of a licence displayed on the car, which was five times higher on cars with a capacity exceeding 16 cv than on those of a lower capacity. It happened that no cars of the higher capacity were made in France, and the Court held that the duty discriminated against products of other Member States (the car in question came from Italy) and was contrary to Article 95.

**11.14** The case law on Article 95(1) has been considerable, dealing with the precise circumstances in which a charge falls under this Article or under Articles 9 and 12, the difficulties principally occurring on the identification of similar national products. This feature was considered in Case 27/67, *Fink-Frucht v. Hauptzollamt München*,[24] where it was held that a guide to similarity was provided by the classification of goods under the same fiscal, customs or statistical heading; the Court also commented that the absence of any item as a domestic product was not of itself a reason why the Member State should not impose a tax on it, even though the only goods to bear the tax would be those of another Member State.

*5. Equal taxation for competing products*

**11.15** Article 95(2), which has also been held to have direct effect,[25] forbids the imposition of internal taxation on the products of other Member States of such a nature as to afford indirect protection to other products. This limb of the article attacks taxes which cannot be said to be imposed on similar domestic products, and it marks the limit of a Member State's freedom to impose taxes at whatever level it wishes where there is no, or no significant, national production of the same item.

**11.16** This is best illustrated by Case 170/78, *Commission v. United Kingdom*,[26] in which the Commission successfully attacked the structure of British excise duties on wine and beer. The Court accepted that the two products were effectively in competition with each other, since consumers might in many circumstances choose to drink either, and it was established that the duty on wine was higher than that on beer. Wine being only to a minimal extent a home product, but beer a major domestic product, it followed that the effect of the level of duty on wine was to protect a domestic product (beer) against a competing product (wine) from other Member States. The taxation of wine produced in the United Kingdom at exactly the same rate as wine from elsewhere in the Community, while

[24] [1968] E.C.R. 223, [1968] C.M.L.R. 228.
[25] *Ibid.*
[26] [1983] E.C.R. 2265, [1983] 3 C.M.L.R. 512.

complying with Article 95(1), did not prevent the indirect protection of beer falling foul of Article 95(2).

*6. Exports*

Article 96 permits repayment of internal tax on goods exported to other Member States, but makes it clear that the repayment must not exceed the amount of the internal taxation borne directly or indirectly. In Case 45/64, *Commission v. Italy*,[27] the term "indirectly" was held not to include taxes borne by the business manufacturing the goods, but to be confined to taxes bearing on the goods themselves. Article 98, however, forbids export rebates (or countervailing charges on imports) of any direct tax, except as may be approved for a limited period by the Council. When full harmonisation is achieved, indirect taxes will be levied on a Community-wide basis and, as with value-added tax after 1996, export rebates and compensating import taxes will become unnecessary in intra-Community trade. Meanwhile, the Court held in Case 142/77, *Statens Kontrol med Ædle Metaller v. Larsen*,[28] that an export tax could infringe Article 95; but pending tax harmonisation, the Treaty contains no effective prohibition on double taxation on goods moving between Member States where, as in this case, domestic production and exports are taxed equally. 11.17

*7. Tax avoidance*

Concern to ensure the neutral application of the tax provisions informed the Court's treatment of anti-avoidance provisions in Joined Cases 138–139/86, *Direct Cosmetics v. Customs and Excise*.[29] Here the question was whether Article 27 of Directive 77/388 ("the Sixth Directive"—see below),[30] allowing Member States to tax certain sales at market value, as opposed to the price at which they actually took place, was applicable. The provision was introduced to enable prevention of certain types of tax avoidance, but the facts of the case showed that the sales pattern in question existed for sound commercial reasons, unconnected with tax avoidance, though the effect was to avoid the full amount of tax that would have been payable but for it. The Court held that the intention of the taxpayer was irrelevant. What mattered was the objective face of avoidance liable to prejudice the design of the tax as one in which the factors which might lead to distortions of competition at national and 11.18

[27] [1965] E.C.R. 857, [1966] C.M.L.R. 97.
[28] [1978] E.C.R. 1543, [1979] 2 C.M.L.R. 680.
[29] [1988] E.C.R. 3937, [1988] 3 C.M.L.R. 333.
[30] [1977] O.J. L145/1.

Community level were to be eliminated, and as a tax to be as neutral as possible covering all the stages of production and distribution.

**11.19** In the field of international travel, where reliefs for travellers from excise and turnover taxes are provided under Directive 69/169,[31] the Court, in Case 158/80, *Rewe v. Hauptzollamt Kiel*,[32] had to consider the effect of "butter cruises" in the Baltic Sea in which the passengers were able to buy butter tax-free and with the benefit of agricultural subsidies, and then to import the goods thus purchased free of tax. It held that the directive must be interpreted as meaning that the reliefs were destined only for travellers coming from third countries and that, in the case of Community travellers, goods would only be eligible for the relief if they had been bought tax paid in a Member State.

**11.20** In Case 81/87, *R. v. H. M. Treasury, ex parte Daily Mail and General Trust plc*,[33] the taxpayer wished, for tax avoidance reasons, to move its residence to the Netherlands but was unable to do so under provisions of United Kingdom tax legislation which forbade a United Kingdom company to migrate outside the United Kingdom without Treasury consent. The Court held that this was not contrary to Articles 52 to 58 (guaranteeing the free right of establishment). Although prima facie a discrimination which was contrary to Article 58, the Court considered that, in the current state of Community law in which no provision had yet been made to regulate such a movement, the national restrictions in question were permissible. The object of the company's change of residence was, in any event, not a purpose for which freedom of establishment was provided. In Community tax legislation generally, for example in Directive 77/388[34] on value added tax, and in Directive 90/434 on company mergers,[35] reference may be found to reliefs not being available or to Member States being entitled take special measures in derogation from the basic legislation to prevent the "avoidance or evasion" of tax. These two concepts, so clearly distinguished in common law jurisprudence, are mentioned as though two aspects of the one phenomenon. The relationship between these notions of Community law and the developed case law on the subject of tax avoidance in the United Kingdom has yet to emerge.

## Claims by taxpayers

**11.21** It has been noted in Chapter 2 that, in relation to taxes and customs duties, the Court has developed a doctrine to deal with claims by taxpayers for

[31] [1969] O.J. L133, as last amended by Dir. 91/191, [1991] O.J. L94.
[32] [1981] E.C.R. 1805, [1982] 1 C.M.L.R. 449.
[33] [1988] E.C.R. 5483, [1988] 3 C.M.L.R. 713.
[34] [1977] O.J. L145.
[35] [1990] O.J. L225.

reimbursement of taxes, etc., paid to Member States but subsequently declared contrary to Community law. The Court affirmed in Case 309/85, *Barra v. Belgium and the City of Liège*,[36] that unless it provides in a judgment indicating a tax's incompatibility with Community law that the judgment is to have prospective effect only, all payments of the wrongly levied tax in the past will in principle be reclaimable. The possibility of reclaim is, however, subject to two limitations.

The first concerns the way of making the repayment claim. This the Court has repeatedly affirmed must be by the national procedure and be governed by national time limits, there being as yet no Community provisions applicable. Nonetheless, Member States may not hedge that procedure round with so many limitations that, as a practical matter, it is impossible, or virtually impossible, for a taxpayer to make a repayment claim, even if the same restrictions apply to repayment claims where no element of Community law is involved: see Case 199/82, *Amministrazione delle Finanze v. San Giorgio SpA*.[37] 11.22

In Case 240/87, *Deville v. Administration des Impots*,[38] the taxpayer, who had imported a car from Italy, had paid tax on import which the Court held was contrary to Article 95; after that decision, national legislation was introduced which had the effect of making back claims more difficult (and in Mr Deville's case impossible). The Court ruled that Member States may not change the recovery rules to the detriment of the taxpayer in the aftermath of a decision by the Court from which it follows that a tax is contrary to Community law. 11.23

The second limitation concerns the doctrine, applicable in all cases of indirect taxation, of "passing on", under which a taxpayer's claim for repayment or remission may be refused by a Member State where the burden of the unlawful tax has been passed on to the taxpayer's customers. Member States are not obliged to adopt such a restriction but, if they do, it will also be subject to the rule that proof that there has been no passing on must not, in practical terms, be so difficult to provide that the right cannot effectively be relied upon. 11.24

This permitted limitation may be affected by the decision of the Court in Case 207/87, *Weissgerber v. Finanzamt Neustadt*.[39] In that case, it was held that an unimplemented provision of the Sixth VAT Directive,[40] 11.25

[36] [1988] E.C.R. 355, [1988] 2 C.M.L.R. 409.
[37] [1983] E.C.R. 3595, [1985] 2 C.M.L.R. 658.
[38] [1988] E.C.R. 3513, [1989] 3 C.M.L.R. 611.
[39] [1988] E.C.R. 4433.
[40] [1977] O.J. L145/1.

exempting credit negotiators from the tax, could be relied upon by the plaintiff as having direct effect. The taxpayer was accordingly not liable to be assessed for tax on credit commission, provided he had not passed the tax on to persons following him in the chain of supply by charging the tax as such. It was thus only in the case of the taxpayer having charged tax on the supply to his customer, and the customer being able to claim an input tax credit, that the taxpayer could be held to have passed on the burden of the tax.

## Duties on capital

11.26 Indirect taxes affecting the movement of capital have been the subject of a considerable degree of harmonisation in regard to duties on capital and share or stock certificates. Directive 69/335[41] abolishes stamp duties on securities and seeks to align provisions throughout the Community on company capital duty with a view to facilitating the free movement of capital and avoiding double taxation. The rules on capital duty apply to capital companies, which are defined as companies incorporated with limited liability, and any other profit-making bodies subjected to capital duty in a Member State.

11.27 The basic principle therefore is that capital duty is payable once only and in one place only. This is to be in the Member State in which a capital company has its effective centre of management at the relevant time. Necessarily there are rules to cover cases in which effective management is outside the Community. Thus, where the company's registered office is within the Community, the State where that office is located is the one in which capital duty is levied; and where a company has a branch within the Community, but has both its registered office and its effective management outside, the State where the branch has capital made available to it is the one in which duty may be levied.

11.28 The events which attract payment of duty in relation to a capital company are: incorporation or an increase in capital; the transfer of either effective management or registered office to the Community, when the other remains in a third country and the company is regarded as a capital company in the place of arrival; the transfer of either effective management from one Member State to another where the company is regarded as a capital company in the State to which transfer has been made, but is not so considered in the first Member State; the transfer, from one Member State to another, of the registered office, where the effective centre of management remains outside the Community, and the com-

[41] [1969] O.J. L249, as last amended by Dir. 85/303, [1985] O.J. L156.

pany is regarded as a capital company in the State to which the transfer has been made, but is not so considered in the first Member State. Certain other operations taxed at 1 per cent. on July 1, 1984 may also continue to be subject to duty (see below).

Articles 5 and 6 of the directive lay down the permissible bases for the calculation of the duty, leaving some latitude to Member States; they are also given discretion with regard to charging duty at higher rates or granting exemptions for reasons of fiscal equality, social reasons or to take account of special situations—in this event, the Commission must be warned, and Article 102 of the Treaty applies. Subject to this, any dutiable event which on July 1, 1984 was exempt, or was taxed at a rate not exceeding 0.5 per cent., is to be exempt thereafter. For the rest, the maximum rate of duty may not exceed 1 per cent., and there are specific optional exemptions for public utility companies controlled by public authorities, and those pursuing only cultural, welfare or educational objectives. **11.29**

Next, the directive prohibits any form of taxation on the creation, issue, or admission to a stock exchange of, or on any dealings with, stocks, shares, or certificates representing them, debentures or other negotiable securities, or in relation to the events which attract capital duty. Article 12, however, permits a number of derogations from these prohibitions.[42] Thus, Member States are allowed to charge duty on transfers of securities (at a flat rate or *ad valorem*); duty on the transfer to a company or firm of businesses or immoveable property situated within the same State; duty on the transfer of any other assets to a company or firm for a consideration other than shares in the business; and duty on the creation, registration or discharge of mortgages or other charges. Also permitted are duties paid by way of fees or dues, and value added tax. The permitted duties may be levied irrespective of where the registered office or effective centre of management of the company or firm is located, provided that such duties are no greater than those applicable to like transactions in the Member State in question. **11.30**

## Value added tax

Value added tax is the harmonised form of the turnover tax now applicable throughout the Community, and it represents the vanguard of the tax harmonisation envisaged in Article 99 of the Treaty. It satisfies the basic criteria of neutrality as between Member States, in that it bears **11.31**

[42] The derogations are exhaustive: see Case 15/88, *Maxi-Di v. Bolzano*: [1989] E.C.R. 1391, [1991] 1 C.M.L.R. 675.

equally on domestic and imported products. It is in contrast both to the previously common "cascade" taxes, in which tax was cumulated at each stage of production or supply, and to single stage taxes or excises. The basic feature of value added tax is that it is economically neutral as between long and short chains of supply from manufacturer to consumer. This is achieved by allowing a set-off at each stage of the tax paid on the supply preceding (input tax) against tax payable on the supply onwards (output tax). In this way, the overall burden of tax is determined by the value of the final taxable supply.

**11.32** The main corpus of Community legislation is to be found in the now much-amended Sixth VAT Directive,[43] referred to in this section as "the directive". The Community law is extensively implemented in the United Kingdom by the Value Added Tax Act 1983, subsequent Finance Acts and orders and regulations made thereunder. Under Article 33 of the directive, value added tax is now the only form of turnover tax permitted in the Community; in Joined Cases 93 & 94/88, *Wisselink*,[44] the Court considered a tax in the Netherlands, chargeable on imported and newly-produced passenger cars—similar to the United Kingdom car tax—and held that, being a single stage tax, it was not a turnover tax and thus escaped the prohibition on other turnover taxes. But in Case C–200/90, *Dansk Denkavit*,[45] a tax to finance social expenditure in Denmark was held to have the nature of a turnover tax and to fall within the prohibition in Article 33; the Danish state was thus liable to refund what had been collected.

*1. Scope*

**11.33** Article 2 of the directive lays down the four elements of the tax as it applies within each country. There must be (a) a supply of goods or services for consideration, (b) within the territory of the country, (c) by a taxable person, (d) acting as such. The tax is also chargeable on the importation of goods to the Community, though not from another Member State. For the United Kingdom, the territory within which the tax is levied as a single area includes the Isle of Man but not the Channel Islands; France includes Monaco, but excludes the overseas territories; Spain excludes the Canaries, Ceuta and Melilla; Germany excludes Heligoland, and there are other minor adjustments to the territorial scope of the tax.

*2. Supplies and consideration*

**11.34** The concept of supply of goods and services is defined at length in Articles 5 and 6 of the directive. A supply of goods is defined as being the

[43] Dir. 77/388, [1977] O.J. L145/1, as last amended by Dir. 92/111, [1992] O.J. L384/47.
[44] [1989] E.C.R. 2671.
[45] Not yet reported.

transfer of the right to dispose of tangible property as owner, and the supply of services covers any transaction which does not constitute a supply of goods. With certain exceptions, tax is only chargeable where consideration for the supply is given. And the directive provides that a number of supplies are or may be treated by national legislation as having been made for consideration, when in reality they have not been. Thus, Article 5 of the directive provides that goods, on whose acquisition by a business input tax was wholly or partly deductible, are deemed to be supplied for consideration if they are applied by the taxable person (see below) for his own private use or that of his employees, or if they are gifted or applied for non-business purposes; an exemption is made for samples or small value business gifts.

The directive also allows Member States to regard as supplies for consid- **11.35**
eration:

(a) self-supplies of goods for use in a business where, if they had been acquired from another taxable person, input tax would not have been wholly deductible,
(b) the retention of goods on the cessation of a business where input tax was deductible on their acquisition, and
(c) the supply of goods in a non-taxable transaction by a taxable person where input tax has been wholly or partly deductible. A similar discretion exists to tax free supplies of services by a taxable person for his private use or that of his employees or for non-business purposes, and to tax as a supply of services the use similarly of business assets on which input tax was wholly or partly deductible.

Although the line between goods and services is to some extent left to **11.36**
Member States' discretion to define, some clarification of doubtful cases is provided in Articles 5 and 6 of the directive. The supply of goods is defined to include the supply of electric current, heat, refrigeration, certain interests in or over immovable property, goods sold on commission and goods sold on hire-purchase. Services include assignments of intangible property, the undertaking of an obligation to refrain from any act or to tolerate any act or situation, and the performance of services under an obligation to a public authority.

It was decided in Case 154/80, *Staatssecretaris van Financien v. CVCA*,[46] **11.37**
that the term "consideration" as used in the directive must be interpreted by the Court as a matter of Community law, and that there must be a connection between the payment made and the supply rendered. In Case 102/86, *CEC v. Apple and Pear Development Council*,[47] the Court held that

[46] [1981] E.C.R. 445, [1981] 3 C.M.L.R. 337.
[47] [1988] E.C.R. 1443, [1988] 2 C.M.L.R. 394.

the (obligatory) payment by producers of a levy to promote the interests of the trade did not constitute consideration for the purposes of the tax. And in Case 230/87, *Naturally Yours Cosmetics v. Customs and Excise*,[48] it was decided that where consideration is partly monetary and partly non-monetary, but capable of being given a monetary value, the total consideration is taxable. The taxable basis is not affected if payment is made by a third party (*e.g.* a credit institution)[49] or if it is deferred and interest is charged on it.[50] The term is defined in relation both to imports and internal supplies in Article 11 of the directive, referred to below.

*3. Taxable persons*

**11.38** The definition of a taxable person in Article 4 focuses on the independent conduct of any number of specified economic activities, irrespective of their purpose or results. They include those of producers, traders and persons supplying services, and cover matters such as mining, agricultural activity and the prices of the professions. The exploitation of tangible or intangible property for the purpose of obtaining income from it is also a relevant activity. The supply, "on an occasional basis", of buildings prior to first occupation or of building land may be treated as a taxable activity.

**11.39** Excluded from the concept of the "taxable person" are employees, and bodies governed by public law[51] in respect of the activities in which they engage as public authorities, whether they collect payment for them or not; but there is again discretion left to the Member States to treat such activities as within the scope of the tax if not to do so would lead to significant distortions of competition. In any event, the supply of telecommunications, gas, water, electricity, steam, and transport of goods or passengers, port and airport services, the supply of new goods manufactured for sale, the transactions of agricultural intervention agencies, trade fairs, warehousing, commercial publicity, travel agency, co-operative type shops and canteens, and the commercial transactions of radio and television bodies are all within the scope of the tax, no matter who carries them out. In Case 286/83, *Rompelman v. Minister van Financien*,[52] it was held that a person who carries out activities preparatory to economic activity is also within the definition, and, in Case C–202/90, *Ayuntamiento de Sevilla*,[53] that privatised tax collectors were taxable persons.

[48] [1988] E.C.R. 6365, [1989] 1 C.M.L.R. 797.
[49] Case C–18/92, *Chaussures Bally*: not yet reported.
[50] Case C–281/91, *Muys'en De Winter's Bouw*: not yet reported.
[51] If transactions are subject to private law, the authority is *pro tanto* a taxable person: see Cases 231/87 & 129/88, *Fiorenzuola*: [1989] E.C.R. 3233.
[52] [1985] E.C.R. 656, [1985] 3 C.M.L.R. 202.
[53] [1994] 1 C.M.L.R. 424.

*4. Place of supply*

Articles 8 and 9 of the directive contain rules determining where a taxable supply has taken place, with a view to establishing its liability to tax in any given Member State. Goods are supplied where, in the Community, they are dispatched to the buyer or installed; if they are not dispatched or transported, they are supplied where they are when the supply takes place. The rules relating to services are more complex. The basic rule is that services are supplied where the supplier taxpayer has established his business, or has a fixed establishment from which a service is supplied or, in default, where he has his permanent address or usual residence. Article 9[54] prescribes different rules for immovable property and building services, transport and entertainment. **11.40**

In the case of disposals of intellectual property, the hiring of moveable property and the supply of a wide range of services to customers or clients outside the Member State where the supplier is established, the Tenth Directive (84/386)[55] prescribed in general that where the customer is outside the Community or is a taxable person in another part of the Community, the place of the supply is where the customer has established his business, has a fixed establishment to which the service is supplied or where he resides. Discretions are given to the Member States to avoid situations of double taxation in respect of these services. **11.41**

*5. Time of supply*

Article 10 of the directive deals with the point at which the tax becomes chargeable. The normal tax points are when goods are delivered or services are performed, but earlier payment on account advances the tax point to the extent of the payment, and periodic supplies give rise to a tax point at the end of the relevant period. Member States are given discretion to provide for further alternative tax points for particular types of transaction or taxpayer which should be, at the latest, the date of issue of an invoice or the receipt of the price, or the passing of a specified period from the basic tax point where there is no invoice. On import, the tax point is the same as that for customs duty or agricultural levies. **11.42**

*5. Basis of assessment*

Article 11A of the directive provides that the total of the consideration given or promised, whether by the purchaser or a third party, is the basis on which the tax is assessed. The purchase price of the goods, the cost **11.43**

[54] As amended by Dir. 84/386, [1984] O.J. L208/58.
[55] [1984] O.J. L208/58.

of the goods or services or their open market value (as defined), are alternative bases in circumstances in which the directive deems there to have been a taxable supply for consideration. Early payment discounts and other rebates allowed at the time of supply together with disbursements made on behalf of customers are not included in the taxable amount, nor is interest awarded by a court on late payment: see Case 222/81, *BAZ Bausystem v. Finanzamt München*.[56] But interest contractually payable is included.[57]

**11.44** Article 27 permits other derogations from the rule of assessment being made on the actual consideration "to prevent certain types of tax evasion or avoidance".[58] In Joined Cases 138–139/86, *Direct Cosmetics v. Customs and Excise*,[59] the Court affirmed the validity of Decision 85/369[60] authorising the United Kingdom to require tax to be assessed on the open market value of a sale by retail in cases where the tax base for the last taxable sale would fall short of that level, as a result of the interposition of a non-registered supplier before the final sale to the customer. By contrast, in Case C–131/91, *"K" Line Air Service*,[61] it was held that Belgian legislation about tax on second hand car sales went further than strictly necessary to prevent avoidance or evasion and departed from the basis of assessment required by Article 11. Other taxes, duties, levies and charges are included in the tax base, along with incidental expenses such as commission, packing and insurance charged by the supplier to the customer.

**11.45** With regard to imports, Article 11B of the directive permits States to treat the tax as a customs duty, for the purpose of reckoning the tax base by reference to the customs valuation provisions in the Community Customs Code. Included in the tax base are taxes, duties, levies and charges due by reason of the importation or imposed outside the Community, and incidental expenses such as commission, insurance and transport costs. Exclusions from the tax base are similar to those applicable to internal supplies.

**11.46** Member States are given wide discretion to provide for bad debts, and it is provided that the taxable amount is to be reduced in cases where payment is refused or orders are cancelled, subject to conditions laid down nationally. Currency conversions necessary for tax on import are calculated by reference to the customs valuation provisions; for tax on internal supplies, optional alternative rules are provided. The cost of

[56] [1982] E.C.R. 2527, [1982] 3 C.M.L.R. 688.
[57] Case C–281/91, see n. 50 above.
[58] These terms appear elsewhere but are neither distinguished nor defined: see para. 11.20.
[59] [1988] E.C.R. 3937, [1988] 3 C.M.L.R. 333.
[60] [1985] O.J. L199/60, now made permanent by Dec. 89/534, [1989] O.J. L280/54.
[61] Not yet reported.

returnable packaging is excluded from the tax base on condition that the packaging is returned.

*7. Tax rates*

Article 12 of the directive requires that the rate applied must be that in force when the taxpoint occurs. The standard rate may not be less than 15 per cent.; up to two reduced rates may be used for restricted categories of goods and services (which include gas and electricity) of not less than 5 per cent. Reduced rates, however, should not result in input tax exceeding output tax. **11.47**

Zero rates (which are described in the Community legislation as exemption with refund of tax at the preceding stage) are for the most part allowed on internal transactions under the directive only on a transitional basis until they are suppressed by the Council acting unanimously. Both the termination of the transitional tolerances laid down in the directive and any new fiscal provisions require unanimity by the Council, under the terms of the directive itself and of Articles 99 and 100 of the Treaty. **11.48**

A condition for the maintenance of zero rates is that they are confined to supplies to the final consumer (or supplies closely connected therewith), and are judged necessary for clearly defined reasons of social policy. In Case 416/85, *Commission v. United Kingdom,*[62] the Court defined the "final consumer" as a person who does not use goods or services in an economic activity, and held that any supply otherwise than directly to such a person (or to a person sufficiently close to him in the supply chain for it to be able to enure to his benefit) may not be zero-rated under this provision. It was held accordingly that a variety of United Kingdom zero rates did not genuinely fulfil these criteria, and appropriate changes were made in the Finance Act 1989 to reflect this. **11.49**

*8. Exports*

Article 15 provides for the zero-rating of goods exported from the Community, of goods for sea-going vessels and for aircraft and of a wide range of services similarly, especially those on moveable property acquired or imported therefor and then re-exported. Article 16 allows suspensions of tax on a similar basis to that applied for import duty, for example for warehousing, inward processing, free zones, temporary importation and Community transit. **11.50**

[62] [1988] E.C.R. 3127, [1988] 3 C.M.L.R. 169.

*9. Deduction of input tax*

**11.51** Supplies within the scope of the tax are either positively rated or exempt; zero-rating, as has been seen, is in effect treated as a positive rate of nil. As also indicated above, the tax paid on supplies to a taxable person (the input tax) is set off against the tax due on supplies made by him (the output tax), and the excess of the latter over the former is alone payable to the tax administration. If the input exceeds the output, the taxable person receives a refund equal to the excess. An exempt input generates no tax credit, and an exempt output generates no tax liability, so that a person who makes nothing but exempt supplies is not liable to account for any tax.

**11.52** The mechanism of offsetting input tax against output tax is dependent on a number of conditions being fulfilled, which are detailed in Articles 17 to 20 of the directive. The usual requirements are that the supply on which the input tax arose is one by another taxable person in the Community of goods or services for the purpose of the taxpayer's taxable transactions, or the tax is payable on import of goods to the Community, or that the taxpayer has made certain self-supplies. The taxpayer must hold a tax invoice for the supply addressed to him, an import document showing him as consignee or importer or comply with requirements laid down by the tax administration. National legislation may not add requirements about tax invoices which make it "practically impossible or excessively difficult to exercise the right to deduct": see Joined Cases 123 & 330/87, *Jeunehomme.*[63]

**11.53** In order to avoid credit being given for input tax on supplies which are not for the purpose of a taxable transaction, there must therefore be a relationship between the taxpayer's inputs and his outputs before the right to set off input tax against output tax will arise. This need occurs in particular when a proportion of the outputs is exempt. In this case, the rule is that only the input tax attributable to taxable (as opposed to exempt) outputs is deductable. Detailed provision is made in Article 19 for the calculation of the deductible proportion of inputs where—as is usual—direct attribution of inputs is not possible. Member States are given wide discretion to provide for mechanisms to attribute inputs to outputs to prevent over-deduction of input tax, and with regard to the deduction of input tax on capital goods. The right to deduct input tax arises when the tax on the supply in question becomes chargeable, but derogations have been given to permit cash accounting schemes. In Case C–193/91, *Mohsche,*[64] it was held to be contrary to Article 6(2) of the

[63] [1988] E.C.R. 4517.
[64] Not yet reported.

directive for a Member State to charge output tax on the private use of a car in respect of which not all the input tax had been recoverable.

The Eighth Directive, 79/1072,[65] provides detailed harmonised procedures for taxable persons established in other Member States to be refunded tax on supplies made to them by taxable persons in the first Member State. It supplements the obligation contained in Article 17(4) of the Sixth Directive to refund tax on supplies to other Community traders. Applications duly made must be decided within six months, and appeals against refusal of an application must be provided for in the Member State in question on the same basis as similar internal appeals. **11.54**

The Thirteenth Directive, 86/560,[66] provides the same in the case of third country traders, but it remains in Member States' discretion to make this conditional on the third country granting reciprocal treatment. Member States may also require third country traders to appoint a tax representative in their territory. Refunds may not be granted under conditions which are more favourable than those applicable to Community traders. **11.55**

*10. Exemptions*

Those supplies which are exempt are defined in Articles 13 and 14 of the directive, and in many cases are subject to compliance with conditions, sometimes selected at the discretion of Member States. Among the most important "public interest" types of exempt supply are: postal services, hospital and medical care, welfare services, education, services to their members by trade unions, political parties, religious bodies, etc., and public service broadcasting. Member States may make these exemptions available to bodies which are not governed by public law subject to the condition that they do not aim systematically to make a profit and are not incidental revenue raising businesses in competition with commercial enterprises. **11.56**

Exemption is also provided for insurance, banking, finance and certain supplies in relation to land, although in certain cases Member States may allow taxpayers the option to elect for tax to be charged on such transactions. In Case 348/87, *Sufa*,[67] the Court held that the exemptions in Article 13, since they constituted derogations from the general principle that turnover tax was charged on every supply of services for a consideration, were to be strictly interpreted. Under Article 13B, Member States are authorised to ıapply further exclusions' from the scope of the exemption, **11.57**

[65] [1979] O.J. L331/11.
[66] [1986] O.J. L326/40.
[67] [1989] E.C.R. 1737, [1991] 2 C.M.L.R. 429.

but in Case C–63/92, *Lubbock Fine*,[68] it was held that they could not take advantage of that freedom in order to bring into tax the surrender of a lease when the rent under that lease was exempt.

*11. Special schemes and simplification procedures*

**11.58** Articles 24 to 26 of the directive allow, at Member States' discretion, provision for special schemes for small undertakings and a common flat-rate scheme for farmers, and lay down special rules in relation to travel agents.

**11.59** Provided there is no reduction in the amount of tax chargeable, simplified systems for charging and collection may, after consultation with the Community's value added tax committee, be provided for small businesses. Similarly, Member States may provide for a regressive system of relief from the charging of tax for small businesses. The states are also given discretion to exempt from the tax altogether businesses whose turnover is below a certain threshold (adjusted by the Council periodically); such businesses are then forbidden to deduct input tax or to show output tax on their invoices. Any business eligible for exemption in this way must have the option of electing for normal taxable status, or of taking advantage of any simplified small business scheme or graduated relief scheme available.

**11.60** A further option, which has now been taken up by the United Kingdom, is granted for the taxation of farm businesses on a flat-rate basis. Travel agents (who include tour operators) are entitled to account for tax only on the margin of their profit on a supply to a client if they satisfy certain conditions laid down in Article 26 of the directive, principally that they make use of services supplied by other taxable persons in the provision of travel services and act in their own name, and not as an intermediary charging clients for specific disbursements. Full deduction of input tax is accordingly not available to agents taxed on this basis.

**11.61** Article 27 allows the Council to authorise derogations by Member States from the directive either for the purpose of introducing simplified procedures or for the purpose of preventing "evasion or avoidance" of the tax. The exercise of this power is subject to the proviso that the measures permitted must not, save to a negligible extent, affect the amount of tax due at the final consumption stage. Reference has been made at paragraph 11.18 above to the Court's approach to the interpretation of this limitation. A number of derogations have been granted under this article

[68] Not yet reported.

to Member States, including the United Kingdom, and are published as decisions in the "L" series of the *Official Journal*.

*12. Liability*

The basic liability for payment of tax is imposed by Article 21 of the directive on taxable persons, in so far as tax due on transactions conducted within a Member State is concerned, and on the person or persons designated as being liable in the case of tax due on import. Where the taxable transaction is effected by a person resident outside the Member State in question, the Member States are given discretion to provide from whom the tax will be due, *e.g.* a tax representative or the customer. Any person who shows value added tax on an invoice is similarly liable for payment. Articles 22 and 23 empower Member States to make detailed provisions regarding the time of payment, the keeping of records and the like. **11.62**

*13. Intra-Community trade*

Between January 1, 1993 and December 31, 1996 a temporary regime is in place to facilitate the operation of the Single Market, but it is intended that at the end of this period the principle under which tax is chargeable by and paid to the State in which a supply originates should be implemented.[69] Meanwhile, Articles 28A–N make detailed provision with regard to intra-Community supplies of goods and services. In very broad terms, supplies by a taxable person in one Member State give rise to an obligation on the part of a recipient in the second Member State who is also a taxable person to account for tax on the supply—known in United Kingdon legislation as the "reverse charge". If the recipient is not a taxable person, tax must generally be charged and accounted for in the State where the supply originates, but there are significant exceptions. The duty-free sales permitted in sea and air travel between States are to continue until June 30, 1999, when they will be suppressed.[70] **11.63**

## Tax and excise duty reliefs on import

Value added tax on the import of goods from outside the Community is chargeable as if the import was a supply, but without any of the other conditions in relation to internal transactions being required. Thus, whether the importer is a taxable person or not, or is or is not making the importation for the purpose of a taxable business carried on by him, **11.64**

[69] Art. 28L of the directive.
[70] Art. 28K of the directive.

tax is chargeable. If tax has been paid in another Member State and not remitted on dispatch of the goods to the State of import the latter must give credit for it to a private importer: see Joined Cases 15/81 & 47/84, *Gaston Schul.*[71] Imports of illegal drugs are not chargeable: see Case 294/82, *Einberger v. Hauptzollamt Freiburg.*[72] Article 14 of the Sixth Directive[73] details the exemptions to be granted on importation from outside the Community. They include cases in which an internal supply would be exempt and cases in which customs duty would not be exigible or be held in suspense, or where the goods would qualify for customs duty returned goods relief.

**11.65** Directive 83/181,[74] however, contains extensive and detailed provision for the exemption from tax on final importation. The main categories for relief cover: personal property imported on a transfer of residence from outside the Community, goods imported on the occasion of marriage, personal property acquired by inheritance, certain property of students, capital goods imported on the transfer of a business, certain agricultural products and products for agricultural use, various medical goods, goods imported for charitable or welfare purposes, importers' samples, items used at trade fairs, etc., and goods for examination, analysis or test purposes. Various other items are included in the lengthy list of exemptions. It will be seen that this list is similar to the list of reliefs applicable in the case of customs duties on import to the Community.

**11.66** Finally, Directive 69/169[75] lays down exemptions from value added tax and excise duties for goods contained in the personal luggage of travellers coming from third countries. The States must set quantitative limits to the relief as it applies to tobacco, alcohol, coffee, tea and perfumes, with minimum age limits of 17, 17 and 15 respectively in the first three cases. The value of these restricted goods does not count towards a person's totals otherwise available for the relief. Directive 78/1035[76] allows exemption from tax and excise duties of small consigments of tax-paid goods of a non-commercial character from third countries not exceeding 70 ECUs in value.

[71] [1985] E.C.R. 1491, [1986] 1 C.M.L.R. 559.

[72] But imports or exports which are *in casu* illegal but may be carried out lawfully receive normal tax treatment—see para. 11.06 above.

[73] Dir. 77/388, [1977] L145/1, as last amended by Dir. 88/498, [1988] O.J. L269/54.

[74] [1983] O.J. L105, as last amended by Dir. 89/219, [1989] O.J. L92.

[75] [1969] O.J. L133, as last amended by Dir. 92/111, [1992] O.J. L384.

[76] [1978] O.J. L366, as last amended by Dir. 85/576, [1985] O.J. L372.

## European Economic Interest Groupings (EEIGs)

EEIGs are provided for by Regulation 2137/85,[77] which is discussed in Chapter 13. They are a new form of business entity set up by enterprises (which may be companies or individuals) in two or more Member States. They may be formed for the purpose of activities which are ancillary to those of the EEIG's members, but not in order to make profits for the grouping itself. The regulation stipulates that national tax law is to apply to an EEIG's activity in a Member State, but that profits or losses are to be taxable only in the hands of its members. Legislation to give effect to those requirements in the United Kingdom are contained in the Finance Act 1990, but operative from July 1, 1989, when the regulation took effect.[78] 11.67

## Direct business taxation

Community harmonisation has now entered the field of direct taxation. In keeping with the Community law objective of neutrality in fiscal matters, Directive 90/434[79] seeks to eliminate the taxation of gains occurring on cross-border reorganisations when assets and shares are notionally realised, differing the taxpoint until the shares or assets acquired are themselves realised. This affects mergers, demergers, joint ventures and takeovers. If one of the principal objectives of the merger, etc., is the evasion or avoidance of tax the reliefs provided for are not to apply. Directive 90/435[80] attacks the problem of parent and subsidiary companies in different Community States in relation to the payment of dividends and provides for Member States to abolish any withholding tax on dividends paid by a subsidiary to its parent, and prevents double taxation of the dividends in the hands of the parent company. 11.68

In an important development affecting double taxation generally, the Member States have entered into a convention providing for mandatory arbitration between E.C. states to prevent the same income being taxed twice. The convention[81] concerns what is known as "transfer pricing" where goods are traded between related companies and the price charged by one to the other is not therefore necessarily the result of an open market, or "arm's length", bargain. In such situations, there is obvious scope for profits to be moved from one jurisdiction to another to suit 11.69

[77] [1985] O.J. L199/1.
[78] Inland Revenue press release, April 13, 1989.
[79] [1990] O.J. L225.
[80] [1990] O.J. L225.
[81] Made on July 23, 1990 and published in [1990] O.J. L225.

the multinational company's advantage. The procedure to be followed under the convention is leisurely, with three years for the taxpayer to file an adminsitrative appeal, two years for the tax authorities concerned to reach agreement if possible, six months for the arbitration committee then to opine and a further six months for the Member States to give effect to its findings. The convention will enter into force three months after the last ratification, and is of five years' duration.

## Intra-Community tax enforcement

11.70 Under Directives 76/308, 77/799, 92/12 and 92/108,[82] provision is made for Member States to render each other mutual assistance in the recovery of value added tax, customs duty, excise duties and agricultural levies, and for the exchange of information in relation to these matters and in relation to direct taxes. Further detailed provision in relation to value added tax consequent upon the creation of the Market is made by Regulation 218/92.[83]

11.71 Exchange of information is governed by Directive 77/799 which is stated to apply to income tax, corporation tax, capital gains tax, petroleum revenue tax and value added tax, but also to any other taxes for the time being levied on income and capital. Member States are to exchange any information that may enable them to make correct assessments, either on the initiative of the State providing the information or at the request of another State. If necessary, enquiries are to be carried out to obtain information requested.

11.72 Information thus exchanged must be kept secret in the receiving State in the same manner as in the sending country, and may not be used other than for the assessment of recovery of tax; and it may only be disclosed at a public hearing if the State supplying the information raises no objection. But information may be used for all purposes for which it could be used in the sending State, if the latter so permits. In any case, information may be refused where its provision would lead to commercial, industrial or professional secrets being disclosed, or the disclosure would be contrary to public policy.

11.73 Directive 76/308 governs the recovery of taxes (agricultural levies, intervention debts, customs duties and value added tax) by one Member State

[82] Respectively [1976] O.J. L73, as last amended by Dir. 79/1071, [1979] O.J. L331; [1977] O.J. L336/15, as last amended by Dir. 79/1070, [1979] O.J. L331, and [1992] O.J. L76/1 and L390/124.
[83] [1992] O.J. L24.

on behalf of another. These are all the duties in which the Community Treasury has an interest. The directive similarly provides for the exchange of information useful in recovery action by any Member State, and there is a saving for information which would disclose commercial, industrial or professional secrets similar to that in the mutual assistance directives. The claims which a State may request another to recover on its behalf must not be contested in the former, and the recovery procedure available there must have been applied first.

It is not necessary for a court judgment for the debt to have been obtained in the requesting State, but only that an instrument permitting the enforcement of the debt in that State should have been in existence. Any dispute arising in the course of recovery action is to be settled according to the procedure of the requesting State, unless it concerns the validity of the procedure in the second State, when it is to be settled in accordance with the procedures of that State. 11.74

Claims may include sums for interest and costs, and are to be recovered in the currency of the requested State, but are not to be treated as preferred debts there. Limitation is governed solely by the law of the requesting State, and the actions of the requested State are accordingly deemed to have occurred in the requesting State for the purpose of reckoning any question of limitation under the law of that State. The requested State may refuse to take recovery action if to do so would create serious social or economic difficulties. Detailed provisions enlarging upon those in the main directive are contained in Directive 77/794.[84] 11.75

United Kingdom implementing legislation is contained in the Finance Act 1977 section 11, the Finance Act 1978 section 77, the Finance Act 1980 section 17 and the Finance Act 1993 section 22. For the recovery of other Member States' claims it is provided that that is to be effected by treating them as if they were Crown debts, and proceeding accordingly. 11.76

[84] [1977] O.J. L333/1, as last amended by Dir. 86/489, [1986] O.J. L283/23.

CHAPTER 12

# FINANCIAL SERVICES: INSURANCE, BANKING, STOCK EXCHANGE, CAPITAL MOVEMENTS AND ECONOMIC AND MONETARY UNION

## INSURANCE

12.01 The only specific mention of insurance in the Treaty is in Article 61, which provides that the liberalisation of banking and insurance services connected with movement of capital shall be effected in step with the progressive liberalisation of movement of capital. This is so because movements of capital are involved in a very large proportion of insurance business.

12.02 The existing Community legislation concerning insurance is based on the provisions of the Treaty covering the freedom of establishment and the freedom to render services. Article 54 of the Treaty calls on the Council to draw up a general programme for the abolition of existing restrictions on freedom of establishment within the Community, and it goes on to mandate the Council to issue directives accordingly. The first requirement of Article 54 is implemented by the enactment of the General Programme for the Abolition of Restriction on Freedom of Establishment of December 18, 1961, and by the enactment of Directive 64/225[1] on the abolition of restrictions on freedom of establishment and on freedom to provide services in respect of reinsurance and retrocession.

[1] [1964] O.J. Spec. Ed. 131.

Article 59 of the Treaty calls for the abolition of restrictions on freedom to provide services and extends the provisions of the chapter on services to nationals of a third country who provide services and who are established in the Community, should the Council so decide (see Article 16(3) of the Single European Act). Article 60, which covers insurance, states that the person providing a service may, in order to do so, temporarily pursue his activity in the State where the service is provided, under the same conditions as are imposed by that State on its own nationals. 12.03

Two directives were enacted dealing with direct insurance. First, Council Directive 73/239,[2] made under Article 57(2), on the co-ordination of laws, regulations and administrative provisions relating to the taking up and pursuit of the business of direct insurance other than life insurance, last amended by Directive 87/343,[3] made the commencement of the business of direct insurance subject to an official authorisation and requirements for obtaining such authorisation. It contained various rules as to the conditions insurance companies must comply with and referred to the solvency margin represented by free assets which insurance companies must maintain. In addition, there is a provision for a guarantee fund equivalent to one third of the solvency margin. The rules also apply to third country insurers operating in the Community, specific rules applying to agencies or branches whose head offices are outside the Community. Directive 87/343 is specifically concerned with credit insurance and suretyship insurance. 12.04

The principles governing the freedom to provide insurance services were considered in Case 205/84, *Commission v. Federal Republic of Germany*,[4] where the requirements of authorisation and of permanent establishment under the German Insurance Supervision Law came under scrutiny. The Court emphasised that authorisation must be granted on request to any undertaking established in another Member State which meets the conditions of the legislation of the State in which the service is provided. The requirement of authorisation under domestic law might be maintained only if it was justified on grounds relating to the protection of policyholders. The Court, however, took the view that it was not in a position to lay down the limits of that distinction with sufficient precision in order to determine individual cases in which the need for protection did not justify the requirement of an authorisation. The necessity for permanent establishment was considered clearly as a negation of the freedom to provide services. Both requirements under the Insurance Supervision Law in relation to Community co-insurance (for authorisation and per- 12.05

[2] [1973] O.J. L228/3.
[3] [1987] O.J. L185/72.
[4] [1986] E.C.R. 3755, [1987] 2 C.M.L.R. 69.

manent establishment) were found to be contrary to Directive 78/473[5] and Articles 59 and 60 of the Treaty. In three other cases considering Directive 78/473 and Community co-insurance, the Court held that France (Case 220/83)[6] Ireland (Case 206/84),[7] and Denmark (Case 252/83)[8] were in breach of the Treaty by requiring that Community co-insurers be established in these Member States in order to provide co-insurance services there as leading insurers.

12.06 The other directive enacted under the General Programme was Directive 73/240[9] abolishing restrictions on freedom of establishment in the business of direct insurance other than life insurance. Further directives following the general tendency to enlarge the freedom of establishment and services are Directive 77/92[10] on measures to facilitate the effective exercise of freedom of establishment and freedom to provide services in respect of the activities of insurance agents and brokers, Directive 78/473 making provisions for Community co-insurance and Directive 87/344[11] dealing with legal expenses insurance.

12.07 The scope of these directives is extended by the Second Council Directive 88/357,[12] as amended by Directive 90/618[13] and Directive 92/49[14] supplementing and amending Directive 73/239.[15] Articles 2 to 4 define "undertaking", "establishment", "Member State where the risk is situated", "Member State of establishment" and "Member State of provision of services" and provide that any permanent presence of an undertaking in the territory of a Member State shall be treated in the same way as an agency or branch, even if it is only an office managed by an undertaking's own staff or an independent person with authority to act. Article 5 is supplementary to Directive 73/239 in that it adds to Article 5 of that directive a definition of "large risks". Article 7 determines the law applicable to contracts of insurance. Article 8 sets out rules whereby insurance undertakings may offer and conclude compulsory insurance contracts. Article 9 abolishes as a general rule the notification of special policy conditions and scales of premiums, subject to various qualifications. Article 10 deals with powers of supervisory authorities and Article 11 with

5 [1978] O.J. L151/25.
6 *Commission v. France*: [1986] E.C.R. 3663, [1987] 2 C.M.L.R. 113.
7 *Commission v. Irish Republic*: [1986] E.C.R. 3817, [1987] 2 C.M.L.R. 150.
8 *Commission v. Denmark*: [1986] E.C.R. 3713, [1987] 2 C.M.L.R. 169.
9 [1973] O.J. L228/20.
10 [1977] O.J. L26/14.
11 [1987] O.J. L185/77.
12 [1988] O.J. L172/1.
13 [1990] O.J. L330/44.
14 [1992] O.J. L228/1.
15 [1973] O.J. L228/3.

transfers of portfolios of contracts. Articles 12 to 26 deal with the provision of services and specific rules which affect the freedom to provide services in the field of insurance. The directive contains transitional provisions for Greece, Ireland, Spain and Portugal. The directive also amends Directive 78/473) so that the criteria defining "large risks" in Article 5 (above) should also define risks to be covered under Community co-insurance arrangements.

The subject of life insurance is tackled by the First Council Directive 79/267,[16] amended by Directive 90/619[17] and Directive 92/96[18] on the taking up and pursuit of the business of direct life insurance. The legislation shows a distinction between life insurance and other insurance and it could well be that it shows a distinction between services connected with the movement of capital and services not so connected, a distinction made by the Treaty itself. Here Directive 88/361[19] on movements of capital becomes relevant by abolishing restrictions on movement of capital in respect of transfers in performance of insurance contracts and dealing with premiums and payments in respect of life assurance (Section X of Annex I of the Directive). 12.08

A separate category seems to be made for automobile liability insurance (Council Directive 72/166[20] as amended by Directive 72/430[21]). National automobile liability insurance is made compulsory on a Community basis and in effect the official associations of insurance companies in each Member State become the agents for all insurance companies from other Member States for the purpose of handling claims. This has done away with the border check of certificates of insurance (the so-called "green cards"). These two directives maintained the existing disparities between the laws of the different Member States concerning the extent of the obligation of insurance cover and so the Second Council Directive 84/5[22] aims at the reduction of such disparities. It lays down the minimum requirements for compulsory insurance cover against damage to property and against personal injury. Member States must establish or authorise a body to provide compensation at least up to the limits of the compulsory insurance obligation in respect of damage or injury caused by unidentified or uninsured vehicles. Member States have to ensure that any statutory provision or any contractual clause contained in an insurance policy issued in accordance with Directive 72/166 which 12.09

[16] [1979] O.J. L63/1.
[17] [1990] O.J. L330/50.
[18] [1992] O.J. L360/1.
[19] [1988] O.J. L178/5.
[20] [1972] O.J. L103/2.
[21] [1972] O.J. L291/162.
[22] [1984] O.J. L8/17.

excludes certain categories of vehicle users from insurance is deemed to be void as against third party accident victims. Members of the family of any person liable under civil law and covered by insurance referred to in this directive must not be excluded from insurance in respect of their personal injuries by virtue of that relationship. Commission Decision 93/43[23] further relates to the application of Directive 72/166. Civil liability in motor insurance is further dealt with in the Third Motor Insurance Directive 90/232[24] which provides that the insurance under Directive 72/166 should cover liability to all passengers other than the driver, and that a single premium should cover the entire territory of the Community. It requires steps to be taken to ascertain promptly the identity of the insurance undertaking involved.

12.10 Directive 91/674[25] on annual accounts and consolidated accounts of insurance undertakings applies the Fourth and the Seventh Company Law Directives to Insurance Companies, aiming at standard disclosure in accounts and greater transparency. It also applies to Lloyds with suitable adaptations.

12.11 Following Case 45/85, *Verband der Sachversicherer v. Commission*,[26] in which the Court confirmed the application of Articles 85 and 86 to the insurance sector, Regulation 1534/91[27] dealt with the application of Article 85(3) of the Treaty to the insurance sector.

12.12 Directive 91/675[28] sets up an insurance committee composed of representatives of Member States and chaired by the Commission, with the object of assisting the Commission in exercising its powers and drawing up new proposals.

## BANKING

12.13 The basis of the existing E.C. legislation in relation to banking and credit institutions rests on the principles of freedom of establishment and of freedom to provide services. The latter assumes the liberalisation of banking and insurance services. This liberalisation connected with movements of capital attaches it in terms (Article 61(2) of the Treaty) to the progressive liberalisation of movement of capital. However, the banking legislation of the Community has its philosophical origins in the aims of

23 [1993] O.J. L175/1.
24 [1990] O.J. L129/33.
25 [1991] O.J. L374/7.
26 Case 45/85, [1987] E.C.R. 405, [1988] 4 C.M.L.R. 264.
27 [1991] O.J. L143/1.
28 [1991] O.J. L374/32.

the Treaty. Article 54(3) of the Treaty, which is cited in the preamble as one of the *vires* for the first directive of consequence 73/183[29] on the activities of banks, talks of priority treatment to be given by the Council and Commission to action where freedom of establishment makes a particularly valuable contribution to the development of production and trade. This directive is on the abolition of restrictions on freedom of establishment and freedom to provide services for self-employed activities of banks and other financial institutions.

The main provisions in Article 3 of the directive require Member States to abolish restrictions which prevent banks from establishing themselves or from providing services in the host country under the same conditions and with the same rights as nationals of that country. The directive goes on to prohibit restrictions existing because of administrative practices which result in treatment being applied to beneficiaries that is discriminatory when compared to that for nationals. The article then deals with specific restrictions in named Member States. The United Kingdom was required to abolish provisions existing in the Prevention of Fraud (Investments) Act 1958, repealed now by the Financial Services Act 1986, and corresponding provisions in Northern Ireland whereby any company which intends to exercise the activity of manager and trustee of a unit trust must be constituted in the United Kingdom. Other provisions of the directive give the right to join professional and trade organisations under the same conditions and with the same rights and obligations as the nationals of the host Member State. The directive also deals with the use of the title "bank", "banker" and "savings bank". The banking sector comprises not only banks but also financial institutions such as finance companies, savings and loan institutions and consortia. Excluded are the activities of stockbrokers and the supply of services by intermediaries who, while remaining established in one Member State, move to another Member State to provide services. 12.14

The decisions of the European Court, since the promulgation of the directive, that articles of the Treaty dealing with freedom of establishment and freedom to provide services are directly applicable go further in their application than the directive. 12.15

The First Council Directive 77/780[30] on the co-ordination of laws, regulations and administrative provisions relating to the business of credit institutions based on Article 57 of the Treaty was the first serious attempt to make it easier to conduct business by eliminating obstructive differences between the laws of the Member States and, as its preamble indic- 12.16

[29] Dir. 73/183, [1973] O.J. L194/1.
[30] [1977] O.J. L322/30.

ates, it was intended only as a first step, to be followed eventually by a variety of additional measures until uniform authorisation requirements applied to comparable types of credit institutions, thus avoiding the need for additional authorisations when credit institutions in one Member State wish to set up branches in another Member State. Article 3 of this directive provides for Member States to require those credit institutions subject to the directive to obtain authorisation before commencing their activities. It lays down the requirements for this authorisation: the credit institution must possess separate and adequate minimum funds of its own and it must be managed by at least two persons who are of good repute and have sufficient experience to perform their duties. It must also submit a programme of operations setting out the types of business envisaged and the structural organisation of the institution.

12.17 The directive also establishes an advisory committee of Member State and Commission representatives, its task being to assist the Commission in ensuring the proper implementation of both this directive and the 1973 directive. The directive does not regulate branches of credit institutions which have their headquarters in third countries but provides that such branches may not receive more favourable treatment than branches of institutions with headquarters in a host Member State.

12.18 The provisions of the directive were implemented in the United Kingdom by the Banking Act 1979. However, the criteria for recognition as a bank and for a full licence under the Act were more stringent than those laid down in the directive. Every person who is a director, controller or manager of the institution must be a fit and proper person to hold that position; thus the "good repute" and "sufficient experience" of the directive were transformed into "fit and proper person". These requirements were further enlarged by the Banking Act 1987.

12.19 The 1977 directive was supplemented by Directive 83/350[31] on the supervision on a consolidated basis of credit institutions. The need for this directive arose from the fact that many banks may be subsidiaries of other banking institutions or own other such institutions and their finances are affected by the financial health of all the related institutions. Under the directive, which is based on Article 57(2) of the Treaty, Member State banking authorities must supervise credit institutions which have a shareholding of at least 25 per cent., in another institution by including in their ambit the financial situation of all such other institutions in which the institution subject to supervision participates. The

[31] [1983] O.J. L193/18.

duty to supervise is imposed upon the Member State where the institution concerned has its head office. A distinction is made between majority and minority shareholdings and the supervisory authority has a wide element of discretion. Directive 89/299[32] further deals with own funds of credit institutions. The issue of supervision is carried further by Directive 92/30[33] on the supervision of credit institutions on a consolidated basis and Directive 93/6[34] on the capital adequacy of investment firms and credit institutions. This last directive extends the field of supervision to all credit institutions and investment funds (going further than own funds of credit institutions dealt with in Directive 89/299) defining in detail all terms involved, providing for initial capital, depending on the type of the institution; it also deals with provisions against risks, introduces monitoring and control of large exposures and provides for supervision on a consolidated basis. Directive 92/121[35] deals specifically with the monitoring and control of large exposures of credit institutions.

E.C. company law legislation (see Chapter 13) formerly allowed Member States to exempt banks from the accounting requirements applied to companies in general. This gap was filled in 1986 by Directive 86/635[36] on the annual accounts and consolidated accounts of banks and other financial institutions. The directive provides that the rules of the Fourth Company Directive are to be followed except in those specified instances where different terminology, valuation rules, contents of items in balance sheets and profit and loss accounts are considered necessary to reflect the special position of banks. Undisclosed reserves are dealt with as well as maturity analyses. 12.20

All these directives have been complemented by the Second Council Directive 89/646[37] which amends the First Directive and deals with harmonisation of authorisation conditions and with conditions for the pursuit of banking business. Freedom of establishment and freedom to provide services are important concerns of the Second Directive. Complementary to it is Directive 89/647[38] on solvency ratios for credit institutions. Directive 93/22[39] deals with investment services in the securities field. It specifies conditions for taking up business, relations with third countries, operating conditions, the right of establishment and the freedom to provide services and authorities responsible for authorisation 12.21

[32] [1989] O.J. L124/16.
[33] [1992] O.J. L110/52.
[34] [1993] O.J. L141/1.
[35] [1992] O.J. L29/1.
[36] [1986] O.J. L372/1.
[37] [1989] O.J. L386/1.
[38] [1989] O.J. L386/14.
[39] [1993] O.J. L141/27.

and supervision. Commission Directive 91/31[40] adapted the technical definition of "multilateral development banks" in Directive 89/647.

**12.22** This directive is supplemented by Directive 89/117[41] on the obligations of branches established in a Member State of credit institutions and financial institutions having their head office outside that Member State, regarding the publication of annual accounting documents. This supplementing directive provides for branches to supply the supervising authorities with copies of the annual report and accounts drawn up by their head office in accordance with the main directive, and it places strict limits on the specific information concerning the branch that foreign bank branches can be required to disclose. It also allows Member States to insist that branches of non-Community banks publish branch accounts, should the accounts of their head office not conform with accounts drawn up in accordance with Directive 86/635.

**12.23** Directive 91/308[42] on the prevention of the use of the financial system for the purpose of money laundering defines money laundering, credit institutions and financial institutions involved and action to combat money laundering.

**12.24** Since banking involves consumer credit, Directive 87/102[43] for the approximation of laws, regulations and administrative provisions of the Member States concerning consumer credit covers all credit agreements made with a consumer, subject to a maximum limit of 20,000 ECUs, except lending for property, short-term agreements and hiring agreements. It deals with advertising, canvassing, written documentation, repossession of goods, rebates for early settlement, negotiable instruments, liability for defective goods or services and licensing requirements. The annual rate of interest must be quoted in all cases, but the directive leaves the rules concerning the true cost-of-credit formula to the Member States pending the introduction of Community methods for calculating the annual rate. The directive also contains provisions for authorisation and monitoring of persons granting credit or offering credit arrangements. It is amended by Directive 90/88[43a] to provide for a Community method of calculating the animal percentage rate for consumer credit. In the United Kingdom the Consumer Credit Act 1974 reflects generally the provisions of the directive.

[40] [1991] O.J. L17/20.
[41] [1989] O.J. L44/40.
[42] [1991] O.J. L166/77.
[43] [1987] O.J. L42/48.
[43a] [1990] O.J. L61/14.

## STOCK EXCHANGE

The liberalisation of banking services and the progressive liberalisation of movements of capital must involve stock exchange activities and Community activity. Securities markets form part of the field of activity connected with freedom of services and so in 1979 the Council adopted a directive co-ordinating the conditions for the admission of securities to official stock exchange listing, Directive 79/279.[44] It specifies in four schedules conditions to be applied by all the Member States, with the object of removing any discrimination between the issuers of securities, also specifying their obligations. This directive is implemented in the United Kingdom by the Financial Services Act 1986 and complemented by Directive 80/390[45] co-ordinating the requirements for the drawing up, scrutiny and distribution of the listing particulars to be published for the admission of securities to official stock exchange listing. This directive was amended by Directive 87/345[46] and Directive 90/211.[47] The Financial Services Act 1986 and Stock Exchange Listing Rules take account of these provisions. 12.25

Directive 82/121[48] specifies information to be published on a regular basis by companies the shares of which have been admitted to official Stock Exchange listing. The directive known as the Interim Reports Directive is again implemented by the Financial Services Act 1986 and Stock Exchange Listing Rules. An important step in the process is Directive 85/611,[49] on the co-ordination of laws, regulations and administrative provisions relating to undertakings for collective investment in transferable securities (UCITS) amended by Directive 88/220.[50] These transferable securities should be freely marketable anywhere in the Community and the directives define the undertakings and specify the transferable securities. Major holdings in a listed company are dealt with in Directive 88/627[51] on the information to be published when such a holding is acquired or disposed of. When the holding reaches a specified threshold the holder must inform the company which in turn must inform the public. The requirements for the drawing up, scrutiny and distribution of the prospectus to be published when transferable securities are offered 12.26

[44] [1979] O.J. L66/21.
[45] [1980] O.J. L100/1.
[46] [1987] O.J. L185/81.
[47] [1990] O.J. L112/24.
[48] [1982] O.J. L48/26.
[49] [1985] O.J. L375/3.
[50] [1988] O.J. L100/31.
[51] [1988] O.J. L348/62.

to the public were co-ordinated in Directive 89/298.[52] Directive 89/592[53] co-ordinated regulations on insider dealing, with the object of establishing a uniform basis for combating such operations within the Community, detailing steps to be taken by each Member State.

## CAPITAL MOVEMENTS

12.27 The programme for the liberalisation of capital movements proposed by the Commission in 1986 looks to the removal of financial and monetary impediments and to the establishment of a Community-wide financial area. In fact the process of liberalisation began in 1960, going through several phases and culminating in the Treaty changes introduced by the Treaty on European Union negotiated at Maastricht. All existing legislation, although intended to be superseded, may remain relevant in view of the derogations involving Member States. Articles 67 to 73 of the Treaty lay down the ground rules for free movement of capital. This area is one in which Community law is less developed than it is in regard to other "freedoms" (free movement of goods, free movement of workers, freedom to provide services and freedom of establishment). In view of its close relationship with the economic policy of Member States, it has to be considered at the same time as the provisions of the Treaty dealing with economic policy, especially Articles 104 to 109. The Single European Act of 1986 replaced the unanimity requirement in Council voting on Article 70(1) (co-ordination of exchange policies of Member States concerning capital movements between those States and third countries), by a system of qualified majority voting.

12.28 Article 67 is the principal source for the provisions on free movement of capital. Article 67(1) provides that Member States during the transitional period and to the extent necessary to ensure the proper functioning of the common market progressively abolish between themselves all restrictions on the movement of capital belonging to persons resident in Member States, and any discrimination based on the nationality or on the place of residence of the parties or on the place where such capital is invested. This of course relates to companies and firms within the definition of Article 58.

12.29 In Case 203/80, *Casati*,[54] the Court of Justice observed that, while Articles 3 and 67 of the Treaty show that the free movement of capital constitutes,

[52] [1989] O.J. L124/8.
[53] [1989] O.J. L334/30.
[54] [1981] E.C.R. 2595, [1982] 1 C.M.L.R. 365.

alongside that of persons and services, one of the fundamental freedoms of the Community, capital movements necessarily have close links with the economic and monetary policy of the Member States; thus at present the possibility exists of complete freedom of movement in relation to capital undermining a State's economic policy or creating an imbalance in its balance of payments and jeopardising the proper functioning of the Common Market. This factor will vary with time and will depend on an assessment of the requirements of the Common Market. This is a matter, first and foremost, for the Council. The judgment therefore means that Member States remain free for the time being to impose control on capital movements, even where there are Community rules requiring the Member States to liberalise such transactions.

The earliest directive implementing Article 67 was the First Directive of May 11, 1960,[55] amended by Directives 85/583[56] and 86/566,[57] designed to complete the first stage of the programme for the liberalisation of capital movements in the Community. The First Directive divides capital movements into four groups listed A to D. **12.30**

List A, as now amended, covers: **12.31**

(a) direct investments,
(b) operations in securities and their admission to the capital market,
(c) investments in real property,
(d) grants and repayments of credits in connection with commercial transactions or the provision of services,
(e) transfers in performance of insurance contracts,
(f) sureties and other guarantees,
(g) personal capital movements such as inheritances, gifts, insurance payments and authors' royalties,
(h) invisible transactions of certain kinds (such as payments of damages and royalties for patents, etc.), and
(i) credits granted in connection with the performance of services

Article 1 of the directive requires Member States to grant the requisite foreign exchange authorisations for capital movements of these kinds at the normal exchange rates. The Monetary Committee set up under Article 105 is entrusted with the task of monitoring the exchange rates applied.

List B covers: **12.32**

[55] [1959-62] O.J. Spec. Ed. 49.
[56] [1985] O.J. L372/39.
[57] [1986] O.J. L322/39.

(a) the acquisition of securities quoted on a stock exchange,
(b) credits in connection with transactions in which no resident is participating, and
(c) other payments not covered by List A.

Article 2 of the directive provides for complete freedom in respect of these transfers, but the monetary conversion safeguard mentioned in Article 1(2) is not included, the Member States being required only to try and ensure that transfers are made at rates which do not differ from those ruling for payments relating to current transactions. The Commission is authorised to make recommendations after consulting the Monetary Committee.

12.33 List C contains a third group of transactions which are only slightly liberalised:

(a) placement of securities on capital markets,
(b) transactions in securities not traded upon securities exchanges, and
(c) the granting of long and medium-term credits.

Article 3 of the directive requires Member States to allow foreign exchange authorisation for List C transactions, but permits Member States to maintain or re-introduce restrictions existing when the directive took effect if the liberalisation of these transactions is likely to interfere with its economic policy.

12.34 Certain transactions have not been liberalised at all and Member States retain freedom of action. They are described in List D and include:

(a) short-term investments in Treasury notes,
(b) the establishment and maintenance of deposits with financial institutions,
(c) the importation and exportation of securities not included in List B and of gold and of means of payment of any kind, and
(d) all other movements of capital not specifically listed elsewhere.

12.35 For List C and D transactions, where the degree of liberalisation reached is at best partial, Article 6 requires Member States to endeavour to impose no new exchange control restrictions affecting capital movements which were free when it came into force, and not to making existing provisions more restrictive. Article 5 of the directive permits Member States to verify the nature and bona fides of transactions and transfers, so that capital frauds may be prevented. The Second Directive 63/21[58]

[58] [1963-64] O.J. Spec. Ed. 5.

removes a restriction upon the liberalisation of transactions in previously issued securities and adds certain "invisible" transactions to List A.

Four more directives must be noted at this stage. The First Directive 63/474[59] liberalised transfers in respect of invisible transactions not connected with the movement of goods, services, capital or persons (not already liberalised under Article 106). Directive 72/156,[60] based on Articles 70 and 103, regulates international capital flows and neutralises their undesirable effects on domestic liquidity. Directives 85/583 and 86/566 amended the First Directive, thus completing the first part of the Commission's 1986 programme to liberalise capital movements in the Community. This further liberalisation relates to long-term credits in commercial transactions, acquisition of securities not dealt on the stock exchange and admission of securities of an undertaking in one Member State to the capital market of another. 12.36

The position changed considerably on July 1, 1990 with the coming into force of Directive 88/361[61] for the implementation of Article 67 of the Treaty and repealing the First Directive of May 11, 1960 and Directive 72/156 with effect from July 1, 1990. Article 1 of Directive 88/361 provides that Member States shall abolish restrictions on movements of capital taking place between residents of Member States. Under Article 4 Member States have the right to take all requisite measures to prevent infringements of their laws and regulations (*inter alia,* in the field of taxation and prudential supervision of financial institutions) or for declaration of capital movements for statistical purposes. 12.37

Capital movements are now classified in accordance with the Nomenclature in Annex I of the directive. It covers: 12.38

(a) direct investments,
(b) investments in real property,
(c) operations in securities normally dealt in on the capital market,
(d) operations in units of collective investment undertakings,
(e) operations in securities and other instruments normally dealt in on the money market,
(f) operations in current and deposit accounts with financial institutions,
(g) credits related to commercial transactions or to the provision of services in which a resident is participating,
(h) financial loans and credits,
(i) securities, other guarantees and rights of pledge,

[59] [1963-64] O.J. Spec. Ed. 45.
[60] [1972] O.J. Spec. Ed. 296.
[61] [1988] O.J. L178/5.

(j) transfers in performance of insurance contracts,
(k) personal capital movements,
(l) physical import and export of financial assets, and
(m) other capital movements.

The annex also contains detailed explanatory notes.

12.39 Article 3 of the directive allows the Community to authorise Member States, in cases of severe strains on foreign exchange markets and movements leading to serious disturbances in the conduct of monetary exchange rate policies, to take protective measures determined by the Commission in respect of capital movements listed in Annex II. Annexes III and IV list special provisions for Spain, Portugal, Greece and Ireland.

12.40 Article 68(1) provides that Member States shall be as liberal as possible in granting such exchange authorisations as are still necessary after the entry into force of the Treaty. Under Article 71, Member States must endeavour to avoid introducing any new restrictions on movements of capital and current payments connected with such movements and must endeavour not to make existing rules more restrictive. Article 71 does not, it seems, impose on the Member States an unconditional obligation which can be relied upon by individuals: see *Casati*.

12.41 Article 68(2) provides that where Member States apply to capital movements domestic rules governing the capital market and the credit system they must do so in a non-discriminatory manner; this appears to be directly applicable. Under Article 68(3) loans for the direct or indirect financing of a Member State or its regional or local authorities may not be issued or placed in other Member States unless the States concerned have reached agreement on this, although this does not preclude the European Investment Bank from borrowing on the capital markets of Member States.

12.42 Article 72 requires Member States to keep the Commission informed of any capital movements to and from third countries which come to their knowledge, and if movements of capital lead to disturbances in the functioning of the capital market in any Member State, the Commission is empowered by Article 73 to authorise Member States to take protective measures in the field of capital movements. In cases of urgency or secrecy a Member State may act on its own initiative, but the Commission has power to direct such measures to be amended or abolished, and both it and the other Member States must be informed of them.

12.43 The Community when dealing with capital movements was conscious of the balance of payments difficulties of its members and provided for a machinery if support for the balance of payments was necessary. Regulation 1969/88[62] establishes a single facility providing medium-term financial assistance for Member States' balances of payments, repealing previous acts. The amount of loans to be granted under this facility is limited to 16,000 million ECUs and the Commission is to contract loans on the capital markets or with financial institutions. This legislation is now repealed and the Commission is to contract loans on the capital markets or with financial institutions. The outstanding amount of loans granted to Member States is limited to 14,000 million ECUs in principal.

The Treaty on European Union replaced as from January 1, 1994, Articles 67 to 73 of the E.C. Treaty by Articles 73b, 73c, 73d, 73e, 73f, 73g and 73h with their wide scope. Article 73b prohibits all restrictions on movement of capital and on payments between Member States and Member States and third countries. Article 73c excludes restrictions applying to third countries under national or Community law which existed on December 31, 1993. Article 73d qualifies the provisions of Article 73b in the field of national taxation and supervision of financial institutions. Article 73e maintains existing derogations and Article 73f allows restriction on movement of capital with regard to third countries in exceptional circumstances. Article 73h deals with the situation generally existing until 1 January 1994. **12.44**

## ECONOMIC AND MONETARY UNION

The annual report of the Commission in 1989 stated that the adoption of Directive 88/361 and Regulation 1969/88 represented a major step towards the completion of the internal market and the monetary integration of the Community. The European Monetary System was created by Regulation 3181/78,[63] supplemented by Regulation 3066/85.[64] The Treaty on European Union provides for economic and monetary union. Article 3a provides for an adoption of an economic policy and Articles 102a to 104c lay down a set of rules on policies. **12.45**

Article 3a specifies that the activities shall include the irrevocable fixing of exchange rates leading to the introduction of a single currency, the ECU, and the definition and conduct of a single monetary policy and exchange-rate policy, the primary objective of both of which shall be to maintain price stability and to support the general economic policies in **12.46**

[62] [1988] O.J. L178/2.
[63] [1978] O.J. L379/2.
[64] [1985] O.J. L290/95.

the Community, in accordance with the principle of an open market economy with free competition.

12.47 Article 4a establishes a European system of central banks and a European Central Bank and Articles 105 and 109 define the task of these banks. Article 109a to 109d lay down provisions governing the institutions. Articles 109e to 109m make various transitional provisions aiming through three stages at attainment of a monetary union and adoption of a single currency. A protocol attached to the Treaty provides that the United Kingdom is under no obligation to move to the third stage unless it notifies the Council that it so intends.

# CHAPTER 13

# COMPANY LAW

## FREEDOM OF ESTABLISHMENT

Community legislation dealing with companies has its background in the provisions of the Treaty concerned with right of establishment. Article 52 calls for abolition of restrictions on the freedom of establishment of nationals of a Member State in the territory of another Member State. This freedom of establishment includes the right to take up and pursue activities as self-employed persons and to set up and manage undertakings, in particular companies or firms within the meaning of the second paragraph of Article 58. Article 58 states that companies or firms formed in accordance with the law of a Member State (and having their registered office, central administration or principal place of business within the Community) shall be treated in the same way as natural persons who are nationals of Member States. In the second paragraph it defines "companies or firms" as companies or firms constituted under civil or commercial law, save for those which are non-profit-making. **13.01**

In Case 81/87, *The Queen v. HM Treasury and Commissioners of Inland Revenue, ex parte Daily Mail and General Trust PLC,*[1] the Court of Justice ruled that in the present state of Community law, Articles 52 and 58 of the Treaty, properly construed, confer no right on a company incorporated under the legislation of a Member State and having its registered office there to transfer its central management and control to another Member State. **13.02**

Article 54 calls for a general programme for the abolition of existing restrictions on freedom of establishment within the Community and for **13.03**

[1] [1988] E.C.R. 5483, [1988] C.M.L.R. 713.

co-ordinating the safeguards which, for the protection of the interests of members and others, are required by Member States of companies or firms within the meaning of the second paragraph of Article 58 with a view to making such safeguards equivalent throughout the Community.

## Company Directives

13.04 These provisions are the basis for Community legislation which commenced in 1968 with the First Directive 68/151[2] concerned with disclosure, validity of company acts and nullity. The directive applies to public and private companies and provides for mandatory publication of certain documents and information, *e.g.* company statutes, names of directors and officers, subscribed capital, the balance sheet and profit and loss account of public companies, details of winding up, liquidators and termination of a liquidation. (The provisions dealing with accounts were further extended by the Fourth Directive 78/660.[3] The First Directive further provides for establishment of company registries in each Member State; validation of obligations entered by companies including a prohibition against the doctrine of *ultra vires* applying against a third party contracting in good faith; and definition of occasions when nullity of a company may be claimed. In Case 136/87, *Ubbink Isolatie BV v. Dak- en Vandtechniek BV*,[4] the Court of Justice held that the rules on the nullity of companies contained in the First Directive do not apply where the acts involved were performed in the name of a private limited liability company which was not registered in the public register because the formalities for incorporation required by national law had not been completed. However, a national court called on to determine a dispute falling within the sphere of application of the First Directive, is obliged to interpret its national law in the light of the wording and purpose of that directive in order to prevent the nullity of a limited liability company from being declared on a ground other than those listed in Article 11 thereof: see Case C–106/89, *Marleasing SA v. La Comercial Internacional de Alimentacion SA*.[5] The First Directive is now implemented in the United Kingdom by section 35 of the Companies Act 1985 (formerly section 9 of the European Communities Act 1972). The doctrine of *ultra vires* is restricted by the Act when it provides that:

(a) in favour of a person dealing with a company in good faith, any transaction so decided on by the directors is deemed to be free

[2] [1968] O.J. L65/8.
[3] [1978] O.J. L222/11.
[4] [1988] E.C.R. 4665, [1990] 1 C.M.L.R. 362.
[5] [1990] E.C.R. 4135, [1992] 1 C.M.L.R. 305.

of any limitation under the memorandum or articles of association; and

(b) a party to a transaction so decided on shall not be bound to enquire as to the capacity of the company to enter into it or as to any such limitations on the power of the directors, and shall be presumed to have acted in good faith unless the contrary is proved. Section 36(4) of the 1985 Act, implementing Article 7 of the directive, establishes liability for contracts entered into prior to the formation of the company by those concerned with its incorporation. The concept of "nullity" in the directive is unknown to United Kingdom law. Section 15(1) of the Companies Act 1948 provided that the certificate of incorporation is conclusive evidence of the due formation of the company.

The Second Directive, 77/91,[6] deals with public companies, their formation and maintenance of their capital. The major requirements of the directive include a minimum capital of 25,000 ECUs, differentiation in name between public and private companies, restrictions on the payment of dividends, virtual prohibition of issuing shares at a discount, the necessity for an expert's report on the value of non-cash consideration to be paid for new shares, sundry provisions relating to share capital and the requirement of a shareholders' meeting if accumulated losses exceed at most 50 per cent. of subscribed capital. This directive was implemented by the Companies Act 1980 (now the Companies Act 1985). A public company is defined as a company limited by shares or guarantee or having a share capital whose memorandum must state it to be a public company. Its name must end with the words "public limited company". The minimum issued share capital in the United Kingdom must be £50,000 (as opposed to 25,000 ECUs in the directive). In defining the non-cash consideration to be paid for new shares the Act employs a concept of money or money's worth in place of the directive's assets "capable of economic assessment". The Second Directive 77/91 was held to have direct effect and may be invoked against public authorities before national courts by an individual. Articles 25 and 41 of the directive are specifically mentioned in this context: see Joined Cases C 134-135/91, *Kerafina-Keramische und Finanz Holding AEG v. Hellenic Republic,*[7] Joined Cases C 19-20/90, *N. Karella and M. Karella v. Minister of Industry, Energy and Technology.*[8] The same point was made with regard to Articles 25(1) and 29(1) of the directive in Case C–381/89, *Syndesmos Melon Tis Elftheras Evangelikis Ekklisias v. Greek State.*[9] 13.05

[6] [1977] O.J. L26/1.
[7] [1993] C.M.L.R. 277.
[8] [1991] I E.C.R. 2691, [1993] 2 C.M.L.R. 865.
[9] Not yet reported.

13.06 The Third Directive, 78/855,[10] applies to public companies and deals with mergers between two companies both subject to the laws of the same Member State. It is intended to pave the way for rules applying to mergers between companies subject to the laws of different states. The term "merger" in the directive relates to a total merger involving the legal transfer of all the assets and liabilities. The provisions of the directive are intended to protect not only shareholders but also creditors and employees. (The interests of employees are specifically dealt with in Directive 77/187[11]). The Sixth Directive 82/891[12] on splitting up of public limited liability companies covers cases where a public company, in the course of reconstruction, divides up and transfers to more than one other company all its assets and liabilities in exchange for the issue of shares in those companies. The detailed provisions of this directive are designed to complement those of the Third Directive. The directives do not embrace most "mergers" as the term is generally understood in the United Kingdom, that is the acquisition for shares of one company by another, but without subsequent transfer of assets and liabilities. The Companies Act 1985 is presumed to cover the rare eventualities arising out of the directives.

13.07 Directive 90/434[13] is concerned with the common system of taxation applicable to mergers, divisions, transfers of assets and exchanges of shares concerning companies of different Member States, defining companies affected, rules applicable to mergers, divisions and exchanges of shares and the special case of the transfer of a permanent establishment. Directive 90/435[14] deals with the common system of taxation applicable in the case of parent companies and subsidiaries of different Member States. Directive 89/666[15] deals with disclosure requirements in respect of branches opened in a Member State by certain types of company (*i.e.* a company to whom Directive 68/151 applies) governed by the law of another State.

13.08 The Twelfth Council Company Directive 89/667[16] on single-member private liability companies adapts existing rules to single-member private liability companies. The type of such a company is listed in Article 1, and in the United Kingdom this is "private company limited by shares or guarantee".

[10] [1978] O.J. L295/36.
[11] [1977] O.J. L61/26.
[12] [1982] O.J. L378/47.
[13] [1990] O.J. L225/1.
[14] [1990] O.J. L225/6.
[15] [1989] O.J. L395/36.
[16] [1989] O.J. L395/40.

The Fourth Directive, 78/660,[17] on annual accounts, applies to public and private companies with the exception of banks and insurance companies. It deals with the layout of annual accounts, valuation methods to be adopted for their preparation, contents of the annual report and provisions concerning publication of the accounts. It does not cover the preparation of consolidated accounts. The directive applies to all limited liability companies, although less strict requirements are imposed on small and medium-sized companies. New thresholds for smaller companies were adopted by the Council in Directive 84/569[18] in place of those in Article 11 of the Fourth Directive. For the purposes of the main directive annual accounts shall comprise the balance sheet, the profit and loss account and the notes to the accounts. The accounts shall give a true and fair view of the company's assets, liabilities and financial position. The directive sets out in considerable detail the information required to be disclosed, and the layout and grouping of balance sheet and profit and loss account headings. It defines in detail the nature of items to be included under certain headings, *e.g.* land and buildings, *etc.* A section dealing with valuation rules sets out certain basic concepts. The directive concerns itself with the rules relating to historical cost accounting. The Court of Justice held in Case C–38/89, *Ministère Public v. Guy Blangernon*[19] that Article 54(3)(g) of the Treaty and the Fourth Directive must be interpreted as meaning that the legislation of Member States intended to implement that directive must be brought into force and applied even if other Member States have not yet adopted measures to implement it. In the United Kingdom the directive is implemented by the Companies Act 1985. Company accounts have to comply with the requirements of Schedule 4. The schedule is based on the directive and Annexes I and II (layout of the balance sheet and layout of the profit and loss account) of the directive. The general principles of the directive are incorporated in the Act. 13.09

The Seventh Company Directive, 83/349,[20] on consolidated accounts covers the areas omitted by the Fourth Directive. It requires the consolidation of financial statements where either the parent undertaking or the subsidiary is established as a public company limited by shares or by guarantee or as a private company limited by shares or by guarantee. The directive exempts from consolidation parent undertakings which are not established as one of the forms of company mentioned above. Member States may exempt financial holding companies (*i.e.* companies which are not involved in the management of the undertakings in which 13.10

[17] [1978] O.J. L222/11.
[18] [1984] O.J. L314/28.
[19] [1990] I E.C.R. 83, [1990] 2 C.M.L.R. 340.
[20] [1983] O.J. L193/1.

they acquire holdings) from the provisions of the directive. The directive deals in detail with the nature and form of consolidated accounts.

**13.11** The Seventh Directive is implemented in the United Kingdom by the Companies Act 1989 (in section 5 and Schedule 2), which inserts new sections 227 to 230 into the Companies Act 1985. The new section 227 contains the obligation to prepare group accounts and prescribes their form; the new section 228 makes exemptions from the obligation; and the new section 229 requires that subsidiary undertakings should be included in consolidated accounts subject to exceptions set out in that section. The new section 230 makes concessions in respect of individual profit and loss accounts where group accounts are prepared. Schedule 2 of the 1989 Act, which will become Schedule 4A to the 1985 Act, lays down the detailed rules for the form and content of group accounts, including the accounting methods and valuation rules prescribed by the Seventh Directive. The Fourth and Seventh Directives on annual accounts and consolidated accounts respectively have made the role of the auditor extremely important.

**13.12** The Eighth Directive, 84/253,[21] deals with the professional qualifications of statutory auditors. Auditing under the directive must be carried out by approved persons only. The directive is mainly concerned with educational and professional training and examination requirements. It has provisions relating to the independent status of auditors and to arrangements for persons entitled to carry out audits who do not fulfil the requirements of the directive. In the United Kingdom the authority to grant approval is regulated by Section 389 of the Companies Act 1985 and the directive is implemented by Part II of the Companies Act 1989.

**13.13** Directive 88/267[22] specifies the information to be published when a major holding in a listed company is acquired or disposed of. When, following acquisition or disposal of a holding, a person or a legal entity holds voting rights exceeding or falling below a specified proportion he has to notify the company and at the same time the competent authority within seven calendar days. Reference ought to be made to the Convention on the Mutual Recognition of Companies and Bodies Corporate signed in 1968 by the original six Member States under Article 220 of the Treaty. The United Kingdom acceded to the Convention under the Act of Accession of 1972, but the original Convention has not entered into force because of failure of the necessary number of ratifications. Since the Treaty itself provides for non-discrimination of Community companies and for all intents and purposes the benefits foreseen by the Conven-

[21] [1984] O.J. L126/20.
[22] [1988] O.J. L348/62.

tion are already available, it is open to doubt whether the Convention will enter into force.

Directive 89/592[23] co-ordinates regulations on insider dealing. The directive defines "inside information" and "transferable securities".

## European Economic Interest Groupings

Pending further developments leading to the harmonisation of company law in the Community, the Council adopted in 1985 Regulation 2137/85[24] on the European Economic Interest Grouping (EEIG), providing for the formation of groupings of firms in the Community, with the aim stated in the regulation "to facilitate or develop the economic activities of members and to improve or increase the results of those activities; its purpose is not to make profits for itself". These firms will co-operate in joint ventures, provide for research and development, join in submission of tenders outside the Community, arrange for bulk purchases and provide joint services. All these activities do not affect the legal and economic independence of the members of the grouping. An EEIG can best be described as a form of incorporated partnership of companies at Community level. It has legal capacity, its formation depends upon a contract drawn up by its members; there is no requirement for any capital and the liability of its members is unlimited. 13.14 13.15

The activity of the grouping must be related to the economic activities of its members and must not be more than ancillary to those activities. It must pursue an activity which each of its members has in common, thus forming a logical basis for the creation of a grouping. Each member must have a link with the Community and carry on an economic activity within the Community, being taxable within the Community by trading through a permanent establishment. EEC subsidiaries of a non-EEC parent may become members. An EEIG should have at least two members from at least two different Member States. The regulation prescribes the terms in which the groupings are formed. The formation contract must be registered in the Member State in which the official address is located; the formation of the EEIG must also be notified in the *Official Journal*. EEIGs must be registered in one Member State and that State may require the number of members to be limited to 20. EEIGs can be formed with or without capital, they may not employ more than 500 people and when employing more than 100 people, a statutory auditor is required. From the date of registration the EEIG has the capacity to 13.16

[23] [1989] O.J. L334/30.
[24] [1985] O.J. L199/1.

have rights and obligations, to enter into contracts and to sue and be sued. It may hold shares but not in any of its members and may not become a member of another EEIG. The acts of managers are binding on the grouping, even if they go beyond the EEIG's objectives. For the purposes of taxes on profits, the regulation provides that an EEIG is to be fiscally transparent. The entity itself will not be taxed but its profit or losses will be apportioned among the members and taxed or relieved in their hands. The headquarters of an EEIG will constitute the permanent establishment in the Member State in which it is located. Hence each member of an EEIG will be exposed to tax in that State. The regulation deals in detail with the contents of the formation contract and with the internal machinery of the EEIG. It further prescribes the procedure of winding up and liquidation which are governed by national law. The regulation applied from July 1, 1989.

# CHAPTER 14

# COMPETITION

The achievement of the conditions of a common market in the original concept of the Treaty, or of the Single Market envisaged by the Single European Act, would be incomplete without the levelling of the playing field between commercial enterprises in terms of their relations in the private law sphere. Thus, Articles 85 to 94 of the Treaty establish a code regulating the conduct of publicly and privately-owned business enterprises. The law divides into three parts: 14.01

(a) the use of unfair commercial practices to restrict competition
(b) the abuse of a dominant position in the market to restrict competition and
(c) the falsification of competition by state aids to particular enterprises or industries.

## UNFAIR COMMERCIAL PRACTICES

### The Principle

Article 85 renders unlawful and therefore void:[1] 14.02

> "all agreements between undertakings, decisions by associations of undertakings and concerted practices which may affect trade between Member States and which have as their object or effect the prevention, restriction or distortion of competition within the common market. . . ."

The purposive nature of this prohibition, in line with the general 14.03

[1] Art. 85(2).

approach of Community law, will be apparent. Thus in Joined Cases 48–57/69, *ICI v. Commission*,[2] the Court held that a concerted practice existed wherever companies knowingly colluded, even informally, to substitute practical co-operation for the risks of competition. Similarly, it has been held that decisions of associations of undertakings include mere recommendations of trade bodies;[3] and that "gentlemen's agreements" are similarly caught by the article.[4] But without prejudice to that broad rule of law, Article 85 goes on to particularise five cases in which the prohibition will be breached.

## The five proscribed activities

**14.04** The specific instances of commercial activity forbidden in Article 85 are:

(a) directly or indirectly fixing purchase or selling prices or any other trading conditions;
(b) limiting or controlling production, markets, technical development or investment;
(c) sharing markets or sources of supply;
(d) applying dissimilar conditions to equivalent transactions with other trading parties, thereby placing them at a competitive disadvantage;
(e) making the conclusion of contracts subject to acceptance by the other parties of supplementary obligations which, by their nature or according to commercial usage, have no connection with the subject of such contracts.

## Businesses affected

**14.05** The term "undertaking" used in the competition articles is not defined, but one of the earliest and clearest descriptions was provided by the Court in Case 19/61, *Mannesman v. High Authority*,[5] when it ruled that the expression referred to an autonomous entity engaged in economic or commercial activities, whether or not for profit. Thus, parents and subsidiaries are generally regarded as the same person, as are principals and agents.[6] But if a company located in a third country has a presence

[2] [1972] E.C.R. 619, [1972] C.M.L.R. 557.
[3] Case 8/72, *Vereeniging van Cementhandelaren v. Commission*: [1972] E.C.R. 977, [1973] C.M.L.R. 7.
[4] Case 45/69, *Boehringer v. Commission*; [1970] E.C.R. 769.
[5] [1962] E.C.R. 357.
[6] Case 170/83, *Hydrotherm Geratebau v. Andreoli*: [1984] E.C.R. 2999, [1985] 3 C.M.L.R. 224.

within the Community its behaviour affecting the Community will be governed by Community law: see Joined Cases 89, 104, 114, 116–117 & 125–129/85, *Re Woodpulp Cartel*.[7] For the Treaty to apply to a situation there must be an actual or probable impact on intra-Community trade.[8] National competition rules therefore continue to apply in relation to matters which do not affect the Community.[9]

## Exemptions

The scope of these rules is so wide that trade would be seriously hindered by uncertainty if some degree of rule of thumb were not to be allowed in applying them. Accordingly, Article 85(3) itself provides for exemptions for agreements, decisions and practices which would otherwise be prohibited, or arguably prohibited, if they contribute to improving the production or distribution of goods or to promoting technical or economic progress. Such agreements, etc., can be sanctioned by the Commission provided that they do not involve unnecessary restrictions on the undertakings concerned or allow the elimination of competition in respect of a substantial part of the products in question. **14.06**

Regulation 17/62[10] provides for the Commission to deal with applications for exemption under Article 85(3). In order to avoid delays in handling large numbers of applications, the Commission is empowered by Regulations 19/65[11] and 2821/71[12] to issue what are known as "block exemptions" which can be prayed in aid by businesses seeking to be sure of not falling foul of Community law. That is done by means of Commission regulations and those issued to date cover a very wide range of topics from exclusive distribution and purchasing agreements to franchising and know-how licensing, and specific sectors such as transport and insurance. In Case C–234/89, *Delimitis v. Henninger Bräu*,[13] it was held that national courts could not extend the scope of block exemptions beyond their strict limits, the exemptions being derogations from the basic prohibitions. **14.07**

[7] [1988] E.C.R. 5193, [1988] 4 C.M.L.R. 901.

[8] Case 56/65, *Société Technique Minière*: [1966] E.C.R. 235, [1966] C.M.L.R. 357; see also Case 42/84, *Remia BV v. Commission*: [1985] E.C.R. 2545, [1987] 1 C.M.L.R. 1.

[9] See Joined Cases 56 & 58/64, *Consten and Grundig v. Commission*: [1966] E.C.R. 299, [1966] C.M.L.R. 418.

[10] [1962] O.J. Spec. Ed. 87, as last amended by Reg. 2822/71, [1971] O.J. L285.

[11] [1965] O.J. Spec. Ed. 35.

[12] [1971] O.J. L285.

[13] [1991] I E.C.R. 935, [1992] 5 C.M.L.R. 210.

14.08 Current block exemptions are provided in relation to exclusive distribution agreements,[14] exclusive purchasing agreements,[15] patent licensing,[16] motor vehicle distribution and service agreements,[17] specialisation agreements[18] research and development agreements,[19] franchising agreements[20] and know-how licensing.[21]

14.09 Individual exemptions are granted in the form of Commission Decisions, which are issued for a limited period and may be subject to conditions. Decisions and regulations are (together with a refusal of an exemption) reviewable by the Court of First Instance.[22] The Commission has also issued informal Notices, which do not have the force of law but which indicate the policy it adopts in applying the Treaty. The most important are the notices on commercial agents,[23] co-operation between enterprises,[24] imports from Japan,[25] subcontracting agreements,[26] exclusive distribution and purchasing,[27] motor vehicle distribution,[28] minor agreements[29] and on co-operation between national courts and the European courts.[30]

## MERGERS AND TAKEOVERS

14.10 Regulation 4064/89[31] establishes Community control over mergers and takeovers which have a Community-wide dimension. Before the regulation was adopted, the Commission did exercise a degree of control in this area pursuant to Article 86 (see below) but matters are now on a

[14] Reg. 1983/83, [1983] O.J. L173 and L281.
[15] Reg. 1984/83, [1983] O.J. L173 and L281.
[16] Reg. 2349/84, [1984] O.J. L219 and [1985] O.J. L113, and Reg. 151/93, [1993] O.J. L21.
[17] Reg. 123/85, [1985] O.J. L15.
[18] Reg. 417/85, [1985] O.J. L53, and Reg. 151/93, [1993] O.J. L21.
[19] Reg. 418/85, [1985] O.J. L53, and Reg. 151/93, [1993] O.J. L21.
[20] Reg. 4087/88, [1988] O.J. L359.
[21] Reg. 556/89, [1989] O.J. L61, and Reg. 151/93, [1993] O.J. L21.
[22] Council decision 88/591, [1988] O.J. L319/1 as amended by Decision 93/350, [1993] O.J. L144/21 and Decision 94/149, [1994] O.J. L66/29.
[23] [1962] O.J. 139; but see Case 311/85, *Re Flemish Travel Agents*: [1987] E.C.R. 3801, [1989] 4 C.M.L.R. 213.
[24] [1968] O.J. C75/3; see also the Notice on Co-operative Joint Ventures at [1993] O.J. C43/2, [1993] 4 C.M.L.R. 328.
[25] [1972] O.J. C111/13.
[26] [1979] O.J. C1/2.
[27] [1984] O.J. C101/2.
[28] [1985] O.J. C17/4.
[29] [1986] O.J. C231/2.
[30] [1993] O.J. C39/6.
[31] [1989] O.J. L395/1 and [1990] O.J. L257/14.

formal legislative footing since the regulation came into force in September 1990.

The test of Community interest in a takeover or merger is defined by reference to a series of quantitative thresholds: if the aggregate worldwide turnover of *all* the undertakings involved is more than 5,000 million ECUs and the aggregate Community-wide turnover of *each* of the undertakings exceeds 250 million ECUs, the case is prima facie one for the Commission rather than the national authorities. There is a let out for cases which satisfy these criteria where two-thirds of *all* the undertakings' aggregate Communitywide turnover is in a single State. **14.11**

Nonetheless, businesses remain in double jeopardy in a restricted class of cases, namely those where issue of public security, media concentrations and the prudential regulation of commerce are raised, and the Commission may refer cases to a Member State if the proposed merger, etc., has consequences for a "distinct market" there. Member States may themselves refer a case below the thresholds to the Commission if trade between Member States is affected. **14.12**

Mergers and takeovers which form the subject of the regulation are described as "concentrations", which are defined as occurring when two or more undertakings merge, or when persons controlling one or more undertakings acquire direct or indirect control of another undertaking. It will be seen that this definition covers a wide range of commercial arrangements and includes many joint venture schemes. Where the arrangements proposed between companies fall short of the scope of the regulation, they are likely to need to be considered in terms of the general prohibitions in Articles 85 and 86. **14.13**

The machinery of the regulation requires that companies proposing a "concentration" are required to notify it to the Commission within a week of the relevant agreement being concluded, the bid being announced or the controlling interest being acquired. The concentration cannot lawfully be put into effect for three weeks unless notified, with a fine of 10 per cent of the aggregate turnover in default. The Commission's initial examination must be completed within one month and may result in one of three conclusions: **14.14**

(a) that the concentration has no Community dimension and is thus outside the scope of the regulation;
(b) that the concentration is compatible with the Common Market;
(c) that the concentration appears not to be compatible with the Common Market and that a further investigation is needed.

14.15 An investigation by the Commission must be concluded within a further four months. Unless the outcome is favourable and the concentration is not opposed, the Commission will then issue a decision either prohibiting completion of the proposals or requiring divestiture, as appropriate; the decision may also approve the concentration subject to modifications agreed with the undertakings concerned. If the Commission fails to take a decision within one month of the notification, or four months of commencing an investigation, as the case may be, the proposed concentration is deemed to have been declared compatible with the Common Market.

14.16 The criteria against which the Commission evaluates notified concentrations are broad and economic in character. They include the need to preserve and develop effective competition in the Community market, the structure of the relevant markets and the current market positions of the undertakings concerned in the proposed concentration. The undertakings must be given the chance to be heard during an investigation as must any other undertakings showing a legitimate interest in the outcome, and the parties directly concerned have access to the Commission's file.

14.17 The Commission can obtain information for the purposes of the investigation, with powers to impose fines in default. It was held in Case C–67/91, *Associación Española de Banca Privada*,[32] that unpublished information obtained by the Commission under Regulation 17/62 could not be used in evidence for the purpose of national competition proceedings by a Member State. Regulation 2367/90[33] detailed the procedural rules to be followed in application of Regulation 4064/89. As with Article 85, informal notices have been published by the Commission on Concentrative and Co-operative Operations[34] and Restrictions Ancillary to Concentrations.[35]

## ABUSE OF A DOMINANT POSITION

14.18 Article 86 completes the series of restrictions imposed by Article 85 and Regulation 4064/89 on the behaviour of commercial undertakings *inter se*. It proscribes any abuse by one or more undertakings of a dominant position within the Common Market, or a substantial part of it, in so far as it affects trade between Member States.

[32] Not yet reported.
[33] [1990] O.J. L219/5.
[34] [1990] O.J. C203/10.
[35] [1990] O.J. C203/5.

## Dominance

It is to be noted that it is the *abuse* of a dominant position rather than the existence of it which is prohibited. Nonetheless, before a dominant position can be abused it must first be held, and the criteria for discerning such a state of affairs are not defined in the Treaty or in legislation. In the case law of the Court, however, the *locus classicus* for the description of this concept is the *Continental Can* case.[36] There, the Court said that a dominant position consisted of the power to behave independently without taking account of competitors, purchasers or suppliers; that occurred when a company had such a share of the market that, with the availability of technical knowledge, raw materials or capital, it had the power to determine prices, or to control production or distribution, for a significant part of the products in question. 14.19

That broad and economic test is given greater focus by the exercise of defining the *relevant market* and calculating the *market share*. These are not matters of legal specification either, but they are frequently used by the Court and by the Commission as yardsticks by which to measure the imponderables of economic activity. The relevant market is discerned by reference to two factors in particular: first, any discrete geographical market in existence, and secondly, the economic market for the product under examination or any product which is functionally interchangeable with it. But whether a dominant position can be said to exist is a question of fact and degree in all the circumstances, and there is no fixed percentage or proportion which is decisive. 14.20

## Abuse

A non-exhaustive catalogue of specific misdemeanours is given by Article 86 which corresponds to (a), (b), (d) and (e) of the Article 85 list given in paragraph 14.4 above, (item (c) of that list being inapplicable to the non-collaborative activities considered by Article 86). Thus, price fixing, the limitation or control of production, applying dissimilar conditions to similar transactions and the imposition of unusual or gratuitous conditions in agreements may all be specific instances of abuse. The vice in every case is the distortion or suppression of the free play of the competitive market. 14.21

In practice the sort of things which lead to an infringement of Article 86 are: price discrimination between retailers, exclusive dealing requirements, practising predatory pricing or maintaining excessively high 14.22

[36] Case 6/72, *Continental Can Co. v. Commission*: [1973] E.C.R. 215, [1973] C.M.L.R. 199.

prices, or refusing to supply dealers with the product, though the mere existence and enforcement of intellectual property rights is not indicative of abuse. It will be seen that some of these practices are incompatible with others—for example, excessive pricing and predatory pricing—if practised at the same time, and it is unsafe to characterise a given practice as necessarily abusive. The fundamental question must always be asked: is this conduct calculated to interfere with the free play of the market by introducing considerations which are not justified in terms of market requirements, such as greater efficiency or improved products?

## PUBLIC UNDERTAKINGS

14.23 Article 90 provides that public undertakings, or undertakings to which Member States grant special or exclusive rights, are to be equally subject to the competition provisions flowing from Articles 85 to 94; likewise, they are to be subject to the general proscription of nationality discrimination in Article 7 of the Treaty. The objects of these further reinforcements of the rules for commercial conduct are evidently national monopolies in public ownership or companies enjoying a degree of monopoly power by reason of public law functions which they are responsible for exercising.

14.24 In Case C–69/91, *Decoster*,[37] the defendant in criminal proceedings in France was charged with the sale of telecommunications terminals without type approval from the Ministry concerned; that Ministry was also engaged in the commercial operation of the public telecommunications network. The Court held that the fact that the business was being conducted by a government department did not prevent it from being regarded as an undertaking within Article 90. As such, it was also subject to Directive 88/301 requiring the body giving such approvals to be independent of every operator offering goods or services in the telecommunications sector. Delivering a wide-ranging judgment, the Court declared that the directive and Articles 86 and 90 of the Treaty precluded national rules prohibiting the import or sale of equipment without approval by a body whose independence of all those operating in the telecommunications sector was assured.

## ENFORCEMENT

14.25 The mechanisms for enforcing Regulation 4064/89 on concentrations have already been mentioned. Article 85(1) states that all agreements,

[37] Not yet reported.

decisions and practices prohibited under Article 85 are "automatically void". The principle enforcement authority is the Commission, which is charged by Regulation 17/62 with imposing fines (which may range from 1,000 ECUs to 1 million ECUs, or 10 per cent. of turnover if greater) for breaches of either Article 85(1) or Article 86. Fines may also be imposed for the supply of false or misleading information or obstructing an investigation. Following an investigation, the Commission may require a company to adopt a course of action designed to remedy any breach of Community law thereby established. Fines imposed are recovered, and the Commission's decisions enforced, by national authorities at the instance of the party concerned.[38]

Complaints to the Commission may be made by interested individuals or undertakings, or by Member States themselves. The Commission may, of its own motion, initiate investigations without waiting for a complaint. Regulation 27/62[39] describes the procedural steps for notifying the Commission of an agreement, etc., which is prima facie prohibited and seeking exemption; that action will have the important consequence of protecting the undertaking from fines and it is common for companies to take the precaution of using a notification to seek "negative clearance" or, in the alternative, an exemption. 14.26

Regulation 99/63[40] lays down the rules of procedure for the conduct of investigations by the Commission. Before making a final decision the Commission is required to consult the Advisory Committee on Restrictive Practices and Dominant Positions, composed of a representative from each Member State. All interested parties must be given an opportunity to be heard and to make submissions and if the Commission intends to grant an exemption under Article 85(3) it must notify its intention in the *Official Journal* and allow the opportunity for comments from interested parties. A refusal to take action on a complaint by a third party must also be notified to him and he must be given the opportunity to offer further written comment. 14.27

## STATE AIDS

Article 92 of the Treaty prohibits "any aid granted by a Member State or through State resources in any form whatsoever" which distorts or threatens to distort competition by favouring certain undertakings or the production of certain goods. So far as it affects trade between the 14.28

[38] Art. 192 of the Treaty.
[39] [1962] O.J. Spec. Ed. 132, as last amended by Reg. 2526/85, [1985] O.J. L240.
[40] [1963] O.J. Spec. Ed. 47; see also Reg. 2988/74, on time limits, [1974] O.J. L319.

Member States, any aid of this kind is incompatible with the Common Market. The Treaty does provide for a number of specific exceptions to this prohibition, some of which are always applicable and others of which are applicable only if the Commission is so persuaded.

**14.29** The mandatory exceptions are:

(a) aid with a social character granted to individuals, if there is no discrimination on the basis of product origin;
(b) aid to make good the damage caused by natural disasters, etc.;
(c) aid to certain areas of Germany affected by the division of that country.

In these cases, the basic prohibition does not apply.

**14.30** In the following cases, the aid *may* be compatible with the Common Market:

(a) aid to promote the economic development of areas where the standard of living is abnormally low or where there is serious underemployment;
(b) aid to promote the execution of an important project of European interest or to remedy a serious disturbance in the economy of a Member State;
(c) aid to facilitate the development of certain economic activities or of certain economic areas, or to promote cultural heritage and conservation, where such aid does not adversely affect trading conditions to an extent contrary to the common interest.

In exceptional cases, the Council of Ministers may approve other categories of aid specified in a proposal made by the Commission, or otherwise,[41] and the Commission is charged generally with keeping all systems of aid under constant review.

**14.31** The all-important question of enforcement of the Community rules is dealt with as follows. Existing aids—that is, those aids in existence when a State joins the Community—should have been notified to the Commission and, pending the latter's review of them, they should not have been increased or extended. Any subsequent investigation by the Commission on the basis that they were incompatible with the Treaty would, unless the Commission were to be convinced to the contrary, lead to the aids being specifically prohibited and conditions set for their termination.[42]

**14.32** For aids introduced after accession, Article 93(3) requires that the State concerned should notify them to the Commission and may not imple-

[41] Art. 93(2).
[42] Art. 93(1).

ment them before obtaining the latter's approval. The Commission then has two months in which to react to the proposal, failing which it may go ahead; alternatively, the Commission may initiate an inquiry into the aid proposed, inviting evidence from other Member States and interested parties, and will announce as a result its approval or disapproval of the aid. That will be published in the *Official Journal*. There is, however, an abbreviated procedure adopted in many cases by which the Commission indicates by way of a brief announcement in the "C" series of the *Official Journal* that it does not oppose a particular aid of which it has been notified by a Member State.

The possibilities for legal action in the event of an illegal aid prejudicing competitors depend upon the facts of the situation. If a proposed aid is being considered by the Commission no action can, in terms of Community law, meanwhile be taken by any interested party, except to offer evidence to the Commission. If an aid is being given which has not been authorised by or reported to the Commission, an interested party may make a complaint to the Commission and matters will take their course from there onwards. An unfavourable decision by the Commission will commonly result in the Member State which granted the illegal aid being required to recover it. **14.33**

If a company is prejudiced by the aid, it may also take advantage of any remedy available to it in the courts of the Member State concerned to prevent the illegal aid being continued, bearing in mind that in general aids are prima facie illegal until authorised. The recent decision of the European Court in joined Cases C 6 & 9/90, *Francovich*,[43] also indicates that businesses have a right of action in damages against a Member State which fails to give effect to Community law; such could be the case with an aid which was not in the event authorised by the Commission. Action would have to be in the courts of the Member State concerned. Both the recipient of the aid and an interested competitor would normally be able to challenge a Commission decision before the European Court under Article 173 of the Treaty (see Chapter 2). **14.34**

The Commission has published information notices on State aids describing its policy and views in the following sectors: Research and Development,[44] Small and Medium-sized Enterprises,[45] Aid Schemes of Minor **14.35**

[43] [1991] I E.C.R. 5357, [1993] 2 C.M.L.R. 66.
[44] [1986] O.J. C83.
[45] [1992] O.J. C213.

Importance,[46] Regional Aid Schemes,[47] Aids to Public Undertakings in the Manufacturing Sector,[48] Aids to the Motor Industry,[49] to Shipbuilding,[50] and Aids to Synthetic Fibres Industries.[51]

[46] [1990] O.J. C40.
[47] [1990] O.J. C40.
[48] [1991] O.J. C273.
[49] [1989] O.J. C123.
[50] Dir. 90/684, [1990] O.J. L380.
[51] [1989] O.J. C173.

## CHAPTER 15

# TRANSPORT

The objectives of the Common Market and the physical nature of the Community combine to make a common transport policy an essential part of the machinery of making the Community work. Article 3 of the Treaty, in defining the activities of the Community, specifies in subparagraph (e) the adoption of a common policy in the sphere of transport. Title IV of Part Two of the Treaty deals with transport in Articles 74 to 84. And so Article 74 states that the objectivies of the Treaty shall, in matters governed by this title, be pursued by Member States within the framework of a common transport policy. The Court of Justice found in Case 13/83, *European Parliament v. Council*,[1] that the council was infringing the Treaty by failing to ensure freedom to provide services in the sphere of international transport and to lay down conditions under which non-resident carriers may operate transport services in a Member State. And in Case C–17/90, *Pinaud Wieger Spedition v. Bundesanstalt fur den Guterfernvekehr*,[2] the Court ruled that under Community law as it stands Articles 59 and 60 of the Treaty do not preclude an undertaking established in one Member State from being prohibited from appointing a carrier in another Member State to provide on its behalf internal transport at rates generally in force in the first Member State using vehicles licensed in the second Member State for goods transport. **15.01**

The common transport policy in relation to rail, road and inland waterways is to be implemented by Article 75 which provides for the Council to lay down common rules applicable to international transport to or from the territory of a Member State, or passing across the territory of one or more Member States, the conditions under which non-resident carriers may operate transport services within a Member State and any **15.02**

[1] [1985] E.C.R. 1556, [1986] 1 C.M.L.R. 138.
[2] [1994] 1 C.M.L.R. 481.

other appropriate provisions. Article 75 constitutes the legal basis for most of the secondary legislation issued in the transport field. In Case 22/70, *Commission v. Council*,[3] the Court ruled that in the areas in which the Community has developed a common policy the competence to negotiate international agreements passed from Member States to the Community. Article 75 is part of this legal authority to negotiate. One of the first steps in developing a common transport policy was the Council decision of March 21, 1962,[4] amended by Decision 73/402,[5] which lays down an obligation by Member States to submit to the Commission draft laws and measures which may substantially affect the implementation of the common transport policy for purposes of consultation and examination. Within two months of the receipt of the draft the Commission must make a recommendation or comment.

## Carriage of goods by road

15.03 Carriage of goods by road lent itself most readily to Community action to liberalise it with the object of enabling foreign firms in Member States to carry goods in the entire Community without requiring authorisation from the Member States involved. The first step along that road was Regulation 1018/68,[6] which allocated to Member States quotas of Community-wide permits. Each permit was valid for one vehicle at one time and enabled the holder to carry goods between Member States. The quota system was intended to permit authorised road hauliers to convey and pick up freight destined for other Member States in the Community, but excluded internal carriage within other Member States. The basic legislation aiming at this effect was contained in Regulation 2829/72,[7] which was extended in Regulation 3164/76.[8] Regulation 3024/77[9] increased the Community quota and simplified record sheets for transport operations. Regulation 3062/78[10] increased by 10 per cent. the Community quota. Quotas were increased again in 1979 when an experimental system of short-term Community authorisation was issued. This was made permanent by Regulation 3515/82[11] with the ceiling of short-term authorisations being 15 per cent. of the total quotas of the Member States. The quotas under Regulation 3164/76 are amended each year.

[3] [1971] E.C.R. 263, [1971] C.M.L.R. 335.
[4] [1962] O.J. Spec. Ed. 23.
[5] [1973] O.J. L347/48.
[6] [1968] O.J. L175/13.
[7] [1972] O.J. Spec. Ed. 43.
[8] [1976] O.J. L357/1.
[9] [1977] O.J. L358/4.
[10] [1978] O.J. L366/5.
[11] [1982] O.J. L369/2.

Regulation 3621/84[12] authorised an increase in quotas for the subsequent five years. Regulation 3677/85[13] amended Regulation 3164/76 to allow for accession of Spain and Portugal. The system worked by annual increases in quotas, pending their replacement by "qualitative criteria regarding market access, containing the basis for future organisation of the market for the carriage of goods by road between Member States" (draft regulation proposed by the Commission in 1983). These annual and additional increases brought extra Community authorisations for 1987, 1988 and 1989. German legislation introducing tax for the use of federal roads and motorways by heavy goods vehicles with its corresponding reduction in the motor vehicle tax gave rise to discrimination contrary to Article 76 of the Treaty between carriers in Germany and those in other Member States: see Case C–195/90, *Commission v. Federal Republic of Germany*.[14]

Again, common rules for international carriage of goods exempt certain types of carriage from any transport quota or exempt other types from quotas but subject them to authorisation (First Council Directive of July 23, 1962).[15] This exemption has been extended several times, last by Directive 84/647,[16] which allows for use of vehicles hired without drivers for the carriage of goods by road. Regulation 1841/88[17] amending Regulation 3164/76[18] increases the Community quota by 40 per cent. for 1988 and 1989 and replaces the present national bilateral and Community quota systems from January 1, 1993 by qualitative criteria for access to the international road haulage market. The system of providing services by non-resident carriers within a Member state (cabotage) by means of quotas in authorisation was continued by Regulation 4059/89 but is now annulled with Regulation 881/92[19] in its place. Regulation 881/92 on access to the market in the carriage of goods by road within the Community to or from the territory of a Member State or passing across the territory of one or more Member State goes further. International carriage shall be carried out subject to Community authorisation which is issued by the competent authorities of a Member State for a renewable period of five years on a form given in Annex 1. The regulation repeals Regulation 3164/76, Article 4 of Directive 75/130, Directive 65/269 and Decision 80/48. Regulation 3118/93[20] entitles a holder of the Community **15.04**

[12] [1984] O.J. L333/61.
[13] [1985] O.J. L354/46.
[14] Not yet reported.
[15] [1962] O.J. Spec. Ed. 70.
[16] [1984] O.J. L335/72.
[17] [1988] O.J. L163/1.
[18] [1976] O.J. L357/1.
[19] [1992] O.J. L95/1.
[20] [1993] O.J. L279/1.

authorisation provided for in Regulation 881/92 to supply on a temporary basis national road haulage services for hire or reward in another Member State without a registered office or establishment therein subject to conditions laid down in this regulation.

*Rate regulation*

15.05 The Common Market calls for some uniformity in rate regulation. Regulation 1174/68[21] introduced a flexible system of rate regulation and a system of compulsory brackets for tariffs for carriage of goods by road. The competent authorities laid down and published bracket tariffs fixing transport rates and conditions, the rate being freely negotiated within the fixed maximum and minimum. The spread of the bracket was to be 23 per cent. of the maximum. Regulation 2831/77[22] replaced this regulation, it being in turn replaced by Regulation 3568/83[23] which was intended to cover the period up to the end of 1988. This last regulation is amended by Regulation 1991/88.[24] Rates here are formed under a system of non-compulsory reference tariffs. Two or more Member States may introduce compulsory brackets for tariffs instead of reference tariffs. This system was prolonged until the end of 1989. From January 1989, however, Member States have agreed to abolish the compulsory tariffs.

## Road passenger transport

15.06 The basic regulation on the carriage of passengers by road is Regulation 117/66[25] which establishes common definitions for international services and a system largely free from authorisation for occasional passenger services. Regulation 516/72[26] deals with shuttle services by coach and bus between Member States and Regulation 517/72[27] with regular and special regular services. Shuttle services are defined as the transportation of previously formed groups of travellers from one point to another point without break and their return transportation at some subsequent time. The agreement on international carriage of passengers by road by means of occasional coach and bus services (ASOR) was signed in 1982 by the Community and certain other European States (Decision 82/505).[28]

[21] [1968] O.J. Spec. Ed. 411.
[22] [1977] O.J. L334/22.
[23] [1983] O.J. L359/1.
[24] [1988] O.J. L516/5.
[25] [1966] O.J. Spec. Ed. 177.
[26] [1972] O.J. L67/13.
[27] [1972] O.J. L67/19.
[28] [1982] O.J. L230/39.

## Drivers' hours

Road transport drivers' hours and records were originally based on Regulation 543/69,[29] amended several times. The position is now governed by Regulation 3820/85,[30] which introduced an element of flexibility. This regulation applies to carriage by road within the Community. The European Agreement concerning the Work of Crews of Vehicles in International Road Transport of July 1, 1970 (AETR Agreement), which entered into force on January 5, 1976, covers Community drivers travelling to or transiting other countries which are signatories to the Agreement, including the journey within the Community, instead of the rule in the regulation. Certain vehicles are exempted from the regulation and AETR. There is an element of discretion left to Member States to exempt vehicles in certain circumstances. Minimum ages are laid down for drivers, for drivers' mates and conductors. Rest periods and total driving periods over specific periods are also stipulated. Payments to wage-earning drivers related to distances travelled or the amount of goods carried are prohibited. In the case of regular services a service timetable and duty roster has to be drawn up. The latter provisions do not apply to drivers of vehicles fitted with tachographs under Regulation 3821/85.[31] This regulation governs the use of tachographs from September 29, 1986 and prescribes in detail the rules of construction, installation, use and testing of tachographs. The definitions used in Regulation 3820/85[32] apply to this regulation and Member States must check on compliance and penalties to be imposed in case of breach. Calculating driving and rest times under this regulation were considered by the Court of Justice in Case C–116/92, *Charlton*.[33] Directive 88/599[34] lays down minimum conditions for checking the correct and uniform application of both regulations. Minimum levels of training for drivers are laid down in Directive 76/914.[35] 15.07

## Qualifications

The occupations of road haulage operator and road passenger transport operator are the subject of Directives 74/561[36] and 74/562[37] respectively. 15.08

[29] [1969] O.J. L77/49.
[30] [1985] O.J. L370/1.
[31] [1985] O.J. L370/8.
[32] *Op. cit.*, above.
[33] Not yet reported.
[34] [1988] O.J. L325/55.
[35] [1976] O.J. L357/36.
[36] [1974] O.J. L308/18.
[37] [1974] O.J. L308/23.

Both specify good repute, appropriate financial standing and technical competence as conditions for the exercise of these occupations. Technical competence involves skills in law, business, financial management, legislation, technical standards and road safety and these subjects are listed in the annexes to the directives. These directives are subject to many amendments, particularly by Regulation 3572/90,[38] while Regulation 2454/92[39] lays down the condition under which non-resident carriers may operate national road passenger transport services within a Member State. Mention should be made of Directive 77/796[40] on mutual recognition of diplomas and other evidence of qualifications for these two kinds of operator. These three directives were amended by Directive 89/438[41] which provides for measures intended to encourage the effectiveness of operators. Directive 80/1263[42] calls for the introduction of a national driving licence based on a Community model. Several aspects of this directive relating to driving tuition were considered in Case C–60/91, *J.A. Batista Morais v. Ministerio Publico*.[43] Directive 91/439[44] repeals as from July 1, 1996 Directive 80/1263, advancing harmonisation of conditions and intending to recognise driving licences throughout the Community irrespective of the holder's State of residence.

**15.09** The Customs Convention on the International Transport of Goods under TIR carnet has been adopted by the Community and Regulation 3237/76[45] as amended by Regulation 2112/78[46] and Regulation 3020/81[47] has transposed the Convention into Community law. The International Convention for Safe Containers is dealt with in Recommendation 79/487.[48] Several steps taken to simplify the formalities involved in the use of carnets became redundant when Regulation 719/91[49] provided that the Community is to be considered a single customs territory in relation to the use of carnets as transit documents. This elimination of formalities was extended to movements under the NATO Convention by Regulation 3648/91.[50] Regulation 4060/89,[51] as amended by Regulation 3356/91,[52]

[38] [1990] O.J. L353/12.
[39] [1992] O.J. L251/1.
[40] [1977] O.J. L334/37.
[41] [1989] O.J. L212/101.
[42] [1980] O.J. L375/1.
[43] [1992] 2 C.M.L.R. 533.
[44] [1991] O.J. L237/1.
[45] [1976] O.J. L368/1.
[46] [1978] O.J. L252/1.
[47] [1981] O.J. L302/6.
[48] [1979] O.J. L308/18.
[49] [1991] O.J. L78/6.
[50] [1991] O.J. L348/1.
[51] [1989] O.J. L390/18.
[52] [1991] O.J. L318/1.

removes frontier control in the field of road and inland waterway transport. The Commission can propose amendments to the arrangements for the transport of dangerous goods and perishable foodstuffs to take account of technological progress.

## Vehicle standards

Vehicles themselves became subject to Community legislation with the passing of Directive 85/3,[53] as amended by Directives 86/360,[54] 86/364[55] on vehicle, plating and 88/218[56] which specifies maximum dimensions and maximum weights for various types of vehicle and associated trailers. Directive 85/3[57] was modified by Directive 89/338[58] in respect of standard weight and size and by Directive 89/461[59] dealing with articulated vehicles. Temporary exemptions have been made for the United Kingdom from the operation of Directive 85/3, the latest derogation being in Directive 89/46.[60] Directive 85/3 was further amended by Directive 91/60[61] and Directive 92/7.[62] Roadworthiness for large vehicles is laid down in Directive 77/143.[63] Tread depth of tyres is the subject of Directive 89/459,[64] and lateral protection (sideguards) of motor vehicles of Directive 89/297.[65] Directive 92/6[66] provides that speed limitation devices are to be installed and used in all heavy vehicles which are newly registered from January 1, 1994 (90km/h for heavy goods vehicles and 100km/h for buses with a maximum weight exceeding 10 tonnes). Directive 91/671[67] provides for the use of a safety belt. Directive 93/91[68] adapted, allowing for technical progress, outstanding legislation relating to interior fittings of motor vehicles. Directives 93/92,[69] 93/93,[70] and 93/94[71] introduced various specifications dealing with two or three-wheel motor vehicles. 15.10

[53] [1985] O.J. L2/14.
[54] [1986] O.J. L217/19.
[55] [1986] O.J. L221/48.
[56] [1988] O.J. L98/48.
[57] *Op. cit.*, above.
[58] [1989] O.J. L142/3.
[59] [1989] O.J. L226/7.
[60] [1989] O.J. L226/5.
[61] [1991] O.J. L37/37.
[62] [1992] O.J. L57/29.
[63] [1977] O.J. L47/47.
[64] [1989] O.J. L226/4.
[65] [1989] O.J. L124/1.
[66] [1992] O.J. L57/27.
[67] [1991] O.J. L373/26.
[68] [1993] O.J. L284/25.
[69] [1993] O.J. L311/1.
[70] [1993] O.J. L311/76.
[71] [1993] O.J. L311/83.

## Railways and waterways

15.11 The Railway systems of the Member States do not, on the whole, operate outside their own country and so there is not much effective competition between them. They do compete with other means of transport, however, and this forces them to co-operate in order to offer effective competition to these other modes of transport. Such co-operation is of importance to the really effective Common Market. A series of resolutions has called for such co-operation. The state of finances of the railways led to Decision 75/327,[72] designed to attain an overall financial balance on the railways, independence on administrative, economic and accounting matters, activity and investment plans and to investigate measures to promote co-operation to integrate at Community level. Regulation 2830/77[73] called for railway undertakings to produce their national accounts in the form of annual accounts as shown in the Annex to the Regulation. Under Regulation 2183/78[74] the cost of international carriage of freight must be calculated in accordance with uniform costing principles. Decision 82/529[75] dealt with the fixing of rates for international carriage of goods by rail between Member States so as to maximise returns and Decision 83/418[76] was concerned with the commercial independence of the railways in management of international traffic. The aims of Decision 75/327[77] gave rise to Recommendation 84/646[78] which contained measures on the commercial management of international services, rail tariffs, train movements, the simplification of frontier crossing procedures and combined transport. Further development of rail transport in the Community took place with the adoption of Directive 91/440[79] which deals with access to and right of transit through the networks of Member States and with financial and accounting autonomy for railway undertakings. Regulation 1893/91[80] is concerned with the obligations inherent in the concept of public service in transport.

15.12 The inland waterway system is an important part of the Community transport system, particularly in relation to heavy industry. The Rhine plays a great part in the system. Directive 76/135[81] provided for mutual recognition of navigability licences issued for vessels using inland water-

[72] [1975] O.J. L152/3.
[73] [1977] O.J. L334/13.
[74] [1978] O.J. L258/1.
[75] [1982] O.J. L234/5.
[76] [1983] O.J. L237/32.
[77] *Op. cit.*, above.
[78] [1984] O.J. L333/63.
[79] [1991] O.J. L237/25.
[80] [1991] O.J. L169/1.
[81] [1976] O.J. L21/10.

ways, if the licence contained the minimum information set out in the directive. Directive 82/714[82] dealt with technical standards for the construction of inland waterway vessels and safety of the crews' accommodation. Directive 87/540[83] lays down conditions for becoming a carrier of goods on the Community waterways. Directive 91/672[84] adopts the reciprocal recognition of national boatmasters' certificate for the carriage of goods and passengers by inland waterway. Regulations 1101/89[85] and 1102/89[86] introduce measures to reduce structural overcapacity of inland waterway vessels. Regulation 3556/91[87] amending Regulation 4060/89[88] eliminates frontier controls in inland waterway transport. Parallel with road transport cabotage rules, Regulation 3921/91[89] specifies conditions under which a non-resident carrier may transport goods or passengers by inland waterway within a Member State. Joined Cases C 184 & 221/91, *Oorburg v. Wasser-und Sciffahrtsdirektion Nordwest, Aurich*,[90] interpreted Article 76 of the Treaty as meaning that a Member State is not precluded from making navigation on its national waterways conditional upon the possession of a Master's Certificate for inland navigation issued in accordance with national law but it does preclude the introduction of new measures which discriminate against carriers from other Member States. Administrative practice may also constitute such modification. Navigation on the Rhine, which involves the Member States and Switzerland, is governed by an international agreement, the Act of Mannheim, which the Community adopted.

## Sea transport

Article 84 of the Treaty, in its first sub-paragraph, applies the provisions of the title dealing with transport to transport by rail, road and inland waterway. Sea and air transport is subject to the second sub-paragraph authorising the Council, acting by a qualified majority, to make appropriate provisions. In addition, following the decision of the Court of Justice in Case 167/73, *Commission v. French Republic*,[91] the general provisions of the Treaty apply to sea and air transport. 15.13

[82] [1982] O.J. L301/1.
[83] [1987] O.J. L322/20.
[84] [1991] O.J. L373/29.
[85] [1989] O.J. L116/25.
[86] [1989] O.J. L116/30.
[87] [1991] O.J. L318/1.
[88] [1990] O.J. L390/18.
[89] [1991] O.J. L373/1.
[90] Not yet reported.
[91] [1974] E.C.R. 359, [1974] C.M.L.R. 216.

**15.14** Sea transport forms the basis of the Community's external trade. This by itself, apart from other factors, would call for action on a Community basis in this sphere. This action started with several decisions dealing with consultation procedures and collection and exchange of information. The United Nations Convention on a code of conduct for Liner Conferences (sharing of cargo) was given effect in the Community by Regulation 954/79.[92] In the area of safety at sea and sea pollution, Directive 79/115[93] deals with pilotage by deep-sea pilots in the North Sea and English Channel and Directive 79/116[94] lays down requirements for tankers entering and leaving Community ports. A considerable step in the field of common sea transport policy is represented by Regulation 4055/86[95] introducing the concept of freedom to provide services to maritime transport between Members States and Member States and third countries. By way of derogation there is a timetable for phasing out unilateral national restrictions: by Regulation 4056/86[96] which lays down rules for the application of Articles 85 and 86 (competition articles) to maritime transport, certain technical agreements and certain agreements between carriers in scheduled services are exempted from the prohibition in Article 85, and conditions are attached to the latter exemption. Decision 78/774[97] is the legal basis for Community monitoring of unfair pricing practices by third country shipowners. Evidence of such practices led to Regulation 4057/86[98] which deals with unfair pricing practices by third-country shipowners which cause disruption of the freight patterns and threaten to cause or do cause injury to Community shipowners and Community interests. In case of major injury redressive duty may be applied by Regulation 4058/86,[99] intended to safeguard the access to cargoes in ocean trade. Details of the procedures relating to competition hearings in relation to sea transport were laid down in Regulation 4260/88.[1] Regulation 613/91[2] facilitates the transfer of ships from one register to another within the Community. Again, Regulation 3925/91[3] eliminates controls and formalities applicable to baggage on an intra-Community sea-crossing (and intra-Community flight), and is implemented by Regulation 1823/92.[4]

[92] [1979] O.J. L121/1.
[93] [1979] O.J. L33/32.
[94] [1979] O.J. L33/33.
[95] [1986] O.J. L378/1.
[96] [1986] O.J. L378/4.
[97] [1978] O.J. L258/35.
[98] [1986] O.J. L378/14.
[99] [1986] O.J. L378/21.
[1] [1988] O.J. L376.
[2] [1991] O.J. L68/1.
[3] [1991] O.J. L374/4.
[4] [1992] O.J. L185/8.

## Air transport

15.15 Case 167/73, *Commission v. French Republic*[5] decided that air transport is subject to the general rules of the Treaty. This was specifically confirmed in Joined Cases 209–213/84, *Ministère Public v. Asjes,*[6] in relation to air tariffs and rules of competition. However, in the absence of specific legislation (Regulation 141/62[7] exempted transport from the application of Regulation 17/62,[8] which forms the basic secondary legislation on the subject of competition), the principle pronounced in Case 13/61, *De Geus v. Bosch,*[9] renders agreements concerning air tariffs valid until a finding that they are contravening Article 85 of the Treaty. Following the judgment in *Asjes* the E.C. Commission officially alleged that Community airlines had infringed Community competition rules and required them to stop the infringements. Other action in the field of air transport is represented by Decision 80/50[10] (consultation procedure), Decision 80/51[11] (limitation of noise emission from subsonic aircraft), and Directive 80/1266[12] (co-operation and mutual assistance in air accident investigations). Directive 83/416,[13] amended by Directive 89/463,[14] deals with scheduled inter-regional air services between Member States. Then in 1987 three important measures were taken in the aviation section, namely Regulation 3975/87[15] laying down a procedure for the application of competition rules to the sector (Regulation 4261/88 passed in December of 1988[16] provides for the procedure on the hearings dealing with such application), Regulation 3976/87[17] applying Article 85(3) of the Treaty (exemptions of certain types of agreement from the competition rules) and Decision 87/602[18] on the sharing of passenger capacity and on access of carriers to scheduled air routes in the Community. Directive 87/601[19] was concerned with fares for scheduled services. Commission Regulations 2671/88,[20] 2672/88,[21] and 2673/88[22] dealt with the applica-

5 [1974] E.C.R. 359, [1974] C.M.L.R. 216.
6 [1986] E.C.R. 1425, [1986] 3 C.M.L.R. 173.
7 [1962] O.J. Spec Ed. 124.
8 [1962] O.J. Spec. Ed. 13.
9 [1962] E.C.R. 45, [1962] C.M.L.R. 1.
10 [1980] O.J. L18/24.
11 [1980] O.J. L18/26.
12 [1980] O.J. L375/32.
13 [1983] O.J. L237/19.
14 [1983] O.J. L226/14.
15 [1987] O.J. L374/1.
16 [1988] O.J. L378/10.
17 [1987] O.J. L374/9.
18 [1987] O.J. L374/19.
19 [1987] O.J. L374/12.
20 [1988] O.J. L239/9.
21 [1988] O.J. L239/13.
22 [1988] O.J. L239/17.

tion of Article 85(3) to agreements concerned with sharing of revenues, computer reservation systems and ground handling services respectively. The exemption of computerised reservation systems from the provisions of Article 85 called in turn for a code of conduct for such systems, which was provided by Council Regulation 2299/89[23] amended by Regulation 3089/93.[24]

Regulations 2671/88, 2672/88 and 2673/88 expired on January 31, 1991 and were replaced by Commission Regulations 82/91,[25] 83/91[26] and 84/91.[27] A major step in the development of air transport policy is represented by Regulation 2343/90[28] dealing with access for air carriers to scheduled intra-Community air service routes and the sharing of passenger capacity between air carriers on scheduled air services between Member States. Regulation 2342/90[29] deals in detail with fares for scheduled air services. (For elimination of controls applicable to cabin and hold baggage see Regulation 3925/91,[30] paragraph 15.14 above). Regulation 295/91[31] established common rules for a denied-boarding compensation system in scheduled air transport.

15.16 All these legislative instruments enacted in 1987 and 1988 were the subject of a decision by the Court of Justice in Case 66/86, *Ahmed Saeed Flugreisen v. Zentrale zur Bekampfung Unlauteren Wettbewerbs eV*,[32] where it was held that bilateral or multilateral agreements fixing tariffs for international flights between Community airports which did not satisfy the conditions for exemption laid down in Regulation 3975/87[33] were automatically void by virtue of Article 85(2) of the Treaty. The application of tariffs arising from bilateral or multilateral agreements to scheduled flights might, in certain circumstances, constitute an abuse of a dominant position where the conditions laid down by Article 86 were fulfilled.

## Investment and co-ordination

15.17 One of the main aims of the common transport policy is co-ordination among Member States, and so the Council created a consultation proced-

[23] [1989] O.J. L220/1.
[24] [1993] O.J. L278/1.
[25] [1991] O.J. L10/7.
[26] [1991] O.J. L10/9.
[27] [1991] O.J. L10/14.
[28] [1990] O.J. L217/8.
[29] [1991] O.J. L36/5.
[30] [1991] O.J. L374/4.
[31] [1990] O.J. L21/1.
[32] [1989] E.C.R. 803, [1990] 4 C.M.L.R. 102.
[33] [1987] O.J. L374/1.

ure for transport infrastructure investment. Under Decision 78/174[34] Member States must inform the Commission of their plans and programmes for developing transport infrastructure and of projects of Community interest. Under Decision 64/389[35] a survey was organised of infrastructure costs in road, rail and inland waterway transport which was followed by Regulation 1108/70,[36] as amended, instituting an accounting system within this decision. There has been a series of regulations granting financial support for infrastructure from 1982 onwards. The Commission monitored the market for the carriage of goods by rail, road and inland waterway and as a result Directive 75/130[37] governs multi-modal (combined road/rail) systems, Member States having to liberalise multi-modal transport transport systems from all quota systems and systems of authorisation, amended by Directive 91/224[38] and Regulation 881/92.[39] Regulation 1738/93[40] calls for an action programme in the field of transport infrastructure with a view to the completion of an integrated transport market. A further important step in this direction is represented by three decisions enacted in 1993 under Articles 75 and 84(2) of the Treaty: Decision 93/628[41] on the creation of of a trans-European combined transport network, Decision 93/629[42] on the creation of a trans-European road network and Decision 93/630[43] on the creation of a trans-European inland waterway network.

The Treaty on European Union replaced the existing Article 75 by new Article 75, which for the purpose of implementing Article 74 and taking into account the distinctive features of transport requires the Council to lay down **15.18**

(a) common rules applicable to international transport to or from the territory of a Member State or passing across the territory of one or more Member States;
(b) the conditions under which non-resident carriers may operate transport services within a Member State;
(c) measures to improve transport safety and
(d) any other appropriate provisions.

34 [1978] O.J. L54/16.
35 [1964] O.J. 102/1598.
36 [1970] O.J. L130/4.
37 [1975] O.J. L48/31.
38 [1991] O.J. L103/1.
39 [1992] O.J. L95/1.
40 [1993] O.J. L161/4.
41 [1993] O.J. L305/1.
42 [1993] O.J. L305/11.
43 [1993] O.J. L305/39.

15.19 An example of another necessary harmonisation is the harmonisation of different national systems for summertime (daylight saving). Directive 88/14[44] on summertime arrangements provides for summertime in 1989 with the United Kingdom and Ireland able to terminate their summertime exceptionally at a later date than other Community States. Similar arrangements applied for 1990–1992 (Fifth Directive 89/47).[45] Sixth Directive 92/20[46] covers the years 1993 and 1994. Another aim of the Community is facilitation of physical inspection and administrative formalities in respect of carriage of goods between Member States which found expression in Directive 83/643[47] with the aim of elimination of certain frontier checks leading ultimately to the completion of the internal market. This directive was amended by Directive 87/53,[48] and Directive 91/342.[49]

## Abolition of subsidies and other distortions to trade

15.20 Until the provisions referred to in Article 75(1) have been laid down, Article 76 introduces a standstill obligation, whereby carriers from other Member States are protected against a worsening of their position in relation to that of domestic carriers. Article 76 allows for subsidies if they meet the needs of co-ordination of transport or if they represent reimbursement for the discharge of certain obligations inherent in the concept of a public service. Article 92 of the Treaty contains a general prohibition of governmental subsidies which may lead to distortion in the Common Market with a list of exceptions. Article 77 provides an independent exception to the principle. The concept of a public service obligation is defined in Regulation 1191/69[50] and in Case 36/73, *NV Nederlandse Spoorwegen v. Minister van Verkeer en Waterstaat*.[51] Regulation 1107/70[52] limits the kinds of subsidies that may be granted in order not to create distortions of competition.

15.21 Article 78 provides that any measures taken within the framework of the Treaty in respect of transport rates and conditions shall take account of the economic circumstances of the carriers. When measures are enacted, consideration must be given not only to the needs of the economy as a whole, but also to the needs of transport enterprises.

[44] [1988] O.J. L6/38.
[45] [1989] O.J. L17/57.
[46] [1992] O.J. L89/28.
[47] [1983] O.J. L359/8.
[48] [1987] O.J. L24/33.
[49] [1991] O.J. L187/47.
[50] [1969] O.J. L156/1.
[51] [1973] E.C.R. 1299, [1974] 2 C.M.L.R. 148.
[52] [1970] O.J. L130/1.

Article 79 calls for the abolition of discrimination which takes the form of carriers charging different rates and imposing different conditions for the carriage of the same goods over the same transport links on the grounds of origin or destination of goods. The article thus eliminates rates adopted for protectionist purposes. Article 79 is implemented by virtue of its sub-paragraph (3) by Regulation 11/60[53] concerning the abolition of discrimination in transport rates and conditions, as amended by Regulation 3626/84.[54] Regulation 2988/74[55] deals with the appropriate sanctions. The burden of showing that their actions do not violate Article 79 is placed on the carriers. 15.22

Another aspect of the defences of the Common Market is contained in Article 80, which prohibits Member States imposing freight rates supporting specific enterprises or industries. Transportation by enterprises on their own behalf falls outside the scope of the article. The Commission may in a specific case grant exemption from the provisions of the article. 15.23

Article 81 demands that charges or dues charged by the carrier in addition to the transport rates on the crossing of frontiers should be at a reasonable level and be progressively reduced by Member States. With the TIR convention this has become much less significant. Article 82 allows the Federal Republic of Germany to take measures to counteract economic disadvantages caused by the division of Germany to the economy of certain areas. Article 83 creates an advisory committee of experts attached to the Commission, to be consulted on transport matters. 15.24

Outside the title of the Treaty dealing with transport there are provisions dealing with the rail, road and inland waterway transport in the ambit of the competition rules. Decision 65/271[56] deals with harmonisation of competition in relation to this kind of transport by aiming at the removal of the differences between Member States in the field of taxation, social legislation and State aids. Double taxation of motor vehicles is abolished, the basis for calculation of goods vehicle taxes is to be harmonised for road and inland waterways and so are the provisions on duty-free import of fuel in vehicle tanks. Directives 68/297[57] and 85/347[58] standardise provisions concerning the duty-free entry of fuel in the tanks of 15.25

[53] [1960] O.J. Spec. Ed. 52.
[54] [1984] O.J. L335/4.
[55] [1974] O.J. L319/1.
[56] [1965] O.J. Spec. Ed. 88.
[57] [1968] O.J. L175/15.
[58] [1985] O.J. L183/22.

commercial vehicles. While Regulation 17/62[59] did not apply to transport, Regulation 1017/68[60] applied competition rules to transport by rail, road and inland waterway.

[59] [1962] O.J. Spec. Ed. 87.
[60] [1968] O.J. L175/1.

CHAPTER 16

# CONSUMER PROTECTION AND THE ENVIRONMENT

## CONSUMER PROTECTION

16.01 The concept of consumer protection is inherent in the principles of the Treaty. The preamble to the Treaty calls for balanced trade and free competition. The objectives of free movement of goods and a common market involve these two requirements and in turn involve measures of harmonisation of standards in manufacture, sale and use of goods, thus eliminating trade barriers and affording consumer protection, and of product liability legislation. Direct specific references to the consumer are in Article 39, where one of the objectives of the common agricultural policy shall be "... to ensure that supplies reach consumers at reasonable prices" and in Article 86, where an abuse of a dominant position may, in particular, consist in "... limiting production, markets or technical development to the prejudice of consumers". Article 129a, inserted by the Treaty on European Union states in terms that the Community shall contribute to the attainment of a high level of consumer protection.

16.02 Most of the legislation in the field of consumer protection is based on Article 100, which provides for the Council issuing directives for the approximation of such provisions laid down by law, regulation or administrative action in Member States which directly affect the establishment or functioning of the Common Market. Again, Article 235 is used in the field of consumer protection when it enables the Council to take appropriate measures if action by the Community should prove necessary to attain, in the course of the operation of the Common Market, one of the objectives of the Community, and the Treaty has not provided the necessary powers. In pursuance of these objectives the Council passed a resolution in 1975 on a preliminary programme for consumer protection and information policy. It was followed by a submission by the Commission of a draft directive and an explanatory memorandum in 1976. The memorandum points to the divergences in law of the Member States when it comes to the extent of liability for defective products and to the nature of compensation for the injured consumer. The divergences may distort competition, and the liability rules imposed on producers of defective products lead to differences in costs for the economies of the various Member States. The draft was finally turned into Directive 85/374[1] on the approximation of the laws, regulations and administrative provisions of the Member States concerning liability for defective products.

## The Product Liability Directive

16.03 This directive is far-reaching in laying down the principle of liability irrespective of fault: Article 1 provides that the producer shall be liable for damage caused by a defect in his product. The definition of "producer" in Article 3 is very wide. It includes the manufacturer of a finished product or of a component part and any person who presents himself as the producer. An importer is deemed to be a producer. When the producer of the product cannot be identified each supplier is treated as its producer; and the same applies in the case of imports if the product does not specify the identity of the importer. The provisions of Article 3 are wide enough to cover undertakings such as mail order firms which have products manufactured by unspecified undertakings and sell them under their own name. Article 2 defines "product" as meaning all moveables, even though incorporated into another moveable or into an immoveable, with the exception of primary agricultural products and game. Product includes electricity. Article 6 of the directive, in defining a defective product, states that a product shall not be considered defective for the sole reason that a better product is subsequently put into circulation. Article 7 provides that the producer shall not be liable as a result of the directive if he proves that he did not put the product into circulation or that having regard to the circumstances it is probable that the defect which caused the damage did not exist at the time when the product was put into circulation by him, or that this defect came into being afterwards. It is a defence if the producer proves that the state of scientific and technical knowledge at the time when he put the product into circulation was not such as to enable the existence of the defect to be discovered. Each Member State may by way of derogation legislate to make the producer liable even if he is covered by this exception (Article 15). The new legislation derogating from Article 7 is subject to the Commun-

[1] [1985] O.J. L210/29.

ity stand-still procedure in order, as the recitals to the directive state, "to raise if possible the level of protection in a uniform manner throughout the Community". The rights of an injured party on grounds other than that provided for in the directive remain unaffected by the directive, which in the recitals refers to the special liability system and the effective protection of consumers in the sector of pharmaceutical products already obtained in a Member State under a special liability system. The directive does not apply to injury or damage arising from nuclear accidents and covered by international conventions ratified by the Member States. The recitals suggest that liability for nuclear injury or damage is already covered by adequate special rules in all Member States. Proceedings for the recovery of damages under the directive are subject to a limitation period of three years. The liability of the producer arising from the directive may not in relation to the injured person be limited or excluded by a provision limiting his liability or exempting him from the liability. The Product Liability Directive is complemented by Directive 92/59[2] on general product safety, to be implemented by June 29, 1994. The directive requires manufacturers to market only products which are safe under normal conditions, to inform consumers of all the possible risks connected with their use and to take steps that consumers are informed of dangers associated with the use of the product.

The directive is implemented in the United Kingdom by the Consumer Protection Act 1987. Part I of the Act under the heading "Product Liability" puts into effect the provisions of the directive and in fact section 1(1) states that "this part shall have effect for the purpose of making such provision as is necessary in order to comply with the Product Liability Directive and shall be construed accordingly." Section 2 re-enacts the provisions of the directive as to the persons liable for the damage and who are deemed to be producers, but goes further than the directive in setting out the steps which may be necessary for the consumer to take in order to identify the person liable. Again section 3, while following the directive, is more explicit in the definition of defect. Section 5 provides that no damages shall be awarded in respect of any loss or damage to property if the amount which would fall to be awarded does not exceed £275. **16.04**

## Misleading advertising

Another aspect of the protection of consumers is seen in Directive 84/450[3] on misleading advertising. Advertising can nowadays be transmit- **16.05**

[2] [1992] O.J. L228/24.
[3] [1984] O.J. L250/17.

ted across frontiers and Community-wide legislation was deemed necessary to protect consumers or trade competitors. The directive defines misleading advertising as any advertising which in any way, including its presentation, deceives or is likely to deceive the persons to whom it is addressed or whom it reaches and which, by reason of its deceptive nature, is likely to affect their economic behaviour or which injures or is likely to injure a competitor. The directive goes into the details to be considered when determining whether an advertisement is misleading. Member States must ensure that adequate and effective means exist for the control of misleading advertising, including ultimate recourse to the courts. In Case C–373/90, *Procureur de la République v. X*[4] the Court of Justice held that the directive must be interpreted as meaning that it does not preclude vehicles from being advertised as new, less expensive and guaranteed by the manufacturer when the vehicles concerned are registered solely for the purpose of importation, have never been on the road and are sold at a lower price because they are equipped with fewer accessories. In the United Kingdom the directive is implemented by the functioning of the Advertising Standards Authority and by enforcement of the Trade Descriptions Act 1968. Sections 20 to 26 of the Consumer Protection Act 1987 on misleading price indications have now replaced section 11 of the Trade Descriptions Act 1968.

## Doorstep selling

**16.06** Directive 85/577[5] deals with the element of surprise inherent in selling away from the business premises (doorstep selling); the consumer is now entitled to have the contract of sale reconsidered. The directive applies to contracts which are concluded during a visit by a trader where the visit does not take place at the express request of the consumer. Traders are required to give consumers written notice of their right of cancellation. This directive was considered by the Court of Justice in Case 382/87, *Buet v. Ministère Public*,[6] when it referred to the preamble of the directive which recognised that Member States might adopt or maintain in force a total or partial ban on concluding contracts outside commercial establishments, and ruled that the application to imported products of a prohibition against door-to-door selling of educational material was not incompatible with Article 30 of the Treaty. The directive was further considered by the Court in Case C–361/89, *Da Pinto*[7] with the ruling that a trader canvassed with a view to the conclusion of an advertising con-

[4] Not yet reported.
[5] [1985] O.J. L372/31.
[6] [1989] E.C.R. 1235, [1993] 3 C.M.L.R. 659.
[7] [1991] I E.C.R. 1189, [1993] 1 C.M.L.R. 399.

tract concerning the sale of his business is not to be regarded as a consumer protected by Directive 85/577; it was also held that this directive does not preclude national legislation on canvassing from extending the protection which it affords to cover traders acting with a view to the sale of their business. Directive 87/102[8] is concerned with consumer credit.[9]

## Package Travel Directive

16.07 Directive 90/314[10] on package travel, package holidays and package tours relates to such packages sold or offered for sale in the Community. Any desciptive matter must not contain any misleading information, brochures are to indicate clearly information regarding specified matters and certain specified information must be given by the retailer or organiser. The contract must contain minimum elements given in the annex to the directive. In the United Kingdom the directive is implemented by the Package Travel, Package Holidays and Package Tours Regulations 1992.[11]

## Unfair Contracts Terms Directive

16.08 Directive 93/13[12] on unfair terms in consumer contracts establishes the principle that consumers are not bound by unfair terms in consumer contracts. The directive is primarily concerned with non-negotiated terms: a non-negotiated clause is to be regarded as unfair where, in spite of the requirements of good faith, it creates a significant imbalance, to the detriment of the consumer, between the rights and obligations of the parties to the contract, the annex to the directive giving examples of terms which may be declared unfair.

## Harmonisation of provisions on health and safety

16.09 The concept of a common market and consumer protection in the Community involves not only the right to protection of economic interests but also the right to protection of health and safety. The right is clearly expressed by the version of Article 129 inserted by the Treaty on European Union. This involves the principle that products (whether manufactured or not) and services in the Community must not constitute a risk

[8] [1987] O.J. L42/48.
[9] See Chapter 12, para. 12.24.
[10] [1990] O.J. L158/59.
[11] S.I. 1992 No. 3288.
[12] [1993] O.J. L95/29.

to health and safety. As a result the Community has adopted a very large number of measures harmonising standards in manufactured goods and eliminating technical barriers to trade. An example of this approach is Community legislation in relation to motor vehicles, represented by a large number of directives covering minute details connected with the safety of the vehicle and creating a Community-type approval procedure. Other examples of this approach are directives harmonising the laws on foodstuffs, *e.g.* dealing with authorised colouring matters, and preservatives, and on medical products, on labelling of paints and on cosmetics. There are many more covering all aspects of safety of consumer products.[13] The common internal market, public health and interests of an individual consumer are inextricably tied up as a reason and basis for the Community legislation. The Community approach is indicated by Decision 84/133[14] providing for exchange of information relating to dangers arising out of use of consumer products. This concept of consumer protection in its widest sense is indicated by the subjects of Community legislation. It falls under the category of health and safety or the internal market. The concept of health and safety is extended to working conditions and, following Directive 89/391[15] on the introduction of measures to encourage improvements in the safety and health of workers at work, Directive 93/104[16] lays down minimum safety and health requirements for the organisation of working time, rest periods, nighttime work and the description of a night worker. The principle of the internal market has called for legislation on motor vehicles, agriculture and forestry, tractors, metrology (measurement), electrical materials, foodstuffs, proprietary medicinal products, cosmetics, dangerous substances, fertilisers and other subjects which call for approximation of laws in the Community. In the field of agriculture there is a large quantity of detailed legislation dealing with approximation of laws in relation to health measures. [17] An example of the approach of the Community is Directive 93/43[18] on the hygiene of foodstuffs and Directives 89/393[19] and 93/44[20] concerned with machinery used for lifting persons. A list of basic legislative instruments in the fields other than those in Chapter 6 is annexed at the end of this chapter.

[13] See the annex to this chapter.
[14] [1984] O.J. L70/16.
[15] [1989] O.J. L183/1.
[16] [1993] O.J. L307/18.
[17] See Chapter 6.
[18] [1993] O.J. L175/1.
[19] [1989] O.J. L183/9.
[20] [1993] O.J. L175/12.

## PROTECTING THE ENVIRONMENT

16.10 The protection of human life and the long-term availability of all the resources which determine the quality of life were considered as part of the objectives of the Community's environment policy (Council Resolution in 1983). Before 1987 the legislation in matters concerning the environment was under the umbrella of the general aims of the Treaty and specifically within the realm of consumer protection. The Single European Act of 1986 introduced a new title to the Treaty, (Title VII), the title on the environment, containing three new articles. Article 130r states that the objectives of action by the Community are to preserve, protect and improve the quality of the environment, to contribute towards protecting human health and to ensure a prudent and rational utilisation of natural resources. Article 130s empowers the Council to take action and Article 130t does not exclude more stringent protective measures compatible with the Treaty being maintained or introduced by any Member State. In Case 302/86, *Commission v. Denmark*,[21] the Court observed that it had already held that environmental protection is "one of the Community's essential objectives" which as such may justify certain limitations to the principle of free movement of goods. In the particular circumstances of the case the Danish system of returnable containers was found in its operation to be disproportionate to the objective pursued, and the restriction to 3000 hl per producer per annum of beer and soft drinks on imports in non-approved containers to be contrary to Article 30 of the Treaty.

16.11 The Treaty on European Union followed in the footsteps of the Single European Act of 1986 and introduced a new version of Articles 130r, 130s and 130t. New Article 130r contains a significant extension of the list of objectives of Community policy by listing the promotion of measures at international level to deal with regional or world-wide enviromental problems. Even before the amending legislation, conservation of wild species was considered another aspect of the protection of the environment. Directive 79/409[22] introduces special conservation measures to ensure the survival and reproduction of wild birds. Sale and transport for sale of live or dead wild birds are prohibited. Certain activities in connection with wild birds legally killed or captured may be authorized and there are derogations for reason of public health, public safety, air safety, protection of flora and fauna and research. The Convention on International Trade in Endangered Species of Wild Fauna and Flora (concluded in Washington in 1973) was applied throughout the Com-

[21] [1988] E.C.R. 4607, [1989] 1 C.M.L.R. 619.
[22] [1979] O.J. L103/1.

munity by Regulation 3626/82,[23] last amended by Regulation 1970/92.[24] The regulation lists in elaborate appendices every kind of endangered species and it became the subject of Case 182/89, *Commission of European Communities v. French Republic*,[25] where the Court considered the interpretation of the regulation in relation to the possibility of issue of import permits for the importation of feline skins of the *felis geoffroyi* and *felis wiedii* species from Bolivia. Wild life is further protected by Directive 92/43.[26]

## Water pollution

16.12 Most of the existing appropriate legislation in relation to the environment was enacted in the field dealing with public health and a good example is water. Drinking water was the concern of Directive 75/440[27] and Directive 80/778.[28] This last directive was the subject of Case 228/87, *Criminal proceedings against persons unknown*,[29] when the Court held that the authorisation to exceed the maximum admissible concentrations of substances shown in Annex I to the directive relating to the quality of water intended for human consumption, as provided by Article 10 of that directive, must be granted only in the event of an emergency in which national authorities suddenly have to cope with difficulties in connection with the supply of water for human consumption; further, such authorisation must be limited to the time normally necessary in order to restore the quality of water affected, must not pose any unacceptable risk to public health and may be granted only if the supply of water for human consumption cannot be maintained in any other way. Again, the Court decided in Case C–337/89, *Commission v. United Kingdom*,[30] that United Kingdom national legislation dealing with water intended for human consumption was not in conformity with the directive. Directive 91/271,[31] the Urban Waste Water Treatment Directive, deals with the collection, treatment and discharge of urban waste water and the treatment and discharge of waste water from certain industrial sectors. It states that, as a general rule, waste water entering the collecting system must be subjected to secondary treatment before being discharged. The stringency

[23] [1982] O.J. L384/1.
[24] [1992] O.J. L201/1.
[25] [1990] I E.C.R. 4337.
[26] [1992] O.J. L206/7.
[27] [1975] O.J. L194/26.
[28] [1980] O.J. L229/11.
[29] [1988] E.C.R. 5099, [1990] 1 C.M.L.R. 716.
[30] Not yet reported.
[31] [1991] O.J. L135/40.

of the treatment depends upon the population of the area into which the waste water is discharged. Fish and shellfish breeding water became the subject of Directive 79/923.[32] Directive 76/160[33] concerns the quality of bathing water and Directive 80/68,[34] the pollution of groundwater. Marine pollution became the subject of Directive 78/176[35] which dealt with pollution caused by waste from the titanium dioxide industry, in addition to a resolution dealing with oil pollution.

## Atmospheric pollution

Air pollution was dealt with by several decisions providing for the exchange of information and data regarding air pollution, and by Directive 84/360,[36] which dealt with air pollution from industrial plants. It listed the most important polluting substances and in accordance with it Directive 88/609[37] established limits of emissions from large combustion plants. Directive 89/369[38] deals with the prevention of air pollution from new municipal waste incinerating plants. Directive 89/427,[39] amending Directive 80/779,[40] prescribes air quality limit values and guide values for sulphur dioxide and suspended particulates. A significant step in this context is Directive 85/210,[41] amended by Directive 87/416,[42] under which Member States must ensure that unleaded petrol is available and distributed from October 1, 1989. This was followed by Directive 88/77,[43] dealing with measures to be taken against the emission of gaseous pollutants from diesel engines in vehicles and Directive 88/76[44] concerned with air pollution by gases from engines in motor vehicles. Measures to be taken against air pollution by emissions from motor vehicles were further considered by Directive 93/59.[45] A far-reaching measure to deal with car pollution is Directive 89/458[46] which after referring to many previous instruments limiting emissions of carbon monoxide and unburnt hydrocarbon, prescribes new standards for emissions from cars 16.13

[32] [1979] O.J. L281/48.
[33] [1976] O.J. L31/1.
[34] [1980] O.J. L20/43.
[35] [1978] O.J. L54/19.
[36] [1984] O.J. L188/20.
[37] [1988] O.J. L336/1.
[38] [1989] O.J. L163/32.
[39] [1989] O.J. L201/53.
[40] [1980] O.J. L229/30.
[41] [1985] O.J. L96/25.
[42] [1987] O.J. L225/33.
[43] [1988] O.J. L36/33.
[44] [1988] O.J. L36/1.
[45] [1993] O.J. L186/21.
[46] [1989] O.J. L226/1.

below 1.4 litres cylinder capacity. These standards apply to new models from July 1, 1992 and all new cars after December 31, 1992. Sulphur content of gas oil was prescribed by Directive 75/716[47] with new levels introduced by Directive 87/219.[48] Decision 93/389[49] deals with monitoring mechanism of $CO_2$ and other greenhouse gas emissions.

## Disposal of waste

16.14 Disposal of waste is another of the subjects which fall within the ambit of public health and other aspects of the environment. Directive 75/442[50] dealt with waste generally, its objectives being specified as being in the area of the protection of health and the environment. The extent of rights conferred by this directive upon individuals was considered by the Court of Justice in Case 380/87, *Enichem Base v. Commune di Cinisella Balsamo*,[51] and further explained in Case C–236/92, *Comitato di Coordinamento per la Defesa della Cava v. Regione Lombardia*[52] where the Court ruled that Article 4 of the directive did not confer individual rights that national courts must safeguard. Directive 75/439[53] dealt with waste oils (which may affect water, soil and air), Directive 76/403[54] with disposal of polychlorinated biphenyls and polychlorinated terphenyls, and Directive 78/319[55] with toxic and dangerous waste. The concept of waste within the meaning of Directives 75/442 and 78/319 was the subject of a ruling by the Court of Justice in Joined Cases C 206-207/88, *Vessoso and Zanetti*[56]. Waste was not to be understood as excluding substances or other objects which are capable of economic reutilisation. The concept does not presume that the holder disposing of the substance or object intends to exclude all economic re-utilisation of the substance or of the object by others. The Court further stated in Case C–359/88, *Zanetti*,[57] that national legislation excluding a substance or object capable of economic re-utilisation is not compatible with the two directives. Directive 84/631[58] introduces the supervision and control of the trans-frontier shipment of hazardous waste, being amended in detail by Commission Directive 87/112.[59] In

47 [1975] O.J. L207/22.
48 [1987] O.J. L91/19.
49 [1993] O.J. L167/31.
50 [1975] O.J. L194/39.
51 [1989] E.C.R. 2491, [1991] 1 C.M.L.R. 313.
52 Not yet reported.
53 [1975] O.J. L194/23.
54 [1976] O.J. L108/41.
55 [1978] O.J. L84/43.
56 [1990] I E.C.R. 1461.
57 [1990] I E.C.R. 1509.
58 [1984] O.J. L326/31.
59 [1987] O.J. L48/31.

Case C–2/90, *Commission v. Kingdom of Belgium,*[60] the Court held that by the prohibition of the disposal of waste originating in another Member State, Belgium was in breach of Directive 84/631. Regulation 1734/88[61] is concerned with the export from and import into the Community of certain dangerous chemicals. Directive 89/428[62] has the purpose of harmonising the programmes for the reduction and eventual elimination of pollution caused by waste from the titanium dioxide industry. The Community joined (Decision 93/98[63]) the Basel Convention on the control of transboundary movements of hazardous wastes and their disposal. Regulation 259/93[64] on the supervision and control of the shipment of waste (within, in and out of the Community) establishes rules to control such movements, giving effect to the Basel Convention.

## Noise

Noise is another subject of Community legislation. As early as 1970 the Council passed Directive 70/157[65] relating to the sound levels and the exhaust systems of motor vehicles, and Directive 78/1015[66] relating similarly to motorcycles. Directive 80/51[67] covers the noise of subsonic aircraft and Directive 84/538[68] the noise of lawnmowers. Directive 86/549[69] is concerned with the airborne noise of household appliances and there is legislation limiting noise of specific items of industrial and road-making machinery. **16.15**

[60] [1992] I E.C.R. 4431, [1993] 1 C.M.L.R. 365.
[61] [1988] O.J. L155/2.
[62] [1989] O.J. L201/56.
[63] [1993] O.J. L39/1.
[64] [1993] O.J. L30/1.
[65] [1970] O.J. L42/16.
[66] [1978] O.J. L349/21.
[67] [1980] O.J. L18/26.
[68] [1984] O.J. L300/171.
[69] [1986] O.J. L344/24.

ANNEX TO CHAPTER 16

# LIST OF PRINCIPAL E.C. DIRECTIVES, INTERNAL MARKET: APPROXIMATION OF LAWS

M indicates an amending instrument
C indicates a supplementary instrument

## GENERAL PROGRAMME

Directive 83/189 on procedure for the provision of information in the field of technical standards and regulations [1983] O.J. L109/8
M by Directive 88/182 [1988] O.J. L81/75

## MOTOR VEHICLES

Directive 70/156 on type-approval of motor vehicles and their trailers [1970] O.J. L 42/1
M by Directive 80/1267 [1980] O.J. L375/34
M by Directive 87/358 [1987] O.J. L192/51
C by Directive 87/403 [1987] O.J. L220/44
M by Directive 92/53 [1992] O.J. L225/1
M by Directive 93/81 [1993] O.J. L264/49

Directive 70/157 on permissible sound levels and exhaust systems of motor vehicles [1970] O.J. L42/16

M by Directive 84/424 [1984] O.J. L238/31
M by Directive 89/491 [1989] O.J. L238/43
M by Directive 92/97 [1992] O.J. L371/1

Directive 70/220 on measures to be taken against air pollution by gases from positive-ignition engines of motor vehicles [1970] O.J. L76/1
M by Directive 83/351 [1983] O.J. L197/1
M by Directive 88/76 [1988] O.J. L36/1
M by Directive 88/436 [1988] O.J. L214/1
M by Directive 89/458 [1989] O.J. L226/1
M by Directive 89/491 [1989] O.J. L238/43
M by Directive 91/441 [1991] O.J. L242/1
M by Directive 93/59 [1993] O.J. L186/21

Directive 70/221 on liquid fuel tanks and rear protective devices for motor vehicles and their trailers [1970] O.J. L76/23
M by Directive 79/490 [1979] O.J. L128/22

Directive 70/222 on the space for mounting and fixing of rear registration plates on motor vehicles and their trailers [1970] O.J. L76/25

Directive 70/311 on steering equipment for motor vehicles and their trailers [1970] O.J. L133/10
M by Directive 92/62 [1992] O.J. L199/33

Directive 70/387 on the doors of motor vehicles and their trailers [1970] O.J. L176/5

Directive 70/388 on audible warning devices for motor vehicles [1970] O.J. L176/12
M by Decision 73/101(01) [1973] O.J. L2/1
M by Directive 87/354 [1987] O.J. L192/43

Directive 71/127 on rear-view mirrors of motor vehicles [1971] O.J. L68/1
M by Directive 86/562 [1986] O.J. L327/49
M by Directive 87/354 [1987] O.J. L192/43
M by Directive 88/321 [1988] O.J. L147/77

Directive 71/320 on braking devices of certain categories of motor vehicles and of their trailers [1971] O.J. L202/37
M by Directive 85/647 [1985] O.J L380/1
M by Directive 88/194 [1988] O.J. L92/47
M by Directive 91/422 [1991] O.J. L233/21

Directive 72/245 on suppression of radio interference produced by spark-ignition engines fitted to motor vehicles [1972] O.J. L152/15
M by Directive 89/491 [1989] O.J. L238/43

Directive 72/306 on measures to be taken against the emission of pollutants from diesel engines for use in vehicles [1972] O.J. L190/1
M by Directive 89/491 [1989] O.J. L238/43

Directive 74/60 on interior fittings of motor vehicles (interior parts of the passenger compartment other than the interior rear-view mirrors, layout of controls, the roof or sliding roof, the backrest and rear part of the seats) [1984] O.J. L38/2
M by Directive 78/632 [1978] O.J. L206/26

Directive 74/61 on devices to prevent the unauthorised use of motor vehicles [1974] O.J. L38/22

Directive 74/297 on the interior fittings of motor vehicles (the behaviour of the steering mechanism in the event of an impact) [1974] O.J. L165/16
M by Directive 91/662 [1991] O.J. L366/1

Directive 74/408 on the interior fittings of motor vehicles (strength of seats and of their anchorages) [1974] O.J. L221/1
M by Directive 81/577 [1981] O.J. L209/34

Directive 74/483 on the external projections of motor vehicles [1974] O.J. L266/4
M by Directive 79/488 [1979] O.J. L428/1

Directive 75/443 on the reverse and speedometer equipment of motor vehicles [1975] O.J. L196/1

Directive 76/114 on statutory plates and inscriptions for motor vehicles and their trailers, and their position and method of attachment [1976] O.J. L24/1
M by Directive 78/507 [1978] O.J. L155/31

Directive 76/115 on anchorage for motor vehicle safety belts [1976] O.J. L 24/6
M by Directive 81/575 [1981] O.J. L209/30
M by Directive 82/318 [1982] O.J. L139/9
M by Directive 90/629 [1990] O.J. L341/14

Directive 76/756 on the installation of lighting and light-signalling devices on motor vehicles and their, trailers [1976] O.J. L262/1

M by Directive 80/233 [1980] O.J. L51/8
M by Directive 82/244 [1982] O.J. L109/31
M by Directive 89/278 [1989] O.J. L109/38
M by Directive 91/663 [1991] O.J. L366/17

Directive 76/757 on reflex reflectors for motor vehicles and their trailers [1976] O.J. L262/32

Directive 76/758 on end-outline marker lights, front position (side) lights, rear position (side) lights and stop lights for motor vehicles and their trailers [1976] O.J. L262/54
M by Directive 89/516 [1989] O.J. L265/1

Directive 76/759 on direction indicator lights for motor vehicles and their trailers [1976] O.J. L262/71
M by Directive 89/277 [1989] O.J. L109/25

Directive 76/760 on rear registration plate lights for motor vehicles and their trailers [1976] O.J. L262/85

Directive 76/761 on motor-vehicle headlamps which function as main-beam and/or dipped-beam headlights, and on incandescent electric filament lamps for such headlamps [1976] O.J. L262/96

Directive 76/762 on front fog lamps for motor vehicles and filament lamps for such lamps [1976] O.J. L262/122

Directive 77/143 on roadworthiness tests for motor vehicles and their trailers [1977] O.J. L47/47
M by Directive 88/449 [1988] O.J. L222/10
M by Directive 91/225 [1991] O.J. L103/3
M by Directive 91/328 [1991] O.J. L178/29
M by Directive 92/54 [1992] O.J. L225/63
M by Directive 92/55 [1992] O.J. L225/68

Directive 77/389 on motor-vehicle towing devices [1977] O.J. L145/41

Directive 77/538 on rear fog lamps for motor vehicles and their trailers [1977] O.J. L220/60
M by Directive 79/138 [1979] O.J. L39/3
M by Directive 89/518 [1989] O.J. L265/24

Directive 77/539 on reversing lights for motor vehicles and their trailers [1977] O.J. L220/72

Directive 77/540 on parking lights for motor vehicles [1977] O.J. L220/83

Directive 77/541 on safety belts and restraint systems of motor vehicles [1977] O.J. L220/95
M by Directive 81/576 [1981] O.J. L209/32
M by Directive 82/319 [1982] O.J. L139/17
M by Directive 90/628 [1990] O.J. L341/1

Directive 77/649 on the field of vision of motor-vehicle drivers [1977] O.J. L267/1
M by Directive 81/643 [1981] O.J. L231/41
M by Directive 88/366 [1988] O.J. L181/40
M by Directive 90/630 [1990] O.J. L341/20

Directive 78/316 on the interior fittings of motor vehicles (identification of controls, telltales and indicators) [1978] O.J. L81/3
M by Directive 93/91 [1993] O.J. L284/25

Directive 78/317 on defrosting and demisting systems for the glazed surfaces of motor vehicles [1978] O.J. L81/27

Directive 78/318 on the windscreen wiper and washer systems of motor vehicles [1978] O.J. L81/49

Directive 78/548 on heating systems for the passenger compartment of motor vehicles [1978] O.J. L168/40

Directive 78/549 on the wheel guards of motor vehicles [1978] O.J. L168/45

Directive 78/932 on head restraints on the seats of motor vehicles [1978] O.J. L325/1

Directive 78/1015 on permissible sound levels and exhaust systems of motorcycles [1978] O.J. L349/21
M by Directive 87/56 [1987] O.J. L24/42
M by Directive 89/235 [1988] O.J. L98/1

Directive 79/490 on the liquid fuel tanks and rear underrun protection of motor vehicles and their trailers [1979] O.J. L128/22
M by Directive 81/333 [1981] O.J. L131/4

Directive 80/780 on rear-view mirrors for two-wheeled motor vehicles with or without a sidecar and on their fitting to such vehicles [1980] O.J. L229/49

M by Directive 80/1272 [1980] O.J. L375/73

Directive 80/1268 on the fuel consumption of motor vehicles [1980] O.J. L375/36
M by Directive 89/491 [1989] O.J. L238/43

Directive 80/1269 on the engine power of motor vehicles [1980] O.J. L375/46
M by Directive 88/195 [1988] O.J. L92/50
M by Directive 89/491 [1989] O.J. L238/43

Directive 81/643 on the field of vision of motor vehicle drivers (amending 77/649/EEC) [1981] O.J. L231/41

Directive 82/244 on the installation of lighting and light-signalling devices on motor vehicles and their trailers (amending 76/756/EEC) [1982] O.J. L109/31

Directive 82/318 on anchorages for motor vehicle safety belts (amending 76/115/EEC) [1982] O.J. L139/9

Directive 82/319 on safety belts and restraint systems of motor vehicles (amending 77/541/EEC) [1982] O.J. L139/17

Directive 84/8 on the installation of lighting and light-signalling devices on motor vehicles and their trailers (amending 76/756/EEC) [1984] O.J. L9/24

Directive 85/3 on the weights, dimensions and certain other characteristics of certain road vehicles [1985] O.J. L2/14
M by Directive 86/360 [1986] O.J. L217/19
M by Directive 88/218 [1988] O.J. L98/48
M by Directive 89/338 [1989] O.J. L142/3
M by Directive 89/460 [1989] O.J. L226/5
M by Directive 89/461 [1989] O.J. L226/7
M by Directive 91/60 [1991] O.J. L37/37
M by Directive 92/7 [1992] O.J. L57/29

Directive 85/647 on the braking devices of certain categories of motor vehicles and their trailers (amending 71/320/EEC) [1985] O.J. L380/1

Directive 86/364 on proof of compliance with Directive 85/3/EEC on the weights, dimensions and certain other technical characteristics of certain road vehicles [1986] O.J. L221/48

Directive 88/77 on measures to be taken against the emission of gaseous pollutants from diesel engines for use in vehicles [1988] O.J. L36/33

Directive 89/297 on the approximation of the laws of the Member States relating to the lateral protection (side guards) of certain motor vehicles and their trailers [1989] O.J. L124/1

Directive 89/459 on the approximation of the laws of the Member States relating to the tread depth of tyres of certain categories of motor vehicles and their trailers [1989] O.J. L226/4

Directive 90/628 adapting to technical progress Council Directive 77/541 on the approximation of the laws of the Member States relating to safety belts and restraint systems of motor vehicles [1990] O.J. L341/1

Directive 90/629 adapting to technical progress Council Directive 76/115 on the approximation of the laws of the Member States relating to anchorages for motor vehicle safety belts [1990] O.J. L341/14

Directive 90/630 adapting to technical progress Council Directive 77/649 on the approximation of the laws of the Member States relating to the field of vision of motor vehicle drivers [1990] O.J. L341/20

Directive 91/226 on the approximation of the laws of the Member States relating to the spray-suppression systems of certain categories of motor vehicles and their trailers [1991] O.J. L103/5

Directive 91/422 adapting to technical progress Council Directive 71/320 on the approximation of the laws of the Member States relating to the braking devices of certain categories of motor vehicles and their trailers [1991] O.J. L233/21

Directive 91/441 amending Directive 70/220 on the approximation of the laws of the Member States relating to measures to be taken against air pollution by emissions from motor vehicles [1991] O.J. L242/1

Directive 91/662 adapting to technical progress Council Directive 74/297 in respect of the behaviour of the steering wheel and column in an impact [1991] O.J. L366/1

Directive 91/663 adapting to technical progress Council Directive 76/756 relating to the installation of lighting and light-signalling devices on motor vehicles and their trailers [1991] O.J. L366/17

Directive 92/6 on the installation and use of speed limitation devices for certain categories of motor vehicles in the Community [1992] O.J. L57/27

Directive 92/21 on the masses and dimensions of motor vehicles of category M [1992] O.J. L129/1

Directive 92/22 on safety glazing and glazing materials on motor vehicles and their trailers [1992] O.J. L129/11

Directive 92/23 relating to tyres for motor vehicles and their trailers and to their fitting [1992] O.J. L129/95

Directive 92/24 relating to speed limitation devices or similar speed limitation on-board systems of certain categories of motor vehicles [1992] O.J. L129/154

Directive 92/61 relating to the type-approval of two or three-wheel motor vehicles [1992] O.J. L225/72

Directive 92/62 adapting to technical progress Council Directive 70/311 relating to steering equipment for motor vehicles and their trailers [1992] O.J. L199/33

Directive 92/97 amending Directive 70/157 on the approximation of the laws of the Member States relating to the permissible sound level and the exhaust system of motor vehicles [1992] O.J. L371/1

Directive 92/114 relating to the external projections forward of the cab's rear panel of motor vehicles of category N [1992] O.J. L409/17

Directive 93/14 on the braking of two or three-wheel motor vehicles [1993] O.J. L121/1

Directive 93/29 on the identification of controls, tell-tales and indicators for two- or three-wheel motor vehicles [1993] O.J. L188/1

Directive 93/30 on audible warning devices for two- or three-wheel motor vehicles [1993] O.J. L188/11

Directive 93/31 on stands for two-wheel motor vehicles [1993] O.J. L188/19

Directive 93/32 on passenger hand-holds on two-wheel motor vehicles [1993] O.J. L188/28

Directive 93/33 on protective devices intended to prevent the unauthorised use of two- or three-wheel motor vehicles [1993] O.J. L188/32

Directive 93/34 on statutory markings for two- or three-wheel motor vehicles [1993] O.J. L188/38

Directive 93/91 adapting to technical progress Council Directive 78/316 relating to the interior fittings of motor vehicles (identification of controls, tell-tales and indicators) [1993] O.J. L284/25

## AGRICULTURAL AND FORESTRY TRACTORS

Directive 74/150 on the type-approval of wheeled agricultural or forestry tractors [1974] O.J. L84/10
M by Directive 82/890 [1982] O.J. L378/45
M by Directive 88/297 [1988] O.J. L126/52

Directive 74/151 on certain parts and characteristics of wheeled agricultural or forestry tractors [1974] O.J. L84/25
M by Directive 82/890 [1982] O.J. L378/45
M by Directive 88/410 [1988] O.J. L200/27

Directive 74/346 on rear-view mirrors for wheeled agricultural or forestry tractors [1974] O.J. L191/1
M by Directive 82/890 [1982] O.J. L378/45

Directive 86/415 on the installation, location, operation and identification of the controls of wheeled agricultural or forestry tractors [1986] O.J. L240/1

Directive 87/402 on roll-over protection structures mounted in front of the driver's seat on narrow-track wheeled agricultural and forestry tractors [1987] O.J. L220/1
M by Directive 89/681 [1989] O.J. L398/27

Directive 89/173 on the approximation of the laws of the Member States relating to certain components and characteristics of wheeled agricultural or forestry tractors [1989] O.J. L67/1

## METROLOGY

Directive 71/316 on common provisions for measuring instruments and methods of metrological control [1971] O.J. L202/1
M by Directive 72/427 [1972] O.J. L291/156

M by Directive 83/575 [1983] O.J. L332/43
M by Directive 87/355 [1987] O.J. L192/46
M by Directive 88/665 [1988] O.J. L382/42

Directive 71/317 on 5 to 50 kg medium accuracy rectangular bar weights and 1 to 10 kg medium accuracy cylindrical weights [1971] O.J. L202/14

Directive 71/318 on gas volume meters [1971] O.J. L202/21
M by Directive 78/365 [1978] O.J. L104/26
M by Directive 82/623 [1983] O.J. L252/5

Directive 71/319 on meters for liquids other than water [1971] O.J. L202/32

Directive 71/347 on measuring the standard mass per storage volume of grain [1971] O.J. L239/1

Directive 71/348 on ancillary equipment for meters for liquids other than water [1971] O.J. L239/9

Directive 71/349 on the calibration of the tanks of vessels [1971] O.J. L239/15

Directive 73/362 on material measures of length [1973] O.J. L335/56
M by Directive 78/629 [1978] O.J. L206/8
M by Directive 85/146 [1985] O.J. L54/29

Directive 74/148 on weights of from 1 mg to 50 kg of above-medium accuracy [1974] O.J. L84/3

Directive 75/33 on cold-water meters [1975] O.J. L14/1

Directive 75/107 on bottles used as measuring containers [1975] O.J. L42/14

Directive 75/410 on continuous totalling weighing machines [1975] O.J. L183/25

Directive 76/764 on clinical mercury-in-glass maximum-reading thermometers [1976] O.J. L262/139
M by Directive 83/128 [1983] O.J. L91/29
M by Directive 84/414 [1984] O.J. L228/25
M by Directive 93/42 [1993] L169/1

Directive 76/765 on alcoholometers and alcohol hydrometers [1976] O.J. L262/143

M by Directive 82/624 [1982] O.J. L252/8

Directive 76/766 on alcohol tables [1976] O.J. L262/149

Directive 76/891 on electrical energy meters [1976] O.J. L336/30
M by Directive 82/621 [1982] O.J. L252/1

Recommendation 76/223 on units of measurement referred to in patent conventions [1976] O.J. L43/22

Directive 77/95 on taximeters [1977] O.J. L26/59

Directive 77/313 on measuring systems for liquids other than water [1977] O.J. L105/18
M by Directive 82/625 [1982] O.J. L252/10

Directive 78/1031 on automatic check-weighing and weight-grading machines [1978] O.J. L364/1

Directive 79/830 on hot-water meters [1979] O.J. L 259/1

Directive 80/181 on units of measurement, and on repeal of 71/354 [1980] O.J. L39/40
M by Directive 85/1 [1985] O.J. L2/11
M by Directive 89/617 [1989] O.J. L357/28

Directive 86/217 on tyre pressure gauges for motor vehicles [1986] O.J. L152/48

Directive 90/384 on non-automatic weighting instruments [1990] O.J. L189/1
M by Directive 93/68 [1993] O.J. L220/1

## ELECTRICAL EQUIPMENT

Directive 73/23 on electrical equipment designed for use within certain voltage limits [1973] O.J. L77/29
M by Directive 93/68 [1993] O.J. L220/1

Directive 76/117 on electrical equipment for use in potentially explosive atmospheres [1976] O.J. L24/45

Directive 79/196 on electrical equipment for use in potentially explosive atmospheres employing certain types of protection [1979] O.J. L43/20

M by Directive 88/571 [1988] O.J. L311/46
M by Directive 88/665 [1988] O.J. L382/42
M by Directive 90/487 [1990] O.J. L270/23

Directive 82/130 on electrical equipment for use in potentially explosive atmospheres in mines susceptible to firedamp [1982] O.J. L59/10
M by Directive 88/35 [1988] O.J. L20/28
M by Directive 91/269 [1991] O.J. L134/51

Recommendation 82/490 on the certificates provided for in Directive 76/117/EEC on electrical equipment for use in potentially explosive atmospheres [1982] O.J. L218/27

Directive 83/447 adopting measures provided for in Art. 3(3) of Directive 76/889/EEC on radio interference caused by electrical household appliances, portable tools and similar equipment, and of Directive 76/890/EEC on the suppression of radio interference with regard to fluorescent lighting fitments fitted with starters [1983] O.J. L247/10

Directive 84/539 on electro-medical equipment used in human or veterinary medicine [1984] O.J. L300/179
M by Directive 93/42 [1993] O.J. L169/1

Directive 88/35 amending 82/130 on electrical equipment for use in potentially explosive atmospheres in mines susceptible to firedamp [1988] O.J. L20/28

Recommendation 88/41 on the involvement and improvement of consumer participation in standardisation [1988] O.J. L23/26

Directive 90/385 on active implantable medical devices [1990] O.J. L189/17
M by Directive 93/68 [1993] O.J. L220/1

Directive 92/75 on the indication by labelling and standard product information of the consumption of energy and other resources by household appliances [1992] O.J. L297/16

## FOODSTUFFS

Directive 62/2645 on colouring matters authorised for use in foodstuffs intended for human consumption [1962] O.J. L115/2645
C by Directive 81/712 [1981] O.J. L257/1
M by Directive 85/7 [1985] O.J. L2/22

Directive 64/54 on preservatives authorised for use in foodstuffs intended for human consumption [1964] O.J. 12/161
M by Directive 85/585 [1985] O.J. L372/43

Directive 65/66 laying down specific criteria of purity for preservatives authorised for use in foodstuffs intended for human consumption [1965] O.J. 22/373
C by Directive 86/604 [1986] O.J. L352/45

Directive 68/420 amending 64/54/EEC on preservatives authorised for use in foodstuffs intended for human consumption [1968] O.J. L309/25

Directive 70/357 on antioxidants authorised for use in foodstuffs intended for human consumption [1970] O.J. L157/31
M by Directive 80/608 [1980] O.J. L170/33
M by Directive 85/7 [1985] O.J. L2/22
M by Directive 87/55 [1987] O.J. L24/41

Directive 73/241 on cocoa and chocolate products intended for human consumption [1973] O.J. L228/23
M by Directive 80/608 [1980] O.J. L170/33
M by Directive 85/7 [1985] O.J. L2/22
M by Directive 89/344 [1989] O.J. L142/19

Directive 73/437 on certain sugars intended for human consumption [1973] O.J. L356/71

Directive 74/329 on emulsifiers, stabilisers, thickeners and gelling agents for use in foodstuffs [1974] O.J. L189/1
M by Directive 85/7 [1985] O.J. L2/22
M by Directive 86/102 [1986] O.J. L88/40
M by Directive 89/393 [1989] O.J. L186/13

Directive 74/409 on honey [1974] O.J. L221/10

Directive 76/118 on certain partly of wholly dehydrated preserved milks for human consumption [1976] O.J. L24/49
M by Directive 83/635 [1983] O.J. L357/37

Directive 76/621 on fixing of the maximum level of erucic acid in oils and fats intended as such for human consumption and in foodstuffs containing added oils or fats [1976] O.J. L202/35

Directive 77/94 on foodstuffs for particular nutritional uses [1977] O.J. L26/55

M by Directive 85/7 [1985] O.J. L2/22
M by Directive 89/398 [1989] O.J. L186/27

Directive 77/436 on coffee and chicory extracts [1977] O.J. L172/20
M by Directive 85/7 [1985] O.J. L2/22
M by Directive 85/573 [1985] O.J. L372/22

Directive 78/142 on materials and articles which contain vinyl chloride monomer and are intended to come into contact with foodstuffs [1978] O.J. L44/15

Decision 78/663 laying down specific criteria of purity for emulsifiers, stabilisers, thickeners and gelling agents for use in foodstuffs [1978] O.J. L223/7
M by Directive 82/504 [1982] O.J. L230/35
M by Directive 90/612 [1990] O.J. L326/58
M by Directive 92/4 [1992] O.J. L55/96

Directive 78/664 laying down specific criteria of purity for antioxidants which may be used in foodstuffs intended for human consumption [1978] O.J. L223/30
M by Directive 82/712 [1982] O.J. L297/31

Directive 79/693 on fruit jams, jellies and marmalades and chestnut purée [1979] O.J. L205/5
M by Directive 88/593 [1988] O.J. L318/44

Directive 79/796 laying down Community methods of analysis for testing certain sugars intended for human consumption [1979] O.J. L239/24

Directive 79/1066 laying down Community methods of analysis for testing coffee and chicory extracts [1979] O.J. L327/17

Directive 79/1067 laying down Community methods for analysis for testing certain partly or wholly dehydrated preserved milks for human consumption [1979] O.J. L27/29

Directive 80/590 determining the symbol that may accompany materials and articles intended to come into contact with foodstuffs [1980] O.J. L151/21

Directive 80/766 laying down the Community method of analysis for official control of the vinyl chloride monomer level in materials and articles which are intended to come into contact with foodstuffs [1980] O.J. L213/42

Directive 80/777 on the exploitation and marketing of natural mineral waters [1980] O.J. L229/1
M by Directive 85/7 [1985] O.J. L2/22

Directive 80/891 on the Community method of analysis for determining the erutic acid content in oils and fats intended to be used as such for human consumption and foodstuffs containing added oils or fats [1980] O.J. L254/35

Directive 81/432 laying down the Community method of analysis for the official control of vinyl chloride released by materials and articles into foodstuffs [1981] O.J. L167/6

Directive 81/712 laying down Community methods of analysis for verifying that certain additives used in foodstuffs satisfy criteria of purity [1981] O.J. L257/1

Directive 82/711 laying down the basic rules necessary for testing migration of the constituents of plastic materials and articles intended to come into contact with foodstuffs [1981] O.J. L297/26
M by Directive 85/572 [1985] O.J. L372/14
M by Directive 93/8 [1993] O.J. L90/22

Directive 83/229 on materials and articles made of regenerated cellulose film intended to come into contact with foodstuffs [1983] O.J. L123/31
M by Directive 86/388 [1986] O.J. L228/32
M by Directive 92/15 [1992] O.J. L102/44
M by Directive 93/10 [1993] O.J. L93/27

Directive 83/417 on certain lactoproteins (caseins and caseinates) intended for human consumption [1983] O.J. L237/25

Directive 83/463 introducing temporary measures for the designation of certain ingredients in the labelling of foodstuffs for sale to the ultimate consumer [1983] O.J. L255/1

Directive 84/500 on ceramic articles intended to come into contact with foodstuffs [1984] O.J. L277/12

Directive 85/7 amending a series of directives on the involvement of the Standing Committee for Foodstuffs [1985] O.J. L2/22

Directive 85/503 on methods of analysis for edible caseins and caseinates [1985] O.J. L308/12

Directive 85/572 laying down the list of simulants to be used for the testing of migration of constituents of plastic materials and articles intended to come into contact with foodstuffs [1985] O.J. L372/14

Directive 85/573 amending 77/436/EEC on coffee and chicory extracts [1985] O.J. L372/22

Directive 85/585 amending 64/54/EEC on preservatives authorised for use in foodstuffs intended for human consumption [1985] O.J. L372/43

Directive 85/591 on the introduction of Community methods of sampling and analysis for monitoring foodstuffs intended for human consumption [1985] O.J. L372/50

Directive 86/424 laying down methods of sampling for chemical analysis of edible caseins and caseinates [1986] O.J. L243/29

Directive 87/524 laying down Community methods of sampling for chemical analysis for monitoring preserved milk products [1987] O.J. L306/24

Directive 88/344 on extraction solvents used in the production of foodstuffs and food ingredients [1988] O.J. L157/28

Directive 88/388 on flavourings for use in foodstuffs and on source materials for their production [1988] O.J. L184/61
M by Directive 91/71 [1991] O.J. L42/25

Directive 89/107 on food additives authorised for use in foodstuffs intended for human consumption [1989] O.J. L40/27

Directive 89/109 on materials and articles intended to come into contact with foodstuffs [1989] O.J. L40/38

Directive 89/396 on indications or marks identifying the lot to which a foodstuff belongs [1989] O.J. L186/21
M by Directive 91/238 [1991] O.J. L107/50

Directive 89/397 on the official control of foodstuffs [1989] O.J. L186/23
C by Directive 93/99 [1993] O.J. L290/14

Directive 89/398 on foodstuffs intended for particular nutritional uses [1989] O.J. L186/27

Directive 90/128 relating to plastic materials and articles intended to come into contact with foodstufs [1990] O.J. L75/19

M by Directive 92/39 [1992] O.J. L168/21
M by Directive 93/9 [1993] O.J. L90/26

Directive 90/650 on transitional measures applicable in Germany in the context of the harmonisation of technical rules for certain products [1990] O.J. L353/39

Directive 90/657 on transitional measures applicable in Germany in the context of the harmonisation of technical rules [1990] O.J. L353/65

Directive 91/321 on infant formulae and follow-on formulae [1991] O.J. L175/35

Directive 92/52 on infant formulae and follow-on formulae intended for export to third countries [1992] O.J. L179/129

Directive 93/10 relating to materials and articles made of regenerated cellulose film intended to come into contact with foodstuffs [1993] O.J. L93/27

Directive 93/43 on the hygiene of foodstuffs [1993] O.J. L175/1

Directive 93/45 concerning the manufacture of nectars without the addition of sugars or honey [1993] O.J. L159/133

Directive 93/77 relating to fruit juices and certain similar products [1993] O.J. L244/23

Directive 93/99 on the subject of additional measures concerning the official control of foodstuffs [1993] O.J. L290/14

## PROPRIETARY MEDICINAL PRODUCTS

Directive 65/65 on provisions relating to proprietary medicinal products [1965] O.J. L22/369
M by Directive 92/27 [1992] O.J. L113/8
M by Directive 93/39 [1993] O.J. L214/22

Directive 75/318 on analytical, pharmaco-toxicological and clinical standards and protocols in respect of the testing of proprietary medicinal products [1975] O.J. L147/1

M by Directive 83/570 [1983] O.J. L332/1
M by Directive 87/19 [1987] O.J. L15/31
M by Directive 89/341 [1989] O.J. L142/11
M by Directive 91/507 [1991] O.J. L270/32
M by Directive 93/39 [1993] O.J. L214/22

Directive 75/319 on provisions laid down by law, regulation or administrative action relating to proprietary medicinal products [1975] O.J. L147/13
M by Directive 89/381 [1989] O.J. L181/44
M by Directive 92/27 [1992] O.J. L113/8
M by Directive 93/39 [1993] O.J. L214/22

Directive 78/25 on colouring matters which may be added to medicinal products [1978] O.J. L11/18

Directive 81/851 on veterinary medicinal products [1981] O.J. L317/1
M by Directive 90/676 [1990] O.J. L373/15
M by Directive 93/40 [1993] O.J. L214/31

Directive 81/852 on analytical, pharmaco-toxological and clinical standards and protocols in respect of testing veterinary medicinal products [1981] O.J. L317/16
M by Directive 87/20 [1987] O.J. L15/34
M by Directive 92/18 [1992] O.J. L97/1
M by Directive 93/40 [1993] O.J. L214/31

Directive 87/22 on the marketing of high-technology medicinal products, particularly those derived from biotechnology [1987] O.J. L15/38
M by Directive 93/41 [1993] O.J. L214/40

Recommendation 87/176 on tests relating to the placing on the market of proprietary medicinal products [1987] O.J. L73/1

Directive 90/657 on transitional measures applicable in Germany in the context of the harmonisation of technical rules [1990] O.J. L353/65

Directive 90/677 extending the scope of Directive 81/851 on veterinary medicinal products and laying down additional provisions for immunological veterinary medicinal products [1990] O.J. L373/26

Directive 91/356 laying down the principles and guidelines of good manufacturing practice for medicinal products for human use [1991] O.J. L193/30

Directive 91/412 laying down the principles and guidelines of good manufacturing practice for veterinary medicinal products [1991] O.J. L228/70

Directive 91/414 concerning the placing of plant protection products on the market [1991] O.J. L230/1
M by Regulation 3600/92 [1992] O.J. L366/10
M by Directive 93/71 [1993] O.J. L221/27

Directive 92/25 on the wholesale distribution of medicinal products for human use [1992] O.J. L113/1

Directive 92/26 concerning the classification for the supply of medicinal products for human use [1992] O.J. L113/5

Directive 92/27 on the labelling of medicinal products for human use and on package leaflets [1992] O.J. L113/8

Directive 92/28 on the advertising of medicinal products for human use [1992] O.J. L113/13

Directive 92/73 widening the scope of Directives 65/65 and 75/319 on medicinal products and laying down additional provisions on homeopathic medicinal products [1992] O.J. L297/8

Directive 92/74 widening the scope of Directive 81/851 on veterinary medicinal products and laying down additional provisions on homeopathic veterinary medicinal products [1992] O.J. L297/12

Directive 93/42 concerning medical devices [1993] O.J. L169/1

## COSMETICS

Directive 76/768 on cosmetic products [1976] O.J. L262/169
M by Directive 87/137 [1987] O.J. L56/20
M by Directive 88/233 [1988] O.J. L105/11
M by Directive 88/667 [1988] O.J. L382/46
M by Directive 89/174 [1989] O.J. L64/10
M by Directive 89/679 [1989] O.J. L398/25
M by Directive 90/121 [1990] O.J. L71/40
M by Directive 91/184 [1991] O.J. L91/59
M by Directive 92/8 [1992] O.J. L70/23
M by Directive 92/86 [1992] O.J L325/18

M by Directive 93/35 [1992] O.J. L151/32
M by Directive 93/47 [1993] O.J. L203/24

Directive 80/1335 on methods of analysis necessary for checking the composition of cosmetic products [1980] O.J. L383/27
M by Directive 87/143 [1987] O.J. L57/56

Directive 82/434 on methods of analysis necessary for checking the composition of cosmetic products [1982] O.J. L185/1
M by Directive 90/207 [1990] O.J. L108/92

Directive 83/514 on methods of analysis necessary for checking the composition of cosmetic products [1983] O.J. L291/9

Directive 85/490 on methods of analysis necessary for checking the composition of cosmetic products [1985] O.J. L295/30

Directive 87/137 adapting to technical progress Annexes II, III, IV, V and VI to Directive 76/768/EEC on cosmetic products [1987] O.J. L56/20

Directive 93/73 on the methods of analysis necessary for checking composition of cosmetic products [1993] O.J. L231/34

## TEXTILES

Directive 71/307 on textile names [1971] O.J. L185/16
C by Directive 75/36 [1975] O.J. L14/15
M by Directive 83/623 [1983] O.J. L353/8
M by Directive 87/140 [1987] O.J. L56/24

Directive 72/276 on certain methods of quantitative analysis of binary textile fibre mixtures [1972] O.J. L173/1
M by Directive 81/75 [1975] O.J. L57/23
M by Directive 87/184 [1987] O.J. L75/21

Directive 73/44 on quantitative analysis of ternary fibre mixtures [1973] O.J. L83/1

Recommendation 87/142 on certain methods for the removal of nonfibrous matter prior to quantitative analysis of fibre mixtures [1987] O.J. L57/52

Recommendation 87/185 on quantitative methods of analysis for the identification of acrylic and modacrylic fibres, chlorofibres and trivilyl fibres [1987] O.J. L75/28

## DANGEROUS SUBSTANCES

Directive 67/548 on the classification, packaging and labelling of dangerous substances [1967] O.J. 196/1
M by Directive 87/302 [1987] O.J. L133/1
M by Directive 87/432 [1987] O.J. L239/1
M by Directive 88/490 [1988] O.J. L259/1
M by Directive 91/325 [1991] O.J. L180/1
M by Directive 91/326 [1991] O.J. L180/79
M by Directive 91/410 [1991] O.J. L228/67
M by Directive 92/32 [1992] O.J. L154/1
M by Directive 92/37 [1992] O.J. L154/30
M by Directive 93/21 [1993] O.J. L110/20
M by Directive 93/72 [1993] O.J. L258/29
M by Directive 93/105 [1993] O.J. L294/21

Directive 73/173 on the classification, packaging and labelling of dangerous preparations (solvents) [1973] O.J. L189/7
M by Directive 80/1271 [1980] O.J. L375/70
M by Directive 82/473 [1982] O.J. L213/17
M by Directive 88/379 [1988] O.J. L187/14
M by Directive 92/32 [1992] O.J. L454/1

Directive 76/769 on restrictions on the marketing and use of certain dangerous substances and preparations [1976] O.J. L262/201
M by Directive 85/467 [1985] O.J. L269/56
M by Directive 85/610 [1985] O.J. L375/1
M by Directive 89/677 [1989] O.J. L398/19
M by Directive 89/678 [1989] O.J. L398/24
M by Directive 91/157 [1991] O.J. L78/38
M by Directive 91/173 [1991] O.J. L85/34
M by Directive 91/338 [1991] O.J. L186/59
M by Directive 91/339 [1991] O.J. L186/64

Directive 78/631 on the classification, packaging and labelling of dangerous preparations (pesticides) [1978] O.J. L206/13
M by Directive 81/187 [1981] O.J. L88/29
M by Directive 84/291 [1984] O.J. L144/1
M by Directive 92/32 [1992] O.J. L154/1

Directive 90/660 on the transitional measures applicable in Germany with regard to certain Community provisions relating to the protection of the environment, in connection with the internal market [1990] O.J. L353/79

Directive 91/157 on batteries and accumulators containing certain dangerous substances [1991] O.J. L78/38
M by Directive 93/86 O.J. L264/51

Directive 91/659 adapting to technical progress Annex I to Council Directive 76/769 on restrictions on the marketing and use of certain dangerous substances and preparations (asbestos) [1991] O.J. L363/36

Directive 93/67 laying down the principles for assessment of risks to man and the environment of substances notified in accordance with Council Directive 67/548 [1993] O.J. L227/9

Directive 93/90 concerning the list of substances referred to in Article 13(1) (5th indent) of Council Directive 67/548 [1993] O.J. L277/33

## FERTILISERS

Directive 76/116 on fertilisers [1976] O.J. L24/21
M by Directive 88/183 [1988] O.J. L83/33
M by Directive 89/284 [1989] O.J. L111/34
M by Directive 89/530 [1989] O.J. L281/116

Directive 77/535 on methods of sampling and analysis for fertilisers [1977] O.J. L213/1
M by Directive 79/138 [1977] O.J. L39/3
C by Directive 87/566 [1987] O.J. L342/32
M by Directive 89/519 [1989] O.J. L265/30
M by Directive 93/1 [1993] O.J. L113/17

Directive 80/876 on straight ammonium nitrate fertilisers of high nitrogen content [1980] O.J. L250/7

Directive 87/94 on procedures for the control of characteristics of, limits for and resistence to detonation of straight ammonium nitrate fertilisers of high nitrogen content [1987] O.J. L38/1
M by Directive 88/126 [1988] O.J. L63/12

## OTHER SECTORS

Directive 68/89 on the classification of wood in the rough [1968] O.J. L32/12

Directive 69/493 on crystal glass [1969] O.J. L326/36
M by Decision 73/101 [1993] O.J. L2/1

Directive 73/361 on the certification and marking of wire-ropes, chains and hooks [1973] O.J. L335/51
M by Directive 76/434 [1976] O.J. L122/20
M by Directive 91/368 [1991] O.J. L198/16

Directive 73/404 on detergents [1973] O.J. L347/51
M by Directive 86/94 [1986] O.J. L80/51

Directive 75/117 on the application of the principle of equal pay for men and women [1975] O.J. L45/19

Directive 75/324 on aerosol dispensers [1975] O.J. L147/40

Directive 76/767 on common provisions for pressure vessels and methods for inspecting them [1976] O.J. L262/153
M by Directive 87/354 [1987] O.J. L192/43
M by Directive 88/665 [1988] O.J. L382/42

Directive 77/728 on the classification, packaging and labelling of paints, varnishes, printing inks, adhesives and similar products [1977] O.J. L303/23
M by Directive 83/265 [1983] O.J. L147/11
M by Directive 86/508 [1986] O.J. L295/31
M by Directive 88/379 [1988] O.J. L187/14
M by Directive 89/451 [1989] O.J. L216/75
M by Directive 92/32 [1992] O.J. L154/1

Directive 84/5 on insurance against civil liability in respect of the use of motor vehicles [1984] O.J. L8/17
M by Directive 90/232 [1990] O.J. L129/33

Directive 84/525 on seamless steel gas cylinders [1984] O.J. L300/1

Directive 84/526 on seamless unalloyed-aluminium and aluminium-alloy gas cylinders [1984] O.J. L300/20

Directive 84/527 on common provisions for lifting and mechanical handling appliances [1984] O.J. L300/72
M by Directive 88/665 [1988] O.J. L382/42

Directive 84/528 on welded unalloyed steel gas cylinders [1984] O.J. L300/84

Directive 84/529 on electrically operated lifts [1984] O.J. L300/86
M by Directive 86/312 [1986] O.J. L196/56
M by Directive 90/486 [1990] O.J. L270/21

Directive 84/530 on common provisions for appliances using gaseous fuels, safety and control devices for these appliances and methods of surveillance of them [1984] O.J. L300/95
M by Directive 87/354 [1984] O.J. L192/43
M by Directive 88/665 [1988] O.J. L382/42

Directive 84/532 on common provisions for construction plant and equipment [1984] O.J. L300/111
M by Directive 84/533-538 [1984] O.J. L300/123-171
M by Directive 88/665 [1988] O.J. L382/42

Directive 86/361 on the initial stage of mutual recognition of type-approval for telecommunications terminal equipment [1986] O.J. L217/21
M by Directive 91/263 [1991] O.J. L128/1

Directive 86/663 on self-propelled industrial trucks [1986] O.J. L384/12
M by Directive 91/368 [1991] O.J. L198/16

Directive 87/54 on the legal protection of topographies of semi-conductor products [1987] O.J. L24/36

Directive 87/372 on frequency bands to be reserved for the co-ordinated introduction of public pan-European cellular digital land-based mobile communications in the Community [1987] O.J. L196/85

Directive 87/404 on simple pressure vessels [1987] O.J. L220/48
M by Directive 90/488 [1990] O.J. L270/25
M by Directive 93/68 [1993] O.J. L220/1

Directive 88/301 on competition on the markets for telecommunications terminal equipment [1988] O.J. L131/73

Directive 89/104 on trade marks [1989] O.J. L40/1
M by Decision 92/10 [1992] O.J. L6/35

Directive 89/106 on construction products [1989] O.J. L40/12
M by Directive 93/68 [1993] O.J. L220/1

Directive 89/336 on electromagnetic compatibility [1989] O.J. L139/19
M by Directive 91/263 [1991] O.J. L128/1
M by Directive 92/31 [1992] O.J. L126/11
M by Directive 93/68 [1993] O.J. L220/1
M by Directive 93/97 [1993] O.J. L290/1

Directive 89/392 on machinery [1989] O.J. L183/9
M by Directive 91/368 [1991] O.J. L198/16
M by Directive 93/44 [1993] O.J. L175/12
M by Directive 93/68 [1993] O.J. L220/1

Directive 89/686 on personal protective equipment [1989] O.J. L399/18
M by Directive 93/68 [1993] O.J. L220/1

Directive 90/396 on appliances burning gaseous fuels [1990] O.J. L196/15
M by Directive [1993] O.J. L220/1

Directive 91/287 on the frequency band to be designated for the co-ordinated introduction of digital European cordless telecommunications (DECT) into the Community [1991] O.J. L144/45

Directive 92/42 on efficiency requirements for new hot-water boilers fired with liquid or gaseous fuels [1992] O.J. L167/17
M by Directive 93/68 [1993] O.J. L220/1

Directive 93/36 co-ordinating procedures for the award of public supply contracts [1993] O.J. L199/1

Directive 93/97 supplementing Directive 91/263 in respect of satellite earth station equipment [1993] O.J. L290/1

Directive 93/98 harmonising the term of protection of copyright and certain related rights [1993] O.J. L290/9

## CONSUMER INFORMATION, EDUCATION AND REPRESENTATION

Directive 71/307 on textile names [1971] O.J. L185/16
M by Directive 83/623 [1983] O.J. L353/8

M by Directive 87/140 [1987] O.J. L56/24

Directive 89/108 on quick-frozen foodstuffs for human consumption [1989] O.J. L40/34

Directive 90/313 on the freedom of access to information on the environment [1990] O.J. L158/56

Directive 90/496 on nutrition labelling for foodstuffs [1990] O.J. L276/40

Directive 92/1 on the monitoring of temperatures in the means of transport, warehousing and storage of quick-frozen foodstuffs intended for human consumption [1992] O.J. L34/28

Directive 92/2 on the sampling procedure and the Community method of analysis for the official control of the temperatures of quick-frozen foods intended for human consumption [1992] O.J. L34/30

## PROTECTION OF HEALTH AND SAFETY

Directive 81/602 on the prohibition of certain substances having a hormonal action and of any substances having a thyrostatic action [1981] O.J. L222/32
C by Directive 88/358 [1988] O.J. L191/46

Directive 85/358 supplementing Directive 81/602 on the prohibition of certain substances having a hormonal action and of any substances having a thyrostatic action [1985] O.J. L191/46
M by Regulation 3768/85 [1985] O.J. L362/8
M by Directive 88/146 [1988] O.J. L70/16

Directive 87/357 on products which, appearing to be other than they are, endanger the health or safety of consumers [1987] O.J. L192/49

Directive 88/146 prohibiting the use in livestock farming of certain substances having a hormonal action [1988] O.J. L70/16

Directive 88/378 concerning the safety of toys [1988] O.J. L187/1
M by Directive 93/68 [1993] O.J. L220/1

Directive 88/379 on provisions relating to the classification, packaging and labelling of dangerous preparations [1988] O.J. L187/14
M by Directive 89/178 [1989] O.J. L64/18

M by Directive 90/492 [1990] O.J. L275/35
M by Directive 92/32 [1992] O.J. L154/1
M by Directive 93/18 [1993] O.J. L104/46

Directive 89/437 on hygiene and health problems affecting production and the placing on the market of egg products [1989] O.J. L212/87
M by Directive 89/662 [1989] O.J. L395/13
M by Directive 91/684 [1991] O.J. L376/38

Directive 89/622 on the labelling of tobacco products [1989] O.J. L359/1
M by Directive 92/41 [1992] O.J. L158/30

Directive 90/35 on the categories of preparations the packaging of which must be fitted with child-resistant fastenings and/or carrying a tactile warning of danger [1990] O.J. L19/14

Directive 90/239 on the maximum tar yield in cigarettes [1990] O.J. L137/36

Directive 90/496 on nutrition labelling for foodstuffs [1990] O.J. L276/40

Directive 91/442 on dangerous preparations the packaging of which must be fitted with child-resistant fastening [1991] O.J. L238/25

Directive 91/477 on control of the acquisition and possession of weapons [1991] O.J. L256/51

Directive 91/498 on the conditions for granting temporary and limited derogations from specific Community health rules on the production and marketing of fresh meat [1991] O.J. L268/105

Directive 92/28 on the advertising of medicinal products for human use [1992] O.J. [1992] L113/13

Directive 92/59 on general product safety [1992] O.J. L228/24

Directive 92/120 on the conditions for granting temporary and limited derogations from specific Community health rules on the production and marketing of certain products of animal origin [1992] O.J. L62/24

Council Directive 93/5 on assistance to the Commission and co-operation by the Member States in the scientific examination of questions relating to food [1993] O.J. L52/18

Directive 93/15 on the placing on the market and supervision of explosives for civil uses [1993] O.J. L121/20

## PROTECTION OF ECONOMIC INTERESTS

Directive 75/106 on the making up by volume of certain prepackaged liquids [1975] O.J. L42/1
M by Directive 79/1005 [1979] O.J. L308/25
M by Directive 85/10 [1985] O.J. L4/20
M by Directive 88/316 [1988] O.J. L143/26
M by Directive 89/676 [1989] O.J. L398/18

Directive 75/107 on bottles used as measuring containers [1975] O.J. L42/14

Directive 76/211 on the making up by weight or volume of certain prepackaged products [1976] O.J. L46/1
M by Directive 78/891 [1978] O.J. L311/21

Directive 79/112 on the labelling, presentation and advertising of foodstuffs for sale to the ultimate consumer [1979] O.J. L33/1
M by Directive 85/7 [1985] O.J. L2/22
M by Directive 86/197 [1986] O.J. L144/38
M by Directive 89/395 [1989] O.J. L186/17
M by Directive 91/72 [1991] O.J. L42/27
M by Directive 93/102 [1993] O.J. L291/14

Directive 79/530 on the indication by labelling of the energy consumption of household appliances [1979] O.J. L145/1
M by Directive 92/75 [1992] O.J. L297/16

Directive 79/531 applying to electric ovens Directive 79/530 on the indication by labelling of the energy consumption of domestic appliances [1979] O.J. L145/7

Directive 79/581 on consumer protection in the indication of the prices of foodstuffs [1979] O.J. L158/19
M by Directive 88/315 [1988] O.J. L142/23

Directive 80/232 on the ranges of nominal quantities and nominal capacities permitted for certain prepackaged products [1980] O.J. L51/1
M by Directive 86/96 [1986] O.J. L80/55
M by Directive 87/356 [1987] O.J. L192/48

Directive 83/463 introducing temporary measures for the designation of certain ingredients in the labelling of foodstuffs for sale to the ultimate consumer [1983] O.J. L255/1

Directive 84/450 on misleading advertising [1984] O.J. L250/17

Directive 85/374 on liability for defective products [1985] O.J. L210/29

Directive 85/577 to protect the consumer in respect of contracts negogiated away from business premises [1985] O.J. L372/31

Directive 87/102 on consumer credit [1987] O.J. L42/48
M by Directive 90/88 [1990] O.J. L61/14

Directive 87/250 on the indication of alcoholic strength by volume in the labelling of alcoholic beverages for sale to the ultimate consumer [1987] O.J. L113/57

Directive 88/314 on consumer protection by indication of prices on non-food products [1988] O.J. L142/19

Directive 89/396 on indications or marks identifying the lot to which a foodstuff belongs [1989] O.J. L186/21
M by Directive 91/238 [1991] O.J. L107/50

Directive 89/451 on the labelling of sparkling wine [1989] O.J. L202/12

Directive 90/314 on package travel, package holidays and package tours [1990] O.J. L158/59

Directive 90/377 concerning a Community procedure to improve transparency of gas and electricity prices charged to industrial end-users [1990] O.J. L185/16
M by Directive 93/87 [1993] O.J. L277/32

Directive 92/75 on the indication by labelling and standard product information of the consumption of energy and other resources as by household appliances [1992] O.J. L297/16

Directive 93/13 on unfair contract terms in consumer contracts [1993] O.J. L95/29

## HEALTH PROTECTION

Directive 77/312 on biological screening of the population for lead [1977] O.J. L105/10

Directive 84/466 laying down basic measures for the radiation protection of persons undergoing medical examination or treatment [1984] O.J. L265/1

Directive 89/105 on measures regulating the prices of medicinal products for human use and their inclusion in the scope of national health insurance systems [1989] O.J. L40/8

Directive 92/109 on the manufacture and the placing on the market of certain substances used in the illicit manufacture of narcotic drugs and psychotropic substances [1992] O.J. L370/76
M by Directive 93/46 [1993] O.J. L159/134

## PROTECTION OF ANIMALS

Directive 86/609 on the protection of animals used for experimental and other scientific purposes [1986] O.J. L358/1

# INDEX